THE GENTLEWOMANS COMPANION
OR, A
GUIDE TO THE FEMALE SEX

HANNAH WOOLLEY

THE
Gentlewomans Companion
OR, A
Guide TO THE Female Sex

THE COMPLETE TEXT OF 1675

WITH AN INTRODUCTION BY
CATERINA ALBANO

PROSPECT BOOKS
2001

This edition first published in Great Britain by Prospect Books in 2001 at Allaleigh House, Blackawton, Totnes, Devon TQ9 7DL.

The Gentlewomans Companion was first published by Dorman Newman in 1673. The present text is that of the second edition, published in London by Edward Thomas, 1675.

British Library Cataloguing in Publication Data:
A catalogue entry for this book is available from the British Library.

ISBN 0907325998

Typeset and designed by Tom Jaine.

Printed and bound at the Cromwell Press, Trowbridge, Wiltshire.

Contents

A Note on the Text

As noted in the introduction by Caterina Albano, the text printed here is that of the second edition, published in 1675. The master copy was that in the British Library (shelfmark 1037e15). It was a great help to have the electronic text of the same edition available through the Women Writers Resource Project found at the website http://chaucer.library.emory.edu.

The text is the same as that first printed except for the substitution of the short for the long 's'. No other changes to spelling, italicization or capitalization have been made. Some misprints or printing errors have been noted where it seemed to help comprehension; the majority have been left to stand as they were. Editorial interpolations are within square brackets. Where possible, the typographical quirks and settings of the original have been followed.

The original text ends with seven pages of advertisement for other books printed for and sold by Edward Thomas. These have not been reproduced in this edition.

Introduction

A conduct book for women as well as household manual, *The Gentlewomans Companion* was announced in November 1672 and first published in 1673 by the bookseller Dorman Newman. It went through four editions (1675, 1682, and a fourth in 1711 with the title of *The Compleat Gentlewoman*), but Newman was only involved in the first. The second was issued by Edward Thomas of Little Britain. The printer, A. Maxwell, was the same in each instance. It is this second edition of 1675 that is reprinted here. There is no substantive difference between the first and second editions.

The author is named as Hannah Woolley. This name was differently spelled on the title-pages of other books by her: *The Cooks Guide* (1664) and *The Queen-like Closet* (1670) both have it Wolley, the spelling preferred by the British Library catalogue. Woolley herself spelled it variously as Woolley, Wolley, Woolly or Wolly. Although her authorship of *The Gentlewomans Companion* is disputed, the fact that the publisher considered it profitable to attach her name to the book testifies to her popularity or drawing-power. She was first professional woman writer of cookery books in England. Indeed, with the exception of the almanac-maker Sarah Jinner, who worked between the years 1658 and 1664, she was arguably the first female professional writer of any sort in the kingdom.[1]

Hannah Woolley was born around 1622–23. At an early age her mother and sisters began to instruct her in domestic skills, particularly how to prepare medicines, a practice in which they were experts themselves. She went to work as a servant to a noblewoman, possibly Lady Anne Wroth, wife of Sir Henry Wroth, to whom she dedicates her second book, *The Cooks Guide*.[2] In 1646 Hannah married Benjamin Woolley who taught at the Free Grammar School in Newport (also called Newport Pond), near Saffron Walden, Essex. To this marriage she bore four sons. Around 1653, the couple moved to Hackney where they kept another boarding school for boys. At both, she was responsible for the care of the pupils, further improving her domestic skills.

In 1661 Benjamin Woolley died, marking the beginning of a difficult period for Hannah. She lost her mainstay and her income, and she suffered a palsy or paralysis from which, it appears, she never fully recovered. Perhaps in response to these setbacks, she published her first two books: *The Ladies Directory* (1661), which she had printed at her own expense and which sold at one shilling; and *The Cooks Guide or rare Receipts for Cookery* (1664). *The Ladies Directory* was announced before the death of her husband and the literary historian Elaine Hobby suggests that he may have been in long decline, prompting her to seek other forms of income before his actual demise. By 1666, she was living in Westminster where she married for a second time: in this instance a widowed gentleman called Francis Challiner or Chaloner. The presumption has to be that wedded bliss was short-lived for, by 1669, she is found making her will, describing herself as a widow, once more under the name of Woolley.

She resumed her career as writer of cookery books. *The Queen-like Closet*, published in 1670, was followed by *The Ladies Delight* in 1672. This was, to epitomize the bibliographer A.W. Oxford, a new edition in a single volume of *The Cooks Guide* and *The Ladies Directory*. However, it was translated into German with the title *Frauen-Zimmers Zeit-Vertreib* in 1674. *The Gentlewomans Companion* appeared in 1673. Although this was attributed to her, Woolley disclaimed her authorship in *A Supplement to The Queen-like Closet* published the following year. In 1675, there appeared a compilation of her earlier work entitled *The Accomplish'd Ladies Delight*. Whatever the origins of the material, the book was issued anonymously (the preface was signed 'T.P.', possibly T. Passinger), as was another book sometimes ascribed to Hannah Woolley, *The Compleat Servant-Maid*, appearing in 1677. Elaine Hobby finds the Bodleian Library catalogue's attribution of this book to Woolley implausible. The British Library catalogue describes it instead as anonymous. *The Compleat Servant-maid* contains culinary and medical recipes, general instructions for servants, and directions for writing and arithmetic. It is possible that it was based on Woolley's books but there are many differences in style and tone from her known writings. The book appears to be the result of what Woolley had initiated in *The Queen-like Closet*.

Although the exact date of Woolley's death is not known, it was presumably around 1675 since there are no later records of her work. An advertisement in the *Supplement to The Queen-like Closet* of 1674 states she is living at Richard Woolley's house in the Old Bailey at Golden Cup Court. He was most likely a son and is recorded as Reader at St Martin's Ludgate and a Master of Arts. The advertisement placed after the 1675 edition of *Gentlewomans Companion* has her living at East Harding Street between Fetter Lane and Shoe Lane, north of Fleet Street. While we may be anxious to claim Hannah Woolley to the ranks of professional writers, these advertisements and other references draw attention to alternative sources of revenue: either the tuition of gentlefolk, their children or their servants in the arts of which she writes, or the sale of pills and remedies.

If we compare this summary of Woolley's life with the auto-biographical account given in *The Gentlewomans Companion*, some details are inconsistent. In the *Companion*, she claims to have been first a schoolmistress and then a governess in a noble household close to the court. Employment as a governess, stewardess and secretary in a second noble household allowed her to improve and refine her skills, moving from cookery to the command of the English and French languages (gained from reading poems, plays, and romances aloud to her mistress). She left this employment when, despite the offer of an aristocratic match, she chose to marry for love. The problem with this sequence of events is that the author seems more concerned with Woolley's refinement than with her practical skills. By contrast, these latter are central to her own version of her life which she recounted a year later in *A Supplement to The Queen-like Closet*, where her tone is more subdued and reflects the pragmatic attitude which characterizes her writing. In *The Gentlewomans Companion*, instead, the importance of love and the role played by reading are stressed as pivotal to her career. The emphasis alludes both to the rise of a modern sensibility and a related mode of fashioning one's identity through the act of reading. These details are also important because they are dealt with in various sections of the text so that the biographical account supports and mirrors the content of the whole manual.

Woolley's education matches her enterprise in becoming a writer, highlighting refinement and the capacity for self-improvement as acquirable skills.

If the actual difficulties of Woolley's life are obliterated in this ideal portrait, it offers an image which is congruent with the aims of the *The Gentlewomans Companion*: an ideal representation of femininity through a codification of the author's social relations and skills. We are told what a woman ought to be like, what she ought to know and, most significantly, how she ought to behave. This should help her become socially mobile and improve her condition. What better example of such a woman than the author herself? The biography in *The Gentlewomans Companion*, though improbable, is integral to the text itself and promotes it by alluding to the exemplary experience of its author. The account, moreover, justifies Woolley's alleged endeavour since the writing is itself the result of her training.

References to personal experience are not unusual in contemporary cookery books. They lent credibility to the author and explained the reasons behind writing. Robert May gives an account of his life in *The Accomplisht Cook* (1660).[3] He refers to his training first in England, then to his service in France, then to his attachment to noble (and often recusant) families during the reign of Charles I and the interregnum. The *curriculum vitae* allows him to position himself politically. He praises the Restoration and sees his project of instructing professional cooks in the latest fashion of cooking as part of the political process of restoring England to its past splendour, of which hospitality was itself a sign. His interest focuses on the upper classes and the protection of 'the professionalized status of the "Art" and "Mistery" of cookery as a male preserve'.[4] May deploys the account of his life to explain who he is and what he has achieved in order to justify the didactic aim of his recipes.[5]

A year after Robert May, William Rabisha introduces *The Whole Book of Cookery Dissected* – also addressed to professional cooks – with his own brief account of his training.[6] He, too, praises the Restoration, linking his endeavour of reviving hospitality to the common good. The problem, of course (though less so to contemporaries), with the analogy between revived hospitality and the improvement of the whole nation is the implicit identification of the common good with the requirements of the upper classes.

(10)

A similar statement, also linking her work to the common good and general utility, is presented in *The Queen-like Closet*. Yet Hannah Woolley's idea of common good differs considerably from that of May and Rabisha because she aims to address a broader and more varied readership:

> I am blamed by many for divulging these Secrets, and again commended by others for my Love and Charity in so doing; but however I am better satisfied with imparting them, than to let them die with me; and if I do not live to have the comfort of your thanks, yet I hope it will cause you to speak well of me when I am dead: The Books which before this I have caused to be put in Print, found so good an acceptance, as that I shall still go on in imparting what I yet have so fast as I can.[7]

The circulation of 'these Secrets' contrasts with May's desire to preserve the art of cookery as the monopoly of a few, which suggests that writing such as Woolley's may have met with some hostility. Woolley markets her books to a readership of non-professionals in the merchant classes and the lower gentry. Food habits were important indicators of class and English society was undergoing a process of redefinition after the Civil War and the restoration of the monarchy. This is evident in Woolley's *Cooks Guide*. Here she sought the patronage of Lady Wroth, a member of one of the most influential royalist families of the time. The title-page of this book is witness to her political affiliations, as well as to a certain self-confidence.[8] It states that it is a collection of recipes for cooking and preserving 'whereby Noble Persons and others in their Hospitalities may be gratified in their *Gusto's*'. Refinement (hinted at by the term *gusto*) is a prerogative of the nobility, which may also appeal and be made available to the undefined others for whom Woolley writes. She further explains that she put out 'this book, to testifie to the scandalous World that I do not altogether spend my time idlely; somewhat of benefit it may be to young Ladies and Gentlewomen; and such I wish it; [however] it may serve to passe away their youthfull time, which otherwaies might be worse employed'. In these few lines, the ideal of accomplishment is linked to virtue and to Woolley's characteristic justification of her writing in terms of improvement and utility, whilst idleness is conventionally condemned.

It is not surprising that in Woolley's statement the private and public dimensions of writing coincide in terms both of personal achievement and the general good. To justify writing in terms of the common good is not unusual, as is the analogy of idleness and moral corruption. Equally familiar is the author's concern with the reception of the book, and in particular the ill-appraisal that the dissemination of secrets may encounter. In the influential *The French Cook* (the English translation of 1653) François de La Varenne states: 'My intention is not to displease or offend anybody, though I doe not doubt, but that some ill-willers, or some envious, will speak of it at randome; but my intention is to serve and succour them who shall stand in need...'[9] As a woman author Woolley adds to these preoccupations that of her reputation: juxtaposing the shame which may derive from revealing the secrets of cookery – as if it were a discrediting act – to the general utility of doing so. Maintaining a language of modesty, Woolley forcefully states her right to challenge the restriction of her sex and render her name as well as her knowledge public and, therefore, useful. Woolley teases with the assumption that to become public for a woman alludes to sexual availability and that the secret of a recipe refers to sensuous gratification. This is the language deployed in the titles of many early-modern collections of recipes. Woolley shifts its meaning, adopting her male colleagues' equation of writing as an improvement of common good.

In these authors' autobiographical references – factual or fictionalized – we see an attempt to present a coherent picture which conforms to a modern attitude of self-improvement and progress. Woolley's life is indicative of her ability to learn and put into practice her knowledge as a means of social advancement. Consequently her life not only validates her enterprise, but represents an example for her readers.

Whilst in *The Gentlewomans Companion* her life-story figures prominently at the beginning of the volume, in the *Supplement* it appears almost accidentally in the middle of the text, as part of what can be learned from browsing through the recipes. In choosing to present herself in this way, Woolley conspicuously stresses her medical skills by reporting how she learned them, and by listing the many ailments she treated.

First, Take notice that my Mother and my Elder Sisters were very well skilled in Physick and Chirurgery from whom I learned a little, and at the age of seventeen I had the fortune to belong to a Noble lady in this Kingdom, till I Married, which was at twenty four years (those seven years I was with her) she finding my genius, and being of a Charitable temper to do good amongst her poor Neighbours, I had her purse at command to buy what Ingredients might be required to make Balsoms, Salves, Oyntments, Waters for Wounds, Oyls, Cordials and the like; besides she procured such knowledge for me from her Physicians and Chirurgions (who were the best that all *England* could afford) and also bought many Books for me to read, that in short time, with the help of those Worthy men before mentioned, I soon became a Practitioner...[10]

These indications are absent from the biographical account in the *Companion* and this disparity is significant in assessing Woolley's endeavour. In justifying her own writing, she points to the most controversial area of women's domestic practices in the early modern period, a time when medical skills were expected in a woman, but male medical professionals showed increasing hostility towards them.[11] Woolley is cautious in her claim to expertise: a family heritage which passed recipes from one generation to the next is paralleled by the teaching of the best physicians and surgeons under the patronage of a noble lady. She also stresses the social importance of women's medical practice as a form of charity outside the medical profession, thus indirectly defining herself in moral and social terms, within a tradition of women belonging to the aristocracy and the middle classes who collected their recipes, especially in manuscript form, and deployed their skills for the welfare of their communities.

It is perhaps not accidental that the title and content of *The Queen-like Closet* bear many similarities with two other influential collections published in the 1650s: *The Queens Closet Opened* (1655) attributed to the Queen Henrietta Maria, and *A Choice Manual of Rare and Select Secrets in Physick and Chyrurgery; collected and practiced by the Right Honourable, the Countess of Kent late deceased* (1653).[12] The choice of the title *The Queen-like Closet* may be clever sales pitch through which the author could reveal possible royalist political sympathies, as well as a more conscious attempt to maintain continuity with the past.

Whether cookery or medicine, Woolley initiates a new practice of women writing and publishing these types of manuals. Although earlier collections had been attributed to women, they were put into print by men who saw the value of the manuscripts. Hannah Woolley's achievement is the product of broader social changes. During the Civil War women's voices had become more prominently heard in public: from members of the upper classes pleading in court or in Parliament, to religious prophetesses who preached across the country. More generally, although 'legally defined only in relation to men, as daughters or wives, women from all walks of life evidently found that the cultural climate of the 1640s and 1650s was conducive to speaking and writing both as women and as socially responsible agents'.[13] Though her subject traditionally belonged to the female sphere, her books chart a new area of writing for women linked to their expected social role.

Woolley offers her expertise to a broad female readership thus connecting to an earlier tradition of cookery manuals addressed to women. The popularity of her books, all of which went through several editions, confirms the existence of an audience. Significantly, she imagines two main types of readers: ladies and gentlewomen who, though already skilled in various domestic practices, may be pleased to learn the latest trends in the preparation and presentation of food; and women of all classes – but especially of the middle and the lower upper – who may wish to learn in order to improve their condition, and earn a living like Woolley herself.

This leads to an appreciation of the value of the biographical information contained in Woolley's books, since only by pointing to her own background could she define her writing as congruous and acceptable. Yet the disparities between the two accounts printed in *The Gentlewomans Companion* and her own *Supplement to The Queen-like Closet* raises problems concerning attribution of the book we have printed here: why the printer might have plagiarized it, and how we can read the text as we find it.

Before considering the *The Gentlewomans Companion* and its relevance, it is important to examine its origin. The literary scholar Elaine Hobby has questioned its attribution on the grounds of Woolley's own repudiation of authorship. According to Woolley's account in *A Supplement* (published in 1674), *The Gentlewomans Companion* was based on an earlier projected book – *The Ladies Guide* – which she agreed with the bookseller and publisher Dorman Newman she should refashion according to his specification. In the event, the rewriting was undertaken by another hand.[14] *The Ladies Guide* is referred to, albeit obliquely, in the opening 'Epistle Dedicatory' of the *Companion*, 'It is near Seven years since I began to write this Book, at the desire of the Bookseller'. Given that the epistle is signed November 1672, that would mean she commenced operations in 1666, around the time of her second marriage (which perhaps saved her from the need to pursue the scheme). Woolley allegedly saw the manuscript and made some changes, but the publisher broke the contract by not introducing the corrections and failing to pay her the agreed amount of money, passing the compilation to another hack-writer. All this is rehearsed by the long-suffering author in her *Supplement to The Queen-like Closet*. Although in the seventeenth century such cases were not uncommon and an author had little control over the manuscript, the controversy surrounding *The Gentlewomans Companion* is significant. From it we may infer that Woolley was quite well-known as a writer of domestic manuals, in particular cookery books, and that her name was considered a good selling-point. No doubt this explains why Dorman Newman used it. Yet this was still an unexpected strategy since the writing of conduct books and similar practical handbooks was not at the time a feminine occupation. From devotional writing to poetry, women's appearance in print was limited, and even if manuscript collections of recipes had previously been ascribed to women, their publication had always been mediated by a man. Woolley seems therefore to initiate a new tradition in a genre which will become increasingly important.

Woolley complains that most of the content of *The Gentlewomans Companion* was inappropriate and although she was allowed to make some changes to the first draft, these were insufficient to avoid, in her view, damage to her reputation:

> I should not speak so much did I not find a prejudice:
> for People of worth do wonder why I would write so;
> and I have vindicated my self to those who told me of
> it, with telling the Truth.[15]

Woolley's objection that her name has been abused – to use her own word – by the inadequacy of the content of *The Gentlewomans Companion* suggests that it was at variance with the intention of her other writing: particularly, it lacked practical effectiveness.

Neither of the original parties to the dispute suggested that *The Gentlewomans Companion* had nothing at all to do with the writings of Hannah Woolley. She accepted herself that her own work formed some sort of basis to the text as we find it. In confirmation, the historian Gilly Lehmann draws attention to the similarity between the recommendations to servants in the *Companion* and in *The Queen-like Closet*.[16]

If, however, we presume that the book was substantively the work of a publisher's hack, there are three important ways it may be distinguished from work we know to be by Hannah Woolley. Elaine Hobby has observed that the overall organization is quite different to Woolley's usual miscellaneous and *pointilliste* approach: the book has structure. She has also noted that syntax and sentence construction are far more Latinate than Woolley's homely prose. Most important of all, the advice tendered to the reader is within the tradition of the conduct book written by a man for women: on the whole it maintains and defines the status quo. Woolley, by contrast, is often seen to be guiding women in climbing the social ladder and attaining a modicum of independence. It should be stressed that the doubts surrounding authorship concern not only the identity but also the gender of the writer. If this is a book written by a man it makes a big difference to our view of it, although this does not diminish the interest of *The Gentlewomans Companion* as a valuable historical and cultural document for understanding the conception of femininity in the second half of the seventeenth century.

The novelty of *The Gentlewomans Companion* may consist in being a book of manners for women based on the example of the many circulating for men. *The Gentlewomans Companion* differs from most earlier advice books for women in dealing in detail with acceptable and unacceptable forms of behaviour, and in extensively merging the traditional moral advice of earlier manuals with collections of recipes.[17]

The Gentlewomans Companion is intended as 'A Guide to the Female Sex: containing Directions of Behaviour, in all Places, Companies, Relations, and Conditions, from their Childhood down to Old Age'. It offers an ideal image of femininity on which women could fashion themselves. Just as Woolley's biographical account is an example of the benefit of education, so the whole book explains what was required and expected of, or suitable for a woman. The book is dedicated to 'To all Young Ladies, Gentlewomen, and all Maidens whatever', and either a 'Lady at court' or a 'Cook-maid in the country' may benefit from it. By addressing women across all age and social groups, the book proposes a unifying category for 'womanhood'. The author may acknowledge differences of social status or age, but presumes a single standard of appearance, behaviour and education. The ideal *gentle-woman* here described is not meant to be representative of either the aristocracy or the lower-classes, but rather of the more mobile middle sort and of the lower gentry.

Woolley's earlier collections of recipes tend to mirror the social changes of the 1660s, with a particular concern for the position of women needing to earn a living because of the impoverishment of their families due to political turmoil. The author of *The Gentlewomans Companion* directly addresses this problem only when dealing with the duties of a governess or in the instructions to servants; otherwise, social issues are erased from the text, just as are references to the difficulties which Hannah Woolley evidently experienced in her own life. This suggests a different approach in the *Companion* from Woolley's own writing. One offers social reassurance; Woolley herself is more pragmatic, more matter of fact. None the less, there are some indications of transformations following the Restoration woven into the *Companion*.

The return of the court meant a reassessment of social standards, and the introduction of new fashions in manners and clothing as well as food. These were the skills and habits which had to be acquired not by the restored aristocracy, rather by those who aspired to mimic it. The court and its manners were not accepted wholesale, nor was the aristocratic way of life. There is the explicit rejection of the complexity of court cookery in the author's comments on the recipe for bisk; and the book alerts the reader to some of the excess of new French vogues in clothing and make-up as inappropriate to a gentlewoman. Equally, the author warns the reader away from the theatre: fit only for occasional visits. The extravagances of the court, and the dangerous example of actresses – who appeared on the English stage with the reopening of the public theatres after the Restoration – are implicitly condemned in defining an urban and refined, yet bourgeois and restrained portrait of femininity.

If some of the plays and novels of the period present a more independent image of femininity, the ideal woman here is a reassertion of traditional decorum and domesticity. The controversies, instabilities, and contradictions of the times are excluded in favour of a comforting presentation of a domestic environment in which class distinctions and gendered roles are carefully maintained. Courtesy functions as the emblem of a re-established social order in need of confirmation.

The Gentlewomans Companion is one of the first examples of conduct books which proposes an educational programme able to fashion a woman and make her desirable for her demeanour and skills as expected attributes of femininity. The consequences of this presentation are far-reaching, especially since towards the end of the century, moral and material soundness were 'a new sexual coin' to be opposed to the sensual manifestations of affection amongst the aristocracy.[18]

The notion of providing an ideal image of femininity seems to be confirmed by the frontispiece engraving which represents a young woman in a fashionable dress and hair-style. Rather than the portrait of any person in particular – supposedly Hannah Woolley but, according to the *Dictionary of National Biography*, one Sarah Gilly – it is instead the visual counterpart of the ideal woman the book aims to fashion. Twice, the author refers to a painter who draws on the features of many different beautiful women to represent the most handsome of all:

> A Painter of old being about a draught of a most absolute beauty, propounded for the accomplishment thereof half a dozen of the most exquisite and wonderful fair Maidens he could find, that he might steal from each those charms and features which he thought were most powerful; but I will assure you, a

greater assistance is required in the framing and fashioning of a Woman, whose behaviour should be such as to please in all companies.[19]

I hope the Reader will not think it much, that as the famous Lymner when he drew the Picture of an exact Beauty, made use of an Eye from one, of a Mouth from another, and so cull'd what was rare in all others, that he might present them all in one entire piece of Workmanship and Frame: So I, when I was to write of Physick and Chyrurgery, have consulted all Books I could meet with in that kind, to compleat my own Experience.[20]

The perfecting of manners requires a more careful creation than the fashioning of physical beauty. The book itself, like the ideal image of a woman, is a compound of many different sources which, along with the personal experience of the author, will enable the reader to resemble the ideal image that both author and painter tried to achieve by taking the best from different models. Womanhood is presented as a malleable, forgeable and adaptable sign, meant to respond to and fulfill the requirements of society. Hence the sections in the text correspond to various forms of social relations: children to parents, scholars to governors, virgins to suitors, wives to husbands, housewives to the house, mistresses to servants, mothers to children, widows to the world.

This range of social relations is charted through the propriety of gestures, clothing, ways of speaking, walking, eating and any other kind of social practice. The latter are categorized according to the expected roles a woman may encounter in her life, mapping a precise course from childhood to widowhood. The emphasis is on the preparation of a young woman for courtship, marriage and motherhood. Reinforcing the traditional presentation of femininity through the categories of virgin, wife, mother and widow, the text – like many other handbooks of the kind – creates a model of femininity which is geared toward domesticity, as part of a social as well as productive system. *The Gentlewomans Companion* further parallels advice on demeanour with instruction in practical skills such as cooking, carving, distilling, dying fabrics, stitching, writing letters, and preparing medicaments, thus bringing together various traditions, especially those of the conduct book, the household manual and the recipe collection. Since the originality of the text consists in this structure of compilation, it is worth considering it – in particular, in relation to conduct books and collections of recipes.

The idea that the individual can be fashioned in accordance with social requirements is crucial to the writing of early-modern conduct books through which 'men and women can be produced'. They may be 'trained for changing social roles; proper instructions can fashion them into successful participants in new social settings and the etiquette belonging to them'.[21] This conception was developed throughout the sixteenth and seventeenth centuries in the writings of influential continental and English authors: Erasmus's *De civilitate morum puerillium libellus* (1530), Baldassar Castiglione's *The Book of the Courtier* (translated into English by Thomas Hoby, 1561), Giovanni della Casa's *Galateo* (translated into English by Robert Peterson, 1576), or Richard Brathwait's *The English Gentleman* (1630) and *The English Gentlewoman* (1630), to mention only a few. Yet, this assumption had different implications in the case of women. Notably, Anna Bryson observes that advice books for women give less concrete detail about behaviour than do the manuals for men.

> This scarcely implies that women were not required to learn basic good manners, for example at table or in salutation, and it seems plausible that the code of elementary civility formulated in works such as *De Civilitate* in many ways applied equally to boys and girls. Conversely, it does not mean that women were not in some circumstances the special object of courtesy, and in others the subject of special restrictions. The problem is that beyond exhortation to modesty and chaste demur, and warnings against feminine vanity of dress and address, advisers for women focus on domestic or purely ethical themes, and precepts for social behaviour are sparse.[22]

In the early modern period, women were ideologically perceived in relation to their sexuality: the great divide was whether they were chaste or unchaste. Chastity not only concerned a woman's sexual conduct, but was more generally expressed through the whole of her appearance and demeanour, in the way she spoke, moved, dressed, thought, and behaved in public and private, in other words according to a code of bodily signs of modesty. The paradigmatic codification of a woman was as chaste, modest, and silent. Her sphere of activities should be indoors, within the confinement of the household. This model is indicative of the ways in which femininity was ideologically monitored and presented in relation to masculinity. This fairly static presentation was expressed in texts as diverse as medical observations and sermons on marriage. The physiological description of gender differences both coincided with and supported the social organization which increasingly focused around the family.

The emphasis on the family as a pivotal economic, moral and social unity allowed an analogy between the king and the head of the family (husband or father), the individual and society at large. The household was economically and politically conceived as a micro-commonwealth whose order engendered the prosperity and proper functioning of the whole country. These ideas were expressed and consolidated in continental and English treatises addressed to the low gentry and middle classes: Alberti's *Della Famiglia* (1514), Tasso's *The Householders Philosophy* (1588), Fitzherbert's *The Book of Husbandrie* (1562), Tusser's *A Hundrethe Good Points of Husbandry, lately married unto a hundrethe good points of Huswifry* (1571), Gouge's *Of Domesticall Duties* (1622), and Markham's *The English Huswife* (1615) are all instances. In these texts the housewife was increasingly seen as responsible for a range of practical duties concerned with the proper management of the household and the diet and health of its members. Both equal and submissive to her husband, according to the contradiction inherent in the Reformation ideology of marriage, she is described as the helper and counterpart of her husband. Yet within this overall picture there were some social differences. Whilst the courtly lady moved in a more public sphere which required refinement and affability together with modesty and chastity, the housewife was the representative of the moral and social stance of the household. 'Domestic discourse linked physical enclosure and household tasks to the purity of women's bodies and...speech. The good wife was constructed as the woman who stays indoors, guarding her chastity as she guards the other property of her husband'.[23]

The making of the early-modern woman is thus conditioned by the perception of a femininity in need of containment. This is exemplified by two equally significant texts whose influence is still evident in *The Gentlewomans Companion*: Markham's *The English Huswife* (1615) and Brathwait's *The English Gentlewoman* (1632). The former, a household manual, concerns 'the inward and outward vertues which ought to be in a compleat woman'.[24] Moral and religious advice is paralleled in this text by cooking and medical recipes, and instructions on dairy, brewing, baking, and preserving. As Ann Jones has observed:

> Markham's recommendations draw together require-
> ments for wifely obedience, bourgeois thrift, and
> patriotic simplicity. He links one obligation to the next
> according to a logic of foresightful and sober acquisition,
> which ends in adducing the housewife's dress and diet
> as proofs of class and national solidarity.... Markham's
> housewife, then, inherited a set of instructions that
> opposed and rewrote earlier class images that had
> included different ideals of womanliness in Europe. He
> transforms the symbolic splendour and public visibility
> through which the noblewoman shored up and
> extended her husband's influence into the practical
> activity of a frugal and energetic preserver of newly
> earned goods and homespun virtues,[25]

Addressed to the lower nobility, Richard Brathwait's *The English Gentlewoman* (1631, republished in a revised edition together with *The English Gentleman* in 1642) also attempts a definition of femininity by analyzing the attributes of a woman emblematically illustrated in the title-page: 'Apparell, Behaviour, Decency, Complement, Estimation, Fancy, Gentility, and Honour'.[26] All attributes centre on the body and bearing as signs of propriety and class. Hence, though condemning the abuse of foreign fashion and its excesses, Brathwait points to the centrality of external apparel in a woman which must correspond to her status and condition (virgin, wife, widow). Clothing is an indicator of distinction and recognition, as are bodily behaviour and speech. For Brathwait, 'Behaviour being an apt composure of the body in arguments of *Discourse* and *Action*, expresseth every person in so faire a Character, that if his brest were transparent, hee could not displayed fuller'. Markham's discreet countenance and conversation for a woman is here shifted to a more urban and refined context which requires unaffected, yet elegant bodily and mental habits (gestures, gait, conversation):

> A *Person* be the *Booke*, your *Behaviour* is the *Index*. Which will require a large *Comment*, if it expresseth it selfe in ought probably incontinent. Now, for as much as nothing better seemes you, more commendably adornes you, or more absolutely accomodates you, then what is native and unaffected, so it by *Education* seasoned: bee your owne Women; dis-value all apish formality; resort not to be Temple to take a patterne of some new fashion: modest discretion blushest at such servile imitation.[28]

Just as an index is the key for understanding the content of a book, so the demeanour of a person (i.e. a woman) is the key to one's own nature (i.e. chastity). Brathwait's 'woman-book' is culturally defined in the exact convergence of her apparel, behaviour, conversation and sexual countenance. She is the product of education which, in the text, corresponds to the delineation of her social and moral requirements in private as well as in public. As a text, she is also fashioned through readable signs of convenience. Hence the specific significance that demeanour had for women as a manifestation of moral and sexual countenance. Yet in creating an ideal image of femininity drafted on precepts of social behaviour *The Gentlewomans Companion* points to a shift in its presentation.

The author of *The Gentlewomans Companion* deploys the same categories mentioned in Brathwait's treatise but enriched by the pragmatic approach of Markham. Whilst Brathwait reinforces the ideological assumptions of aristocratic gentility, the author of *The Gentlewomans Companion*, like Markham, focuses on the making of a gentlewoman who has to show both the household skills of Markham's housewife and the civility of Brathwait's gentlewoman. This is perhaps due to the need in the restoration period to accommodate the aspirations and ideology of two different groups which, though supportive of the reinstated monarchy, resented its flamboyant excess: for instance preferring more restrained costumes which had to convey a sense both of material prosperity and moral soundness.

The return of the king meant the validation of ideals of kingship and patriarchal authority. This contrasted with the economic empowerment of the middle classes and the greater independence and equality that women had acquired during the republican years. Women from all social ranks had gained a more public role, by petitioning, preaching or as helpers in their husbands' business.[29] Woolley is a good example: she first collaborated with her husband in the running of his schools, then succeeded in her own right in a field which was mainly a male domain. Although Woolley's writing concentrates on the household and on women's role within it, she shows an acute awareness of social change and the difficulties due to political transformations. We may say that Woolley succeeds in transposing this awareness into the idiom of domestic practices. Hence, in *A Supplement to The Queen-like Closet,* instruction in the most appropriate and fashionable dishes matches her advice not to be wasteful and how to prepare a tasty dish with leftovers.

The worlds of mercantile expansion and traditional thrift merge in her writing, and testify to the domestic economy of those classes in which frugality and consumption could coexist. Consumption – 'the active seeking of personal gratification through material goods' – developed in the early modern period, accelerating the acquisition of goods such as foodstuffs, textiles, household objects and books, and the enjoyment of affability, politeness and wit.[30] Good manners and pleasant conversation were also commodities, so that instruction in manners, or advice on how to dress were equally a recipe for civility. *The Gentlewomans Companion* can be set at the dawn of this process, and offers an insight into the negotiation of different tendencies of behaviour.

Conduct books register social and economic change by merging diverse forms of literature previously written for women such as household manuals, books on marriage, advice books for children, treatises on femininity and collections of recipes. This is already evident in Robert Codrington's *The*

Education of a Woman, The Second Part of Youths behaviour, or Decency of Conversation amongst Women (1664), a conduct book written for women as the complement of one published for men in 1646. This is probably the closest parallel to *The Gentlewomans Companion*, both in aim and content. *The Education of a Woman* also offers an ideal image of femininity – this is suggested by the portrait in the frontispiece, on which the one in Woolley's text is presumably based.[31] The book is dedicated to Ellinor Partiger, 'true mirror of her sex', and Elizabeth Washington (both belonged to the middle classes) and fosters education for women as a boost to beauty. The education from the age of seven to sixteen endorsed by the text is a reaffirmation of traditional attributes of femininity adapted from earlier and quite diverse material. The emphasis is still on domesticity, from needle work to the knowledge of spices and the homely practice of medicine. Codrington refers to *The Queens Delight* and *The Compleat Cook*, *The Queens-Closet*, Dr. Burges' *Vade Mecum*, Markham's *The English Huswife*, and May's *The Accomplisht Cook* – all popular texts – as indispensable reference books. Like Markham, he underlines the importance of diet as a manner of living, a notion already developed in the sixteenth century and further deployed as a sign of bourgeois propriety, pointing to sobriety in diet as a natural quality in a gentlewoman:

> Temperance which is a Regular ordering of the Diet, and a certain Moderation in our Meat, and Drink, is a Divine Vertue, and such as brings Strength, and Vigour, both to Mind and Body....
> It will furnish young Gentlewomen, and especially persons who addict themselves to Piety, with such a way and manner of Living, as with more ease, and cheerfulness, and fervency, they may the better apply themselves to Devotion, and to the faithful service of God.

The moral rigour of these lines is equalled in the presentation of etiquette, which the text addresses more in terms of a moral discussion than as a series of precepts. The book, for example, ends with a section on new fashions in clothing which merely considers the legitimacy of clothing and adornment. More innovative is the section dedicated to epistolary examples. This section and the inclusion of monthly bills of fare are prelude to the contents of *The Gentlewomans Companion*.

Codrington's manual covers most of the same categories as Brathwait's. Moral awareness and practical advice merge in the text, fashioning the gentlewoman of the title according to a precise aesthetic. Codrington discusses apparently unrelated topics – which *The Gentlewomans Companion* will also deal with – such as the importance of 'ornament and apparel', or the contested reading of romances, which he recommends to young women as exemplary.[32] Appearances and moral education are both considered part of the same code of social practice which moulds the correct behaviour of a gentlewoman. He also advocates moderate exercise, music, limning and dancing as suitable forms of recreation, but his conventional advice to his readers is not to indulge in the staging of plays or going to the theatre. Finally, he examines the appropriate modes of conversation and deportment in a woman, for which discretion, lack of affectation and modesty are the golden rules:

> ...to enter into discourse with strangers doth argue Lightness and Indiscretion: if I might advise, their Carriage in this Nature should not be too loose, nor too precise. The simpring Countenances, and such kind of Antick Gestures, are more suitable to the Condition of Chamber-maids, than Gentlewomen.
>
> ...yet a Vertuous and Discreet Gentlewoman by her Resort unto publick places, may confer no less Benefit to such as see her behaviour, than she doth profit to her Family over whom she is an Overseer; for many of them in publick places have been observed to express such a well-becoming Garb, that every Action hath deserved her applause and Imitation of all that were in her Company, her Conceits were many, and tempered with lightness, her Jests innocent, and seasonable, without the least Capriciousness, Her Discourse free without niceness, her whole Carriage delightfull, and flowing with a seeming carelessness...[33]

Codrington's gentlewoman offers a new synthesis of courtly refinement and unaffected simplicity, her naturalness the product of her education, a way of fashioning her body and countenance. The homespun attributes and modest decorum are now insufficient to the requirement of a more worldly and refined life-style. Codrington condemns artificial moles, but encourages garments for young women which enhance their beauty, provided these are not above their rank.

The new model of femininity presented in *The Education of a Woman* can also be found in *The Lady's New-years Gift: or Advice to a Daughter* (1688), by George Savil, Marquis of Halifax, and in the increasingly numerous conduct books published towards the end of the century. Although intended for a female readership, the authors are men. In content, *The Gentlewomans Companion* does not differ from them, yet the attribution to Hannah Woolley shifts the emphasis to a more intimate relation between the author and the reader. The discourse meant to shape femininity acquires a feminine voice, even if fictitious, to validate it.

This consideration of *The Gentlewomans Companion* as a conduct book explains its content as well as the way it deals with its material. The text can be divided into two. The first concerns the proper demeanour of a gentlewoman, as a girl then as an adult: gestures, conversation, and all kinds of rules concerning civility, clothing, table manners and conversation, as well as touching on her pastimes, courtship and marriage. The second focuses on domestic activities (cooking, carving, distilling, the preparation of medicaments, instructions to the servants in a household) and examples of how to write letters. Through this range of topics the book attempts to chart all the activities and requirements of a woman. When compared with the earlier tradition of advice books, the first part covers a similar range of topics. It restates conventional ideas about a wife's duty and the excellence of housewifery tasks, thus pointing to a continuity in the cultural expectations concerning womanhood, and the social roles of women. The book, however, differs in taking a new approach by addressing civility from a female point of view and in using a female voice claiming to be the product of a woman author's experience and reading. This raises the problem of authorship discussed above, and the way we read and examine the book itself.

There is a shift between contrasting registers which makes it difficult to identify the author as a well-defined personality. This may partly be the result of the derivative nature of the book: it mimics the tone as well as the examples of the different sources it draws upon. It may also be due to the way in which the author variously identifies with the reader by using the first person plural – 'we', that is 'our sex' – or the second or third person plural – 'you', that is 'ladies' – thus distancing himself or herself from the audience. Class, gender, and experience alter the flow of the writing, creating a disparity between the writer and the addressee. Whilst we are invited to assume that the author is a woman who talks to other women in order to create a more direct and intimate relation with the reader, the text defies this assumption, reinforcing instead an ideal presentation of femininity. The use of the first person – which we are meant to believe is Hannah Woolley – is too contrived to sound true, or at least true to the Hannah Woolley of her other books. Woolley may have inspired *The Gentlewomans Companion*, and she is integral to the text as the embodiment of its aim, yet it is hard to recognize her as the author, the text probably the result of assembling and editing.

In the dedicatory letter, the author advertises the book's uniqueness and usefulness, as a 'Universal Companion and Guide to the Female Sex'. Nothing similar has been written before, it claims, and it is an aid to women in every circumstance, age and condition. Although questionable whether *The Gentlewomans Companion* satisfies this aim, nevertheless the idea of offering such a guide to women is indicative of a need to chart femininity according to social rules in a way which is different from that for men. In the Erasmian tradition of conduct books, *The Gentlewomans Companion* sets guidelines upon familial and social duties, and sketches a narrative of gestures which, by endorsing a relation between appearance and morality, moulds both the body and the mind. As the author of *The School of Good Manners* suggested in 1595, 'the manners are lively represented in the habit of the minde and disposition of man', functioning as signs on which a person is judged and credited.[34] Through the discussion of manners, the early-modern definition of femininity and feminine attributes merges with rules of proprieties similar to those which we can find in conduct books for men as parameters of civility. The notion of civility thus becomes crucial to the presentation of the ideal gentlewoman and her etiquette both as a form of self-definition and mediation of the self to social requirements.

At the outset, the text discusses the daily routine at school and home of a young gentlewoman, and her duties towards her parents and governess. Then, the author turns the attention to a 'Gentlewomans civil Behavior to all sorts of people in all places'. The section begins conventionally by alluding to the most desirable qualities in a woman, 'Discretion, Silence, and Modesty'. It refers to the importance of conversation as fundamental to society, but also to its danger when language creates unsuitable relations or betrays inappropriate feelings or a wrong countenance. The general advice of this section unfolds in two sections on speech and rules of conversation, building a meticulous relationship between words and gestures. The author advises the reader to be neither too talkative, nor too reserved, and suggests a middle way by inviting the gentlewoman to entertain with pleasant conversation, adequate to the circumstance and interlocutor. As words are a sign of civility, so are gestures:

> It is an easie matter to gather a disposition of our heart, by the dimension of our Gait. A light carriage most commonly discovers a loose inclination; as jetting and strutting, shew haughtiness, and self-conceit. Were your bodies transparent, you could not more perspicuously display your levity than by wanton Gesticulations.

In dealing with manners, our author pays particular attention to the way in which the ideal gentlewoman moves in public spaces and in society. The domestic sphere of a woman's activities is here mediated in a variety of social occasions in which the key rule of civility is that 'a certain Modesty or Pudor required in all your actions' should be visible as an inner as well as outward disposition. The eye can be thus equally revealing of a person's inclination:

> [As] the Eye entertains it self not with more Objects than the Invention furnisheth the Tongue with Subjects; and without Speech, no Society can subsist; so by it we express what we are; as Vessels discover themselves best by the sound.

Discretion, moderation and lack of affectation are crucial for a woman's most suitable appearance, gestures and conversation. Through a symmetry of inner inclinations and countenance, the book gradually unfolds a vocabulary of gestures 'to please all companies'. Acts are focused on the relationship between the individual and the other, and on the acceptability of the behaviour itself, in order to be socially agreeable and avoid slander, derision, or affectation – possibly the worst fault of all. This is an art which can be learned, as proved by the training the text wishes to impart:

> Civility, or the gentle plausibility, of which I intend to give you information; is in my slender judgement nothing else but the modesty and handsome decorum, to be observed by every one according to his and her condition, attended with bonne grace, and a neat becoming air.

The 'gentle plausibility' suggests both pleasantness of manner and the applause that such agreeableness deserves. It links the actor and the observer in a shared knowledge and appreciation of decorum.

Instructing good table manners, the author warns the reader:

> Gentlewomen, the first thing you are to observe, is to keep your Body strait in the Chair, and do not lean your Elbows on the Table. Discover not by any ravenous gesture your angry appetite; nor fix your eyes too greedily on the meat before you, as if you would devour more that way than your throat can swallow, or your stomack digest.

The control of appetite is indicative of the more general emphasis on restraint. By juxtaposing a language of decorum to one of excess and animality the text sketches table manners according to rules of precedence, acceptability, and seemliness – 'avoid clapping your fingers in your mouth'. Although techniques of carving are addressed in the sections devoted to food, there are also suggestions as to the best way to serve food in that part which concentrates on manners. A ritual of elegant and precise gestures should bear no sign of effort – fie on a hostess who sweats when carving for a guest! Outward gesture is reinforced by inner knowledge, imbibed from advice on the correct choice of the cuts of meat and the rules of precedence in helping oneself. As to quantity, the author states:

> If you have a stomach, eat not voraciously; nor too sparingly, like an old-fashioned Gentlewoman I have heard of.... Eat not so fast, though very hungry, as by gormandizing you are ready to choak yourself. Close your lips when you eat; talk not when you have meat in your mouth; and do not smack like a Pig, nor make any other noise which shall prove ungrateful to the company.

These are traditional instructions, derived from earlier advice books written for men. As for all other activities, such as walking, looking and dancing, they are indicative of the use of pauses and a just measure of the movements to make the body itself a text that articulates the canons of civility. Old fashions are counterbalanced by new, more socially acceptable behaviour to avoid ridicule; forms of restraint and censorship function as means of politeness, for instance one should clean the spoon each time before helping oneself, in order not to offend 'some squeamish stomacks'. By the same token, one ought not show dislikes or behave with ridiculous affectation such as the gentlewoman who ate peas one by one, cutting each in two as she did so.

Instructions on table manners are typical of the book's ethos. Restraint and lack of affectation are essential, just as discretion and wisdom should be guides in the choice of entertainment. What the author has to say offers an insight into the debate surrounding reading, the theatre, and other artistic pursuits. Music and dancing are central to the upbringing of a gentle-woman, and the author is concerned with the best ways to perform them. When it comes to plays and reading (of ballads or novels), the reader is no longer performer but audience. Plays and ballads are condemned as dangerous. Novels, by contrast, are held to be educational. The emergence of the novel as an influential genre, from the late seventeenth century, will help fashion a new sense of individuality, especially for women.

Vanity, excusable in a court lady, is otherwise condemned as feminine weakness. The common attack on the excess of foreign fashion, or of over-dressing, echoes the analogy between external manners and innermost thoughts: 'the use of Apparel is to dignifie the Wearer'; 'misconceived ornaments are meer deformities to virtuous minds'; 'proportion your Clothes to your shape, condition, and age'. Clothing is a sign; impropriety in dress means moral or psychological 'deformity'. Echoing Markham's distinction of the outward and inward qualities of a perfect housewife, the author of *The Gentlewomans Companion* consistently stresses order and cleanliness as both physical and moral attributes.

As these examples suggest, the text unfolds a mutuality based on the gaze between the reader as the actor and a hypothetical observer. In this relationship, civility is manifest as a shared language of gestures. In 1576, the translator of *Galateo* by Giovanni della Casa already argued the importance of manners and countenance for social acceptance, claiming that the lack of manners renders all the other qualities of a person 'lame', 'wheare this civilitie and courtesie, without other releese or patrimonie, is riche of it self, & hath substance enough, as being a thing that standeth in speache and gestures alone'.[35] With an implicit attention to an urban social setting and its life-style, *The Gentlewomans Companion* rephrases the traditional idea of civility for a female readership.

In *The Gentlewomans Companion*, civility is defined both as 'the framing and adapting our actions to the satisfaction of other People', and as 'a Science for the right understanding of our selves, and true instructing how to dispose all our words and actions in their proper and due places'. The self is fashioned according to social requirements. This has obvious implications, since the book presents us with a conventional ideal of femininity for which a woman is forged in order to fulfill her role as wife, mother and runner of the household, able to conform to the desires of others – whether men or social superiors – through her gestures and attitudes. The (auto)biographical account of Hannah Woolley at the beginning of the book exemplifies this moulding of one's persona by education. Woolley describes the improvement in her manners, her capacity for languages and mastery of appropriate ways of speaking, as well as her general knowledge, from listening to the conversation of her employer, transcribing her letters, reading poetry and fiction, medical handbooks and manuals on letter-writing. Woolley prioritizes imitation and the act of reading in her effort at self-improvement. This may be mimicked by the reader of *The Gentlewomans Companion* as he or she reads and attempts to emulate the advice of the book.

Examples of letter-writing and of polite conversation are found in the closing sections. Like manners and clothing, they are another instance of self-fashioning and 'of the properly sensible and delicate consciousness with which to live in the world'.[36] As Ruth Perry observes, by following the conventions of letter-writing, women 'tailored a self to suit expectations and desires of the audience' and, not unlike conduct books, manuals on the subject provided a means to forge the reader's sensibility and etiquette, 'since their intention was to exhibit an exemplary consciousness for the reader to emulate, their success depended on creating believable ideals'. *The Gentlewomans Companion* extends this aim to all the other spheres of social practice. Through its ideal gentlewoman, the text points to a further example of civility to emulate. Yet, this emulation can also be recognized as one of self-awareness, since the individual shapes his or her identity according to a social model. Etiquette becomes a way of mediating an individual's own desires and broader social expectations, generating a complex relation between culture and the forging of one's individuality.

In the light of this we can read the oft-quoted introduction to *The Gentlewomans Companion*, in which the author stresses the importance of education for women:

> The right Education of the Female Sex, as it is in a manner every-where neglected, so it ought to be generally lamented. Most in this depraved later Age think a Woman learned and wise enough if she can distinguish her Husbands Bed from anothers.... Vain man is apt to think we were meerly intended for the Worlds propagation, and to keep its humane inhabitants sweet and clean; but, by their leaves, had we the same Literature, he would find our brains as fruitful as our bodies. Hence I am induced to believe, we are debarred from the knowledg of humane learning, lest our pregnant Wits should rival the towring conceits of our insulting Lords and Masters.

Pardon the Severity of this expression, since I intend not thereby to infuse bitter Rebellion into the sweet blood of Females; for know, I would have all such as are enter'd into the honourable state of Matrimony, to be loyal and loving Subjects to their lawful (though lording) Husbands. I cannot but complain of, and must condemn the great negligence of Parents, in letting the fertile ground of their Daughters lie fallow, yet send the barren Noddles of their Sons to the University, where they stay for no other purpose than to fill their empty Sconces with idle notions to make a noise in the Country.

Like Robert Codrington's *The Education of a Woman*, the book echoes the early-modern debate on the decline of women's education, rephrasing the progressive assertion of the need for women to be offered a good training within the discrete parameters of the household and an accomplished social life-style. In the same year that *The Gentlewomans Companion* was issued, Bathsua Makin (sister of the mathematician John Pell) published *An Essay to Revive the Ancient Education of Gentlewomen, in Religion, Manners, Arts and Tongues*. One of the most learned women of her time, Makin had been tutor to the daughters of Charles I, and in 1673 she was running a school for girls at Tottenham High Cross.[37] In her essay she advocates the importance of instructing young women in various literary and scientific disciplines together with the more traditional pursuit of music and dance, and practical skills such as cooking and limning. Her syllabus – described in her treatise – is more comprehensive than that endorsed by *The Gentlewomans Companion*, which is still centred mainly on a woman's position within the household.

Makin was influenced by the Dutch scholar Anna Maria van Schurman (1607–1678) – also mentioned in *The Gentlewomans Companion* – who believed in the importance of women's learning as a form of moral perfecting: 'that both her self may be more vertuous and the more happy, and that she may (if that chargebly upon her) instruct and direct her Family, and also be useful, as much as may be to her whole Sex'. Schurman was one of the most renowned female scholars of her time. Although she restricts her arguments in favour of education to upper-class women whose leisure from work presented them with a duty of profitably employing their time, she none the less sees learning as a fundamental, natural need. She recommends the study of languages (especially Greek and Hebrew), history, classical literature, rhetoric, logic and theology, though this should not, in her view, undermine women's traditional tasks.[38]

Compared with Makin's and Schurman's positions, the praise of women's education in *The Gentlewomans' Companion* sounds almost ironic, since it is not mirrored by the rest of the book which is still content to present a traditional image of femininity. Education was central to Woolley's own social and professional advancement, but it is implausible, in my view, to trace the authorship of this introduction to Woolley herself. There is no evidence in Woolley's other work of a wish to debate the nature of womanhood; it is mainly concerned in imparting practical advice and helping women in their domestic tasks. In *The Gentlewomans' Companion*, the biographical account shows the importance of learning and indirectly addresses the issue of women's education. However, while the beginning of the passage quoted above claims the need for education, the rest deals with moral virtue and the need for mothers to be living examples to their daughters. Perhaps the real preoccupation of these paragraphs lies in the loose sexual customs condemned at the outset, rather than in the attempt to offer an educational programme.

The meaning of this praise for women's education becomes clearer from the reference to classical examples of learned women and the apology for the careful raising of children which follows it. As the Roman exemplars testify – the familiar ones of Portia, Cornelia and Sulpitia – learning is an enhancement of morality, piety and chastity. The whole drift of the book, the moral imperative if you will, is to buttress a conventional image of femininity: praise of education only serves to reinforce it. The accomplished gentlewoman is 'like a Star' whose five rays represent the attributes fostered by advice books: 'Devotion, Modesty, Chastity, Discretion and Charity'. Learning is geared to the achievement of civility. If there is a tension between the opening phrases of the *Companion*'s introduction in praise of education and the actual aims and content of the text as a whole, it derives from an unresolved attempt to mediate between the tradition of advice books for women with the new tendencies of the Restoration.

Our author attempts a similar compromise between a romantic notion of marriage (modern) and a woman's duty to obey her husband and win his favour in any circumstances (traditional). Classical examples are again used to support views which offer little variation on a long tradition of writing on the subject. But there are dim reflections of an attempt to reassess the institution of marriage: a pivotal social issue, as some of the literature and drama of the time testifies. Women can choose their spouse, mainly in terms of making a reasonable and profitable choice which negotiates passion and status, yet they are denied independence from their husbands. In conceiving an ideal gentlewoman, the book guides her through her courtship and marriage by pointing to the most appropriate attitudes. No less than other social circumstances, attention focuses on the creation of a ritual of convention and control, far removed from the witty exchanges and marital negotiations of Restoration comedy. In the delineation of an ideal which suited the middle rather than the upper classes, the text is perhaps telling of a gradual adjustment in social practices in which the old and the new converged. The homespun virtues of Markham's housewife still hold true for the ideal portrait of a courteous gentlewoman who ought to be able to move and talk in society yet preserve her modesty and patient tolerance.

As already mentioned, two of the most influential cookery books published in the second half of the seventeenth century – Robert May's *The Accomplisht Cook* (1660) and William Rabisha's *The Whole Body of Cookery Dissected* – were written for professional cooks and reflected the tastes of the aristocracy.[39] Yet, from the 1550s, a succession of cookery books – most of which went through several reprintings and were still popular in the 1670s – had been written for a female readership, usually belonging to the lower gentry and the middle classes. Woolley's earlier books can be traced to this tradition. *The Gentlewomans Companion* has sections on cookery, distillation and preserves and medical receipts. While not, therefore, at odds with Woolley's other known works, these parts of the *Companion* are quite concise and bear little resemblance to the disorderly assembling and practical comments which characterize her other collections.

This may be a further sign of alternative authorship and raises the question why a writer of cookery books would not devote more space to cooking in a book aimed to instruct women. Alternatively, we may ask why the author of a book on manners would include a section on food.

A possible answer lies in the cultural importance of food as part of the ideal of civility sponsored by the book. Cookery books and dietary prescriptions point up food's symbolic value.[40] They sketch a moral and social picture of food habits while dealing with the qualities and proper ordering of food, its preparation and consumption. Regimens of health, in particular, provide medical advice on diet as part of a general life-style regulating a person's bodily activities according to season, age and physiological predisposition. The ideal of temperance sponsored in these treatises was illustrated in a fairly diversified diet which corresponded to the bills of fare contained in early-modern cookery books.

The tradition had its origins in medieval collections of secrets and bills of fare. They were part of a broader range of manuals on husbandry and gardening, herbals or medical handbooks which were meant to divulge techniques and teach skills. They pragmatically instruct how to do something:

> It is a prescription for taking action: *recipe* is the Latin imperative 'take'. Because it prescribes an action, a means for accomplishing some specific ends, the recipe's 'completion' is the trial itself. A recipe is...an experiment, a 'trying out'.[41]

An early example of the genre is the English translation *The Secretes of the Reverende Maister Alexis of Piemont* (1558) which contains recipes for cosmetic powders and medicaments, for distilling, preserving and candying. This text was influential and much copied, a common tendency with any book of this type. Like many before her, Hannah Woolley cared little about originality or repetition.

Whilst books of secrets contain recipes for many sorts of thing, cookery books may be more focussed. Often, they are organized according to diverse manners of cooking (boiling, roasting, baking), with bills of fare suggesting ways to organize meals for various occasions. The instructions given by the recipes illustrate a sequence of actions whose accomplishment can only be discovered in the 'trying out', as William Eamon observes. Quantities do not always appear, nor the time taken in preparation, nor lists of ingredients. In this sense, early-modern recipes are sketched guidelines for an audience familiar with the techniques of cooking. C. Anne Wilson has observed that bills of fare probably functioned as *aides-mémoire* proposing a choice of dishes from which a meal might be composed.[42] This notion may also apply to recipes: they reminded the reader of the right procedure as a sequence of actions.

In 1661, William Rabisha advised that:

> whereas the dishes of meat may seem too big in most, or all Receipts to some; that makes no matter to the teaching of them that have occasion to have them less; it is reminded in taking an equal proportion of each ingredient, according to the quantity as you intend to dress, whether half, or a quarter, or so as the Receipt.[43]

He counselled further to add salt, when omitted from the receipt, and to remove the 'faggot' of herbs before taking the dish to the table. Moreover, 'Let not the Reader think that the Bills of Fare be too big, but consider, if he intends to have fewer dishes, what an advantage he hath to have his choice out of so many'. Rabisha referred to common practice, which he restated in keeping with the clarity proper to his systematic approach, but which he implicitly suggested was superfluous. The early-modern reader of cookery books, familiar with the laborious practice of cooking, could creatively deploy the instructions of cookery books, adapting them to his or her need.

This is significant if we think of cookery books in relation to the broader range of handbooks popular at the time, and in particular of books of manners like *The Gentlewomans Companion*. Instructions for demeanour may function like recipes, as guidelines to be followed and adapted according to occasion and circumstance. The reader engages actively with the text by being reminded of what is acceptable as well as of what ought to be done, and by being asked to perform what he or she has learned. Like recipes, these instructions are secret tips of civility which need to be acquired and performed by the reader who can then make them his or her own secret. Yet, as in the case of conduct books, the writing of cookery books for a female reader-ship has further implications.

I have already suggested that cooking, preserving, candying and preparing medicaments belonged to a female sphere of activity. As Gervase Markham puts it:

> To speak then of outward and active knowledge which belong to our English housewife, I hold the first and most principal to be a perfect skill and knowledge in cookery, together with all secrets belonging to the same, because it is a duty really belonging to a woman; and she that is utterly ignorant therein may not by law of strict justice challenge the freedom of marriage, because indeed she can then but perfume half her vow; for she may love and obey, but she cannot cherish, serve and keep him with that true duty which is ever expected.[44]

As an indispensable attribute to their expected social role, women were supposed to be able to cook, and mothers probably instructed their daughters. Although there was an active seventeenth-century tradition of men collecting recipes out of gastronomic and antiquarian curiosity, for example Sir Kenelm Digby or John Evelyn (as well as Sir Hugh Plat before them), other manuscripts testify to women annotating their recipes and passing them from one generation to the next. In charge of the many activities in a kitchen, women were responsible for the well-being of the household and proper hospitality. Correct preparation and presentation of food reflected the economic and social status of the family, as well as attaining the ideal of civility through actively performed social norms.

In *The Gentlewomans Companion*, if a woman is ignorant in the art of cooking and carving she is 'insignificant'. As in Markham, moral and social values are ascribed to the preparation of food and to the role of women as nurturers. The book offers its readers only recipes 'à la mode', organized alphabetically irrespective of whether sweet or savoury. However, the brevity of the recipe section prevents a full range of dishes being offered or discussed. What is more, the receipts which are included are to a large extent derived from other cookery books, particularly Robert May's *The Accomplisht Cook*.

The collection is completed by monthly bills of fare, each meal being of two courses with between five and seven dishes in each (except January's which is unconsciably long). These menus correspond quite closely to actual meals of the period. That for the month of June consists of a first course of 'Neats-tongue, or Leg of Mutton and Colliflowers'; 'Steak-Pye'; 'Shoulder of Mutton'; 'fore-quarter of Lamb'; and a 'Dish of Pease'. The second course is, 'Sweet-bread-Pye'; 'Capon'; 'Goose-berry-Tart'; 'Strawberries and Cream. Or Strawberries, White-wine, Rosewater and Sugar'. Twenty-five years later, the Bedfordshire gentlewoman Diana Astry records a June dinner of 1703: 'wee had for diner a supe, a ham & chicking, a coople of green geeas, a legg of mutton rosted, peas, 2 coople of rawbits rost, cherry and gosebery tarts, whip sulebubes, a custard pudding the 3 dish'.[45] Markham illustrates the arrangement of such meals in detail: the dishes of each course placed on the table in front of the guests to help themselves, first the salads then, 'Next them all sorts of roast meats, of which the greatest first, as chine beef or sirloin, the gigot or legs of mutton, goose, swan, veal, pig, capon, and such like'. This aspect of dining is not touched upon by *The Gentlewomans Companion*, save by implication in the author's advice on manners at table.

Carving is considered in greater detail. The prescribed way of cutting and serving was a ritual within the ritual of the meal itself. Brief instructions remind the reader of the appropriate gestures required to minimize effort and not to spoil the dish. The choicest cuts were intended for the guests of honour and it was an act of delicacy not to take them unless invited to do so. The carved pieces were put on a plate and care taken, in order to avoid dirtying oneself, by careful use of the napkin.

Order and hygiene are the main signs of propriety at table as well as in the kitchen, but economy also entered the equation. The instructions to a cook-maid warn: 'And as you must know how to dress Meat well, so you must know how to save what is left of that you have dressed, of which you may make both handsome and toothsome Dishes again, to the saving of your Masters purse, and the credit of his Table. Be as saving as you can, and cleanly about everything.' This advice to be frugal is rare in the book, but recurs when encouraging a gentlewoman to prepare her own banquet-stuff, since it is cheaper and more delicious. Woolley does refer to economy (with reference to this self-same banquet course) in other places. In *The Queen-like Closet* she advises the reader to put any sweetmeats left over into a box to preserve them. Thrift agrees with the overall emphasis on moderation, the proper measure of civility. Equally, thrift suggests an attempt to negotiate the increasing social value ascribed to consumption with an ability to produce material goods without indulging in waste. Rather than being a denial of luxury, frugality here suggests a striving for fashionable patterns of consumption:

> Now because you will have frequent occasions for Banquets, in the entertaining of persons of Quality, I think it not unfit for a Gentlewoman to learn the art of Preserving and Candying, of which I shall, according to the Profession I make thereof, give you an ample account or instruction in some Chapters following. Frugality will perswade you to learn these excellent Arts, for in constant use of the product thereof, you will save much for Sweetmeats, you will make much cheaper than you can buy them, and more commendable.

As in conduct books, tradition and innovation merge in a social practice in which food functions as a symbol of affluence, etiquette, and moral propriety. One of most significant innovations in Renaissance eating was the introduction of the banquet, a course of sweetmeats served separately in the banquet-room or house at the end of a meal. It had been initiated with the introduction of continental delicacies to the 'subtilties', spiced confections and sweetened wines which traditionally ended medieval feasts. Recipes for the banquet were conceived as 'secrets', precious conceits or rare curiosities for the preparation of exotic and titillating dainties. Originally, they were not clearly distinguished from receipts for remedies, cordials, or pills. Sweet confections were intended to help digestion and purify the breath, since both sugar and spices had important medical properties. By the sixteenth century, sugar was more easily available, though still expensive and affordable only by a minority.[46] Like spices and citrus fruits, other ingredients essential to the banquet, sugar began to be seen as a commodity denoting the diet and culinary habits of the English upper classes.[47]

Sugar, though still considered a medicament, was increasingly used for confectionery and preserving. The merging of its medical properties with the preparation of sophisticated sweet-meats created a kind of foodstuff which was pleasurable as well as healthful. It could, therefore, function as a complex sign of social and physical wholesomeness (even if there were some who questioned the benefits to health of too great an ingestion of the stuff). Courtly appreciation of the classical world is mirrored by elaborate sculptures of animals or buildings made of marzipan in imitation of those previously consumed in medieval feasts which had helped to validate the aristocracy's power through a display which carried a concrete economic as well as symbolic meaning.[48] Because of the rarity and supposed wholesomeness of their ingredients, sweetmeats rendered the banquet course a precious key to status. Yet, as William Hart suggests, they were also considered an indulgence, the sophisticated and sensual filling of an idle and effeminate society.[49] Effeminacy and gluttony are both forms of excess or transgression which threaten to generate ambiguity. This adds complexity to the meaning of sweetmeats as a social signifier contrasting the allusion to decorum to one of disorder, sensuality and intemperance.

This ambivalence is evident in contemporary cookery books or compilations of secrets which intimate in their titles the opening of a 'lady's closet' and present the preparation of banquet-stuffs as a 'gentlewoman's delight' and 'daily exercise'. Sir Hugh Plat's *Delightes for Ladies* (1609), for example, offers a rich collection of recipes for confectionery such as a 'sugar paste' for casting 'Rabbets, Pigeons, or any other little birde or beast, either from the life or carved molds'.[50] Pleasure and practice are united in a class-defined performance of rank in which the economic capacity to acquire is translated into essential skills of preserving and candying. At the same time, the refinement of the banquet course can also suggest seduction, indulgence, and femininity. Cookery books describe it as necessary to the proper accomplishment of a housewife, often directly identifying the recipes with a lady or gentlewoman, as later collections testify.[51] In terms of food and cookery, the banquet course is probably the best example of the early-modern ideal of civility since it is both the result and performance of accomplishment. Beyond the ceremonious display enacted by the banquet course, a space of free individual interaction is granted, thus allowing the recipe to become again a feminine secret.[52] To discover and reveal this secret collection of recipes lures the reader into taking part in the opening of a lady's cabinet or closet, which contains her recipes like precious jewels or, as the author of *The Gentlewomans Companion* describes them, 'These are Curiosities which are not only laudible, but requisite and necessary in young Ladies and Gentlewomen'.

The Gentlewomans Companion only offers a few recipes for sweetmeats or preserves, without any detail on how to present a banquet course. In these, the language is factual and precise and lacks the visual vividness met in works more certainly from the pen of Woolley herself. In *The Queen-like Closet* she enters into much greater detail. For example, to a guest in the afternoon – 'if no greater, or so great as the Person who entertains them' – she recommends:

> one or two Dishes of Cream only, and a whipt Sillibub, or other, with about four Dishes of Sweet-meats served in, in like manner as at Dinner, with dishes of Fruit, and some kind of Wine of you own making; at Evenings, especially on Fasting Days at Night, it is fit to present some pretty kind of Creams, contrary from those at Dinner, or instead of them some Possets, or other fine spoon Meats, which may be pleasant to the taste, with some dry Sweetmeats, and some of your fine Drinks, what may be most pleasing.

She goes on to describe how, after a meal, a variety of creams, fruits – fresh and dry, or candied in winter – sweetmeats and jellies can be served. Vine leaves and flowers may be used to embellish the dishes and fruits and sweetmeats arranged according to their colours. The plates for the banquet course, preferably silver or china, should be placed on a painted tray made of light wood. The ritual of the banquet comes alive here in the attention to detail.

If the ability to cook is indispensable to a woman, medical skills are equally essential to prove her 'usefulness'. Through the practice of medicine, a woman was valuable to both household and the community at large, fulfilling her charitable duty to the poor. Early-modern women's journals testify to their commitment in curing wounds, setting bones, or providing remedies for the most diverse ailments. In A.L. Wyman's words:

> The lady of the manor might be the unofficial doctor of the village. The example was followed by the wives of wealthy burgers and others of lower degree. At the other end of the social scale, 'wise women' used such empirical knowledge as they had to help those around them, but for the 'professionals' as we might term them, we must look at the wives and daughters of the tradesmen and craftsmen.[42]

Hannah Woolley may have been one of these 'professionals'. This is certainly how she presents herself in *A Supplement to The Queen-like Closet*. A tension exists, however, between women's expected medical skills and their practice, which was increasingly subject to the resistance of physicians, surgeons and apothecaries. The dual tradition of medical treatment, either male or female, is represented by the authorities cited in our *Companion*: Culpeper, Gerard, Parkinson and Riolanus among the men; *A Choice Manual of Rare and Select Secrets in Physick and Chirurgery* (1653), or *The Queens Closet Opened* (1655) standing on the distaff side (even if interpreted by male pens). Woolley's own *Queen-like Closet*, also containing medical remedies, is a robust example of the female tradition.

These recipes reflect humoral medicine and traditional, popular forms of remedies. We may doubt the effectiveness of goose and chicken dung for the treatment of cancer or gunpowder wounds, but it would be dangerous to dismiss completely their significance. The demarcating line between official and unofficial medicine cannot always be easily drawn, treatment with herbs constituted an important aspect of the medical practice of the time. Knowledge of the properties of herbs belongs to an ancient tradition which survives in today's alternative medicine.

In the early-modern kitchen, the distillation of waters and making cordials and other remedies merged with the preparation of banqueting-stuff and daily cooking. A single ingredient could be used for a cordial, flavouring a dish or making a jelly. In *The Gentlewomans Companion*, the medical recipes are prefaced by a description of the properties of some of the most common spices and herbs, honey and sugar (condemned as the most prevalent cause of consumption). The kitchen can be seen as a space devoted to all those activities concerning the wholesomeness of a household, in physical as much as social terms. Recipes seem to echo the bustle of the kitchen, where nothing was wasted but transformed, preserved and recycled.

Quite unusual in *The Gentlewomans Companion* is a long contemplation on the necessity of hygiene and the importance of changing a patient's bed linen, whereas the common prejudice was that this may be dangerous, risking a chill. Similarly, the author advises keeping the teeth clean to prevent stinking breath and gives the recipe for a dentifrice. This preoccupation with cleanliness is recurrent. It is symptomatic of a general awareness of order as a bodily, social and moral sign of propriety and well-being: yet more versions of its central ideal of civility.

Janet Todd, referring to the number of topics dealt with by the *Companion*, observes that 'the incongruous effect of this list on a modern reader comes in part from its apparent heterogeneity. But perhaps it is also the result of our unfamiliarity with past advice books intended to advance women's economic capability rather than what might be called their traditional femininity.' As I have attempted to suggest, it is through this seeming miscellany that the text offers us a picture of early-modern femininity.

As a work which eludes straightforward attribution, the text is itself an 'artefact' (created when the bookseller chose to link it to the name of Hannah Woolley) which aims to create a 'social artefact': the ideal gentlewoman of the title. Beyond the derivative nature of the writing and the impossibility to ascribe it to a consistent feminine voice, it coherently illustrates an ideal of civility. As a mode of self-improvement, civility becomes a way of defining the individual, and in particular women, in relation to society in order to fulfil that society's requirements.

The instructions on conduct and manners bear an underlying similarity to the receipts for cookery, preserving and medicine in that they all describe sequences of actions which can be performed according to specific conditions and circumstances. Although the moral and didactic tone may differ from the way we write today, the book is not a too dissimilar in intent from current magazines which still deal with issues such as fashion, social relations, cooking, and health by giving the reader useful tips. The value of *The Gentlewomans Companion* thus consists in sketching a cultural model of femininity. The text does not question the meaning of being a woman, but discusses what a woman ought to be in relation to the external world.

In this picture of courtesy and social relations, domestic skills are presented as essential. Accomplishment and utility are the two hinges on which womanhood is constructed. The (auto)biographical account of Woolley confirms and exemplifies this portrait. She is the embodiment of the qualities the manual professes. Through reading books and her own experience, she has achieved the intention of *The Gentlewomans Companion*. In her example the reader can recognize herself by the same act of reading. Reading thus becomes a performative act, a mode of being and acting. Whether understood in terms of cooking recipes or instruction in manners, *The Gentlewomans Companion* educates the reader to act in certain ways, in order to be or to become a 'gentle-woman', as the perfect embodiment of femininity for a developing bourgeois society which praises accomplishment and self-achievement as forms of social acceptability, national prosperity, and individual self-definition.

Caterina Albano
London, 2001

NOTES TO THE INTRODUCTION

[1] Elaine Hobby, *Virtue of Necessity: English Women's Writing 1646–1688* (London: Virago Press, 1988), 181–2. HW's career is discussed in this book at pp. 166-76, as well as in Elaine Hobby, 'A Woman's Best Setting out is Silence: The Writings of Hannah Wolley', in Gerald Maclean, ed., *Culture and Society in the Stuart Restoration: Literature, Drama, History* (Cambridge: Cambridge University Press, 1995), 179–200. I am most grateful to Ms Hobby for her comments, and for the information about Hannah Woolley contained in these works. For another resumé of Woolley's life, see Matthew Hamlyn, *The Recipes of Hannah Woolley* (London: Heinemann Kingswood, 1988).

[2] Hannah Woolley, *The Cooks Guide or Rare Recipes for Cookery* (London: 1664). In her dedication Woolley deferentially manifests her gratitude to Lady Wroth. The tone of the letter is conventional, yet, in further addressing Anne Wroth's daughter, Mary, a note of affectionate familiarity comes across in her words 'your practice will be my content, and I doubt not your own....this book I hope will afford you something; and whatever else you know in me to serve you, be pleased freely to command; I shall always be ready to express my self' (dedicatory epistle).

[3] Robert May, *The Accomplisht Cook* (London: 1660; see the Prospect Books facsimile of the 1685 edition, Totnes 2000).

[4] Gerald Maclean, 'Literature, Culture, and Society in Restoration England', in Gerald Maclean, ed., *Culture and Society in the Stuart Restoration*, 3–27, 18.

[5] Felicity A. Nussbaum, *The Autobiographical Subject: Gender and Ideology in Eighteenth Century England* (Baltimore and London: Johns Hopkins University Press, 1989), 53. See also Anthony Fletcher, *Gender, Sex and Subordination in England 1500–1800* (New Haven and London: Yale University Press, 1995), 378–84.

[6] William Rabisha, *The Whole Book of Cookery Dissected* (London: 1661; see also the facsimile edition, Prospect Books, Totnes, forthcoming).

[7] *The Queen-like Closet*, p. 341.

[8] In the title-page of *The Ladies Directory*, Woolley advertises herself as having cooked for the late king Charles I. Already in this first book, the pretence of a link with the aristocracy is ambiguously deployed both as a selling pitch and an indirect allusion to political sympathies.

[9] François de La Varenne, *The French Cook*, translated by I. D. (London: 1653). La Varenne's book is not exclusively intended for a professional readership and contains a broad range of recipes.

[10] *A Supplement to The Queen-like Closet*, pp. 10–11.

[11] See Lucinda McCray Breier, *Sufferers & Healers: The Experience of Illness in Seventeenth Century England* (London and New York: Routledge and Kegan Paul, 1987), 211–47; Doreen G. Nagy, *Popular Medicine in Seventeenth Century England* (Bowling Green: Bowling Green State University Popular Press, 1988), 54–70.

[12] The author of *The Gentlewomans Companion* mentions both these texts as sources.

[13] Maclean, op. cit., p. 12.

[14] There are no surviving records of this book.

[15] *A Supplement*, pp. 132–3.

[16] Gilly Lehmann, *The British Housewife*, Prospect Books, Totnes, forthcoming.

[17] In the fifteenth and early sixteenth century, general advice on educating girls, considerations on how to behave as a wife or as a servant may appear in practical manuals addressed to women. See Suzanne Hull, *Chaste, Silent and Obedient: English Books for Women 1475–1640* (San Marino, Calif., Huntington Library, 1982), 31.

[18] Maclean, op. cit., p. 10.

[19] Below, p. 88.

[20] Below, p. 56.

[21] Ann Rosalind Jones, 'Nets and Bridles: Early Modern Conduct Books and Sixteenth Century Women's Lyrics' in Nancy Armstrong and Leonard Tennenhouse, eds., *The Ideology of Conduct: Essays on Literature and the History of Sexuality* (New York and London: Methuen, 1987), 41.

[22] Anna Bryson, *From Courtesy to Civility: Changing Codes of Conduct in Early Modern England* (Oxford: Clarendon Press, 1998), 39.

[23] Jones, op. cit., p. 52. The Puritan writers John Dod and Robert Cleaver offer the following exemplary guidelines for the proper government of a household: 'Husband: Get goods; Travel, seek a living; Get money and provisions; Deal with many men; Be "entertaining"; Be skillful in talk; Be a giver; Apparel yourself as you may; Dispatch all things out of doors. Wife: Gather them [goods] together and save them; Keep the house; Do not vainly spend it [money]; Talk with few; Be solitary and withdrawn; Boast of silence; Be a saver; Apparel yourself as it becomes you; Oversee and give order within'. John Dod and Robert Cleaver, *A Godly Forme of Householde Government* (London: 1614).

[24] Gervase Markham, *The English Huswife* (1615), title-page.

[25] Jones, op. cit., p. 63.

[26] Richard Brathwait, *The English Gentlewoman* (London: second edition 1632, third and compiled edition 1642) the corresponding attributes for a men are youth, disposition, education, vocation, recreation, acquaintance, moderation, perfection. The discrepancy in emphasis in the two lists is evident. Men's attributes regard more capacities and dispositions than physical and moral propriety as for women.

[27] Brathwait, op. cit., p. 285.

[28] Brathwait, op. cit., p. 301.

[29] Janet Todd, *The Sign of Angelica: Women, Writing and Fiction, 1660–1800* (London: Virago, 1989), 14–20. Towards the end of the seventeenth century women's economic position changed due to a shift from a fundamentally household-based economy to a more capitalistic system which removed from the household activities such brewing and millinery, originally a feminine domain.

[30] Joyce Appleby, 'Consumption in early modern social thought' in John Brewer and Roy Porter, eds., *Consumption and the World of Goods* (London and New York: Routledge, 1993), 162–73.

[31] The two images are almost identical in the expression of the face. The wilder hair and larger décolleté of the figure in *The Gentlewomans Companion* are indicative of a shift in fashion as well as of a more open licentiousness.

[32] Codrington does not condemn the reading of romances as either a cause of corruption or unsuitable for a young woman.

[33] Codrington, 33, 38, sig. d1r, d3v.

[34] Anonymous, *The Schoole of Good Manners, or A new Schoole of Vertue*, translated from the French by W. Frison (London: 1595), sig. A4.

[35] *Galateo of Maister John della Casa, A Treatise of manners and behauiours, it behoueth*

a man to use and eschewe, in his familiar conuersation, translated by Robert Peterson (London: 1576), 4.

[36] Ruth Perry, *Women, Letters, and the Novel* (New York: New York AMS Press), 88.

[37] The syllabus of the school included the learning of languages (Latin and French, to which may be added Greek, Hebrew, Italian, and Spanish), science and an introduction to anatomy, geography, history and arithmetic, dancing, music, singing, writing and the keeping of accounts and the teaching of domestic skills (i.e. limning, preserving, cooking and baking), Bathsua Makin, *An Essay to Revive the Ancient Education of Gentlewomen, in Religion, Manners, Arts and Tongues* (1673), 42–43.

[38] See Caroline van Eck, 'The First Dutch Feminist Tract? Anna Maria van Schurman's discussion of women's aptitude for the study of arts and sciences', in Mirjam de Baar, Macheteld Loewensteyn, Marit Monteiro and A. Agnes Sneller, eds., *Choosing the Better Part: Anna Maria van Schurman (1607–1678)* (Dordrecht, Boston and London: Kluwer Academic Publishers, 1996), 43–53.

[39] Both these books were indebted to La Varenne's *The French Cook* (English translation, 1653). Also highly influential was *The Closet of Sir Kenelme Digby Opened* (1669, Prospect Books edition, Totnes, 1999) which contains both medical and cookery recipes.

[40] The importance that food had in the life of early modern men and women can also be gathered in the inventories of household objects in which cooking equipment and tablewares feature conspicuously. See Lorna Weatherill, 'The meaning of consumer behaviour in late seventeenth- and early eighteenth-century England', in *Consumption and the World of Goods*, op. cit., 206–27, 211–17.

[41] William Eamon, *Science and the Secrets of Nature: Books of Secrets in Medieval and Early Modern Culture* (Princeton: Princeton University Press, 1994), 131.

[42] C. Anne Wilson, 'Ideal Meals and their Menus from the Middle Ages to the Georgian Era', in C. Anne Wilson, ed., *The Appetite and the Eye: Visual Aspects of Food and its Preparation within their Historical Context* (Edinburgh: Edinburgh university Press, 1991), 92–122.

[43] William Rabisha, *The Whole Body of Cookery Dissected* (1661), 'To the Reader'.

[44] Markham, op. cit., p. 49.

[45] Bette Stitt, ed., 'Diana Astry's Recipe Book c. 1700', *Bedfordshire Historical Record Society*, vol. XXXVII, 1957, 166.

[46] Lynette Hunter, 'Sweet Secrets', in C. Anne Wilson ed., *'Banquetting Stuffe'* (Edinburgh: Edinburgh University Press, 1991), 36–37.

[47] See Sidney Mintz, *Sweetness and Power: The Place of Sugar in Modern History* (New York: Viking Penguin, 1985), 74–150. In describing the luxurious abundance of food at the table of the gentry and merchants on the occasion of a feast, William Harrison refers to the spectacular display of banquet-stuffs: 'In such cases also geliffes [jellies] of all colours, mixed with a variety in the representation of sundry flowers, herbs, trees, forms of beasts, fish, fowls, and fruits, and thereunto marchpane wrought with no small curiosity, tarts of divers hues and sundry denominations, conserves of old fruits, foreign and homebred, suckets, codiniacs, marmalades, marchpane, sugarbread, gingerbread, florentines, wild fowl, venison of all sorts, and sundry outlandish [foreign] confections, altogether seasoned with sugar..., do generally bear the sway, besides infinite devices of our own not possible for me to remember'. Harrison, *Description of England*, quoted by Mintz, p. 129.

[48] Mintz, *Sweetness and Power*, op. cit., 86–92.

[49] William Hart, *KLINIK* , *or the diet of the diseased* (London, 1633), chap. XXII, 96–97.

[50] Hugh Plat, *Delightes for Ladies* (London: 1602). The 1609 edition was edited by G.E. & K.R. Fussell, London 1948, the reference is on p.23.

[51] *The Ladies Companion* (London: 1652), brings together recipes of several ladies and gentlewomen; John Shirley, *The Accomplished Ladies Rich Closet of Rarities* (London: 1687); *The Queen's Closet Opened* (London: 1655); Kenelm Digby, *The Closet of Kenelm Digby* (London: 1669).

[52] Kim F. Hall, 'Culinary Spaces, Colonial Spaces: The Gendering of Sugar in the Seventeenth Century', in Valerie Traub, Lindsay Kaplan, Dympna Callaghan, eds., *Feminist Readings of Early Modern Culture* (Cambridge: Cambridge University Press, 1996), 168–190, 176.

[53] A.L. Wyman, 'The Surgeoness: The Female Practioner of Surgery, 1400–1800', *Medical History* 28 (1984), 22–41, 23.

The frontispiece to the 1675 edition (the title page is opposite). Due to the condition of the original (courtesy of the British Library), the image has been cropped of its border as well as of the signature of the engraver, W. Faithorne.

THE
Gentlewomans Companion;
OR, A
GUIDE
TO THE
Female Sex:

CONTAINING

Directions of Behaviour, in all Places, Companies, Relations, and Conditions, from their Childhood down to Old Age :

VIZ. As,

Children to Parents.	Huswifes to the House.
Scholars to Governours.	Mistresses to Servants.
Single to Servants.	Mothers to Children.
Virgins to Suitors.	Widows to the World.
Married to Husbands.	Prudent to all.

With LETTERS & DISCOURSES

upon all Occasions.

Whereunto is added, *A Guide for Cook-maids, Dairy-maids, Chamber-maids*, and all others that go to Service. *The whole being an exact Rule for the Female Sex in General.*

By *HANNAH WOOLLEY*

LONDON, Printed by *A. Maxwell* for *Edward Thomas*, at the *Adam* and *Eve* in *Little-Brittain*, 1675.

(53)

To *all Young Ladies, Gentlewomen, and all Maidens whatever.*

I have formerly sent forth amongst you two little Books; the first called, *The Ladies Directory*; the other, *The Cooks Guide* Both which have found very good Acceptance. It is near Seven years since I began to write this Book, at the desire of the Bookseller, and earnest intreaties of very many worthy Friends; unto whom I owe more than I can do for them. And when I considered the great need of such a Book as might be a *Universal Companion* and *Guide* to the Female Sex, in all *Relations, Companies, Conditions*, and *states* of Life even from *Child-hood* down to *Old-age*; and from the Lady at the *Court*, to the Cook-maid in the *Country*: I was at length prevailed upon to do it, and the rather because I knew not of any Book in any Language that hath done the like. Indeed many excellent Authors there be who have wrote excellent well of some particular Subjects herein treated of. But as there is not one of them hath written upon all of them; so there are some things treated of in this Book, that I have not met with in any Language, but are the Product of my Thirty years Observations and Experience.

I will not deny but I have made some use of that Excellent Book, *The Queens Closet*; *May's Cookery*; *The Ladies Companion*; my own *Directory* and *Guide*; Also, the second part of *Youth's Behaviour*, and what other Books I thought pertinent and proper to make up a Compleat Book, that might have an Universal Usefulness; and to that end I did not only make use of them, but also of all others, especially those that have been lately writ in the *French* and *Italian* Languages. For as the things treated of are many and various, so were my Helps.

I hope the Reader will not think it much, that as the famous Limner when he drew the Picture of an Exact Beauty, made use of an Eye from one, of a Mouth from another; and so cull'd what was rare in all others, that he might present them all in one entire piece of workmanship and Frame: So I, when I was to write of Physick and Chirurgery, have consulted all Books I could meet with in that kind, to compleat my own Experiences.

If any shall wonder why I have been so large upon it, I must tell them, I look upon the end of Life to be Usefulness; nor know I wherein our Sex can be more useful in their Generation than having a competent skill in Physick and Chirurgery, a competent Estate to distribute it, and a Heart will thereunto.

The like Apology I have for my Prolixity about Cookery and Carving, which being essential to a true Housewife, I thought it best to dwell most upon that which they cannot dwell without, unless they design to render themselves insignificant, not only in the world, but in those Families where they are.

As for what concerns *Gentlewomans Behaviour*, I have the concurrent advice and directions of the most able Professors and Teachers, both here and beyond the Seas; yet durst not be so airy and light in my Treatise about Ladies Love and Courtship as some of the *French* Authors have been, but have taken out of them what I found most taking with our *English* Gentry. The like I may say for Habits and Gesture; I am not ignorant of the vanity of some Mens stiles upon these Subjects; and that young Ladies are too apt to take what may gratifie their Fancies, and leave what may better their Judgments about true Behaviour.

I know I may be censured by many for undertaking this great Design, in presenting to all of our Sex a compleat Directory, and that which contains several Sciences: deeming it a Work for a *Solomon*, who could give an account from the Cedar to the Hysop. I have therefore in my Apology to the Bookseller, declared how I came to be of Ability to do it, reciting to him the grounds of my knowledg in all those Sciences I profess; and also what practice and experience I have had in the World, lest any should think I speak more than I am able to perform. I doubt not but judicious persons will esteem this Essay of mine, when they have read the Book, and weighed it well; and if so, I shall the less trouble my self what the ignorant do or say.

I have now done my Task, & shall leave it to your candid Judgments and Improvement; your *A*cceptation will much encourage

Your

Most humble Servant,

London, Nov.
   10. 1672.

Hannah Woolly.

THE
T A B L E

A Table

A Table

A Table

A Table

THE

Introduction.

The right Education of the Female Sex, as it is in a manner everywhere neglected, so it ought to be generally lamented. Most in this depraved later Age think a Woman learned and wise enough if she can distinguish her Husbands Bed from anothers. Centainly Mans Soul cannot boast of a more sublime Original than ours; they had equally their efflux from the same eternal Immensity, and therefore capable of the same improvement by good Education. Vain man is apt to think we were meerly intended for the Worlds propagation, and to keep its humane inhabitants sweet and clean; but, by their leaves, had we the same Literature, he would find our brains as fruitful as our bodies. Hence I am induced to believe, we are debarred from the knowledg of humane learning, lest our pregnant Wits should rival th[e] towring conceits of our insulting Lords and Masters.

Pardon the Severity of this expression, since I intend not thereby to infuse bitter Rebellion into the sweet blood of Females; for know, I would have all such as are enter'd into the honourable state of Matrimony to be loyal and loving Subjects to their lawful (though lording) Husbands. I cannot but complain of, and must condemn the great negligence of Parents, in letting the fertile ground of their Daughters lie fallow, yet send the barren Noddles of their Sons to the University where they stay for no other purpose than to fill their empty Sconces with idle notions to make a noise in the Country.

Pagans of old may teach our Christian Parents a new lesson. *Edesia*, an infidel, taught her Daughters Learning and Morality. *Cornelia*, hers (with the *Greek* Tongue) piety. *Portia*, hers (with the learning of the *Egyptians*) the exemplary grounds of Chastity. *Sulpitia*, hers (with the knowledg of several Languages) the precepts of conjugal Unity. These, though *Ethnicks*, were excellent informers of youth; so that their Children were more bound to them for their breeding than bearing, nurturing than nursing. Emulation of goodness is most commendable; and though you cannot hang up the pictures of these worthy persons, so that their memories may live with you; however, imitate their Virtues, that their memories may live fresher in you. All memorials, being materials, be they never so durable, are subject to frailty; only the precious monuments of Virtue survive time, and breath eternity.

Thus as ye take good example from others, be ye Mother-patterns of Virtue to your Daughters: Let your living actions be lines of their direction. While they are under your command, the error is yours not theirs, if they go astray. Their honour should be one of the chiefest things you are to tender, neither can it be blemish'd without some soil to your own credit.

I have known some inconsiderate Mothers, and those none of the lowest rank and quality, who either out of the confidence of their Daughters good carriage, or drawn with the hopes of some rich Suitors to advance their Marriage, have usually given too free way to opportunity, which brought upon their Daughters name a spreading infamy. Suffer not then those who partake of your image, to lose their best beauty. Look then to your own actions, these must inform them; look to your own examples, these must confirm them: Without you, they cannot perish; with you they may. What will you do with the rest that is left, when you see a part of your self lost.

There is no instruction more moving, than the example of your living. By that line of yours they are to conform their own. Take heed then lest the damp of your own life extinguish the light of your Childrens. As you are a kind Mother to them be a careful Monitor about them; and if your business will permit, teach them your self, with their letters, good manners. For there is an in-bred, filial fear in Children to their Parents, which will beget in them more attention in hearing, and retention in holding what they hear. But if it be inconsistent with your conveniency, and that you must commit the Tutelage and Education of your Children to a Governess, give me leave to inform you what she ought to be.

The duty and qualification of a Governess to Gentlemens Children.

THey who undertake the difficult Employ of being an Instructress or Governess of Children, should be persons of no mean birth and breeding, civil in deportment, and of an extraordinary winning and pleasing conversation. They should not be harsh in expression, nor severe in correcting such as are under their charge; but instruct them with all mildness, cheerfully incouraging them in what they are injoin'd to perform; not suddenly striking, nor startling them with a loud rebuke, which causeth in some an aversness to what they should love, imbittering all the former delight they had in learning. Whereas if you wooe them with soft words, you will soon find them won by the testimony of their good works.

There is so much servility in rigor and restraint, that of consequence there can be no greater enemy to Ingenuity and good nature. Fools are to be always bauld upon, and blows are fitter for beasts than rational creatures; wherefore there can nothing more engage an ingenious generous soul, than cheerfulness and liberty; not over-frightned. I have often observed the many ill consequences which attends an unadvised severity. A Gentlewoman of my acquaintance, who was well-born and bred, and every way accomplisht for a Tutoress to young Ladies, lost all her employment in that fa[c]ulty, by her irresistible passion. Another in *Dorsetshire* being somewhat aged, and suspecting her strength was not able to grapple with active youth call'd up her maid to her assistance, with whose help she so cruelly chastised a young Gentlewoman for some fault she had committed, that with grief and shame she died in a little time after. Many more instances I could insert, but I shall forbear to publish further the shame of such inconsiderate rashness.

As I must condemn the insolent severity of such a Governess, so I must not let pass without reproof the tyranny of some

Mothers, whose presence makes their Children tremble, without the commission of a fault; by which means they many times with their imperiousness frighten their love into an abhorrency of their sight; to be sure they make them tell many a lye to excuse their negligence, (which otherwise they would not do) only that for that time they might escape the rigor of their punishment. Yet I would not have any mistake me in my perswading young Gentlewomen to be used mildly, and tenderly, that I intend thereby their over-indulgence, so as to let their tender age rust in sloth and vanity; all that I would have a Mother do, is, that she would be moderate in the correction of an offence, lest by correcting one she commit another, and so transgress that positive command in holy Writ, *Parents provoke not your children to wrath.*

A Governess is to study diligently the nature, disposition, and inclination of those she is to teach; and so by suiting their humours, make their study the more facile, by how much it is more pleasant to them, praising such and such of their own age, that are thus and thus qualified, which will breed in them an emulation to tread in their footsteps. If she finds any addicted to reading, let her ask the question, What she thinks of such a Book she hath read? by the answer she may easily conjecture at the strength of her Intellect: If she find her a lover of conversation, it will not be amiss to ask what she thinks of such a Gentlewoman or Gentleman whose Virtues she hath a great esteem for; when she hath return'd an answer to the demand, let the Governess require a reason for her so saying; which in the approving or condemning will not only make the Scholar cautious of what she delivers, but give a great insight both into her disposition and understanding.

Whatever she doth, let her have a special care in obstructing the growth of evil manners, and ingraft the good, stifle in the very birth those corruptions which will grow in the purest natures without an indefatigable circumspection.

Countenance not an untruth by any means, especially if they stand in it; this is a very great Vice, and argues an inclination impudently vicious: There is a fault contrary to this, and shall be reckoned in the number of infirmities, when by an over-modesty, and too much bashfulness, a young Maid cannot hold up her head when spoken to; and if askt a question, would blush, as if by some gross miscarriage she had lately contracted a guilt. This sudden alteration of the countenance may breed an underserv'd suspition, and therefore it ought to be corrected discreetly with good instruction. Favour not obstinacy by any means, for flattery in this case will spoil the Gentlewoman.

Be the incessant tormentor of her sloth, lest by proving burdensome to others, she at length becomes so to her self, by which means her understanding starves, and her body contracts an Hospital of Diseases. This you may remedy by suffering her not to sleep over long, lest the spirits be over-dull'd, as well as by too little rest.

If the season be dry, walk them in the fields; if not, some moderate exercise within doors, which will be instrumental in keeping them from the knowledg of the Physician. And now since Nature only gives us a being; and Education, a well-being; the Parent or Governess ought to have a special care how she seasons youth with what is most conducible to the orderly and prudent management of the concerns of this life; let such a Foundation be therefore laid which may sufficiently promise the Parents a happy issue, when their Children shall arrive to maturity of age.

Letters undoubtedly is the first step to the perfection of knowledg, by which means they come to improve their own understandings by the help of others: Reading furnisheth them with agreeable discourse, and adapts them for the conversation of the most ingenious, without which I know not how the fancy can be supplied with what is acceptable to the Auditor. How little would conversation signifie, did not reading on all occasions find matter for discourse. The want of which hath made so many Country Gentlewomen stand like so many Mutes or Statues when they have hapned into the company of the ingenious; their quaint expressions have seem'd to them *Arabian* sentences; and have stared like so many distracted persons, in that they should hear the sound of *English*, and yet understand but here and there a word of their own language. The consideration hereof is sufficient one would think to make the preposterous suspitions of some to vanish, who vainly imagine that Books are Womens Academies, wherein they learn to do evil with greater subtilty and cunning; whereas the helps of Learning, which are attained from thence, not only fortifies the best inclinations, but enlargeth a mean capacity to a great perfection.

Having thus proved, That the reading Books doth much conduce to the improving the understanding of young Gentlewomen, it behoveth the Governess to be careful in her choice of them. In the first place let them read some choice pieces of Piety, which may inflame their hearts with the love of God, and kindle in them ardent desires to be early followers of the Doctrine of Christ Jesus. Let there be a strict watch to keep unviolated the two gates of the Soul, the Ears and Eyes; let the last be imployed on good and proper Subjects, and there will be the less fear that the Ears should be surpriz'd by the converse of such who delight in wanton and obscene discourses, which too often do pleasantly and privately insinuate themselves into the Ear, carrying with them that unwholsome air which infects and poysons the purity of the Soul.

I know it will be expected what sort of Books of Piety, I would recommend to the perusal of these Gentlewomen; *London* affords such plenty of them, I know not which to pitch on. Not to trouble you with too many, take these which follow: Bishop *Ushers* Body of Divinity. Mr. *Swinnocks* Christian-calling. Mr. *Firmins* Real Christian. Mr. *James Janeways* book, Intituled, *Acquaintance with God betimes*; and his *Token for Children* when they are young.

Some may imagine, that to read Romances after such practical Books of Divinity, will not only be a vain thing, but will absolutely overthrow that fabrick I endeavoured to erect: I am of a contrary opinion, and do believe such Romances which treat of Generosity, Gallantry, and Virtue, as *Cassandra*, *Clelia*, *Grand Cyrus*, *Cleopatra*, *Parthenissa*, not omitting Sir *Philip Sydney's* Arcadia, are Books altogether worthy of their Observation. There are few Ladies mention'd therein, but are character'd what they ought to be; the magnanimity, virtue, gallantry, patience, constancy, and courage of the men, might intitle them worthy Husbands to the most deserving of the female sex. Thus having qualified them for reading, you should so practice them in their pen, as not to be ignorant in a *Point de Venice*, & all the Productions of the Needle, with all the curious devices of *Wax-work*, *Rock-work*, *Moss work*, *Cabinet-work*, *Beugle-work*, &c. and in due time let them know how to Preserve, Conserve, Distil; with all those laudable Sciences which adorn a compleat Gentlewoman.

Having thus characteriz'd in part, what a Governess ought to be, I shall with your leave and patience give you some account of my self.

A Short account of the life and abilities of Authoress of this Book.

I Would not presume to trouble you with any passages of my life, or relate my innate qualifications, or acquired, were it not in obedience to a Person of Honour, who engag'd me so to do, if for no other reason than to stop the mouths of such who may be so maliciously censorious as to believe I pretend what I cannot perform.

It is no ambitious design of gaining a Name in print (a thing as rare for a Woman to endeavour, as obtain) that put me on this bold undertaking; but the meer pity I have entertain'd for such Ladies, Gentlewomen, and others, as have not received the benefits of the tythe of the ensuing Accomplishments. These ten years and upwards, I have studied how to repair their loss of time, by making publick those gifts which God hath bestow'd upon me. To be useful in our Generation is partly the intent of our Creation; I shall then arrive to the top of the Pyramid of my Contentment, if any shall profit by this following Discourse. If any question the truth of what I can perform, their trial of me I doubt not but will convince their infidelity.

The things I pretend greatest skill in, are all works wrought with a Needle, all Transparent works, Shell-work, Moss work, also cutting of Prints, and adorning Rooms, or Cabinets, or Stands with them.

All kinds of Beugle-works upon Wyers, or otherwise.

All manner of pretty toyes for Closets.

Rocks made with Shells, or in Sweets.

Frames for Looking glasses, Pictures, or the like.

Feathers of Crewel for the corner of Beds.

Preserving all kind of Sweet-meats wet and dry.

Setting out of Banquets.

Making Salves, Oyntments, Waters, Cordials; healing any wounds not desperately dangerous.

Knowledg in discerning the Symptomes of most Diseases, and giving such remedies as are fit in such cases.

All manner of Cookery.

Writing and Arithmetick.

Washing black or white Sarsnets.

Making sweet Powders for the Hair, or to lay among Linnen.

All these and several things beside, too tedious here to relate, I shall be ready to impart to those who are desirous to learn.

Now to the intent I may increase your wonder, I shall relate how I came to the knowledg of what I profess. When I was fourteen years old, I began to consider how I might improve my time to the best advantage, not knowing at that age any thing but what reason and fancy dictated to me. Before I was Fifteen I was intrusted to keep a little School, and was the sole Mistress thereof. This course of life I continued till the age of Seventeen, when my extraordinary parts appear'd more splendid in the eyes of a Noble Lady in this Kingdom, than really they deserv'd, who praising my works with the appellation of curious pieces of Art, was infinitely pleas'd therewith. But understanding withal, that I understood indifferently the smoth *Italian*, and could sing, dance and play on several sorts of Musical Instruments, she took me from my School, and greedily entertained me in her house as Governess of her only Daughter. Unto this honourable Person I am indebted for the *basis*, or ground-work of my Preserving and Cookery, by my observation of what she order'd to be done. By this Ladies means I came acquainted with the Court, with a deportment suitable thereunto.

The death of this Lady gave me a fit opportunity to be entertain'd by another no way inferiour to the former, with whom I lived seven years. At first I was Governess to those of her Children, whose forward virtue sufficiently declared the goodness of the stock from whence they came. Time and my Ladies good opinion of me, constituted me afterwards her Woman, her Stewardess, and her Scribe or Secretary. By which means I appear'd as a person of no mean authority in the Family. I kept an exact account of what was spent in the house. And as I profited in Externals; so I treasured up things necessary for my understanding, having an happy opportunity so to do, not only by hearing that ingenious and agreeable discourse interfac'd between my Lady and Persons of Honour, but also by inditing all her Letters; in the framing and well-fashioning of which (that I might increase my Ladies esteem) I took indefatigable pains. There were not any who both wittily and wisely had publisht their Epistles to view of the world, whom I had not read, and on all occasions did consult: those which I placed in my greatest esteem were the Letters of Mr. *Ford*, Mr. *Howel*, Mr. *Loveday*, and Monsieur *Voiture*.

But that which most of all increast my knowledg was my daily reading to my Lady, Poems of all sorts and Plays, teaching me as I read, where to place my accents, how to raise and fall my voice, where lay the *Emphasis* of the expressions. Romances of the best sort she took great delight in; and being very well verst in the propriety of the *French* Tongue, there was not any thing published by the *Virtuosi* of *France*, which carefully and charge-ably she procur'd not; this put me upon the understanding of that Language, she was so well experienc'd therein, which is as great an Ornament for young Ladies as those learned Tongues, of which the Academical *studioso* boasts a more than common understanding.

Here as I learned hourly courtly phrases and graces, so how to express my self with the attendency of a becoming air. And as I gather'd how to manage my tongue gracefully, and dis-creetly; so I thought it irrequisite to let my hands lye idle. I exercise then daily in carving at Table. And when any sad accident required their help in Physick and Chyrurgery, I was ready to be assisting; in those two excellent arts in this place I acquired a competent knowledg.

In short time I became skilful, and stayed enough to order an house, and all Offices belonging to it; and gained so great an esteem among the Nobility and Gentry of two Counties, that I was necessitated to yield to the importunity of one I dearly lov'd, that I might free my self from the tedious caresses of a many more.

In the time I was a Wife, I had frequent occasions to make use of all, or most of my aforenamed qualities; and what I exercised not within my own roof, I used among my neighbours, friends and acquaintants.

That which qualified me as a Governess for Children as well as anything yet I have mention'd, was the great knowledg I had in the humours, inclinations, and dispositions of Children, having often had at one time above threescore in number under my tuition.

Besides, as I have been the Mistris of many Servants, so I have qualified them with my instructions to be Mistress to others; the major part of them living very comfortably in a married condition.

As I have taken great pains for an honest livelihood, so the hand of the Almighty hath exercised me in all manner of

Afflictions, by death of Parents when very young, by loss of Husband, Children, Friends, Estate, very much sickness, by which I was disenabled from my Employment. Having already given you an account of the duty, and requisite endowments which ought to be in a Governess, and how qualified I was my self in that troublesome concern; I shall now proceed in giving young Ladies such Rules which long experience and obser-vation have taught me, which may be as their perfect guide in all ages and conditions, the practise whereof will assuredly imbalm their names here: let their stedfast faith in Jesus Christ only crown them with glory hereafter.

Good Instructions for a young Gentlewoman, from the age of Six to Sixteen.

I Shall suppose your Parents have not been so remiss in their duties as not to furnish your tender age with what it is capable of understanding; and therefore do not question but that you can read well, sow and write indifferently; but I would have, long before you arrive at your teens, your first age water'd with the wholsome and sound doctrine of fearing God. *Remember thy Creator in the days of thy youth*, that thou mayst have, with *David*, in thy later days, this comfortable testimony of thy self, *From my youth up have I loved thy Law.*

I cannot bewail enough the careless neglect of Parents in this matter, who think neither God nor Nature doth tye them to further regard of their Children than to afford them food, and make them strut in the fashion, learn them to dance and sing, and ['and' repeated] lastly lay up a considerable sum for some person whom they value by his greatness, not his goodness; but how far that care falls short of what is required from Parents, I appeal to the sad effects thereof, profaneness towards God, and a contempt of his People and not only a daily breach of his holy Laws, but the Laws of a civil Society.

Above all things, let the fear of God be improved in you. Omit not by any means the duty of Prayer, Morning and Eve-ning; and forget not to read some portion of the Scripture every day.

Be very cautious in the choice of your Companions, and when your age adapts you for Society, have a care with whom you associate. If you tender your repute, you must beware with whom you consort, for report will bruit what you are by the company which you bear. Would you then preserve those precious odours of your good name? consort with such whose names were never branded, converse with such whose tongues for immodesty were never taxed. As by good words evil manners are corrected; so by evil words, are good ones corrupted.

Make no reside there where the least occasion of lightness is ministred; avert your ear when you hear it, but your heart especially, lest you harbour it.

It is proverbially said, *Maids should be seen, not heard*; not that they should not speak, but that they should not be too talkative. A Traveller sets himself out best by discourse, but a Maid is best set out by silence.

For your carriage, let it be in a Mediocrity, neither too precise, not too free. These simpring, made-faces, partake more of Chamber-maid than Gentlewoman.

Being grown up, you may possibly be wooed to interchange Favours; Rings or Ribbinds may seem trifles, yet trust me they are no trifles that are aim'd at in those exchanges. Wherefore let nothing pass from you that may any way impeach you, or give others advantage over you. It is probable that your innocent credulity may be free from the conceit of ill as theirs from the intention of good? but these intercourses of Courtesies are not to be admitted, lest by this familiarity an entry to affection be opened which before was closed. It is dangerous to enter parley with a beleaguring-enemy; it implies want of weakness in the besieged.

Presuming on your own strength is a great weakness; and the ready way to betray your self to dangers, is to contemn them. Presumption is a daring sin, and ever brings out some untimely birth, which, Viper-like, is the destruction of its Parent. I shall desist here in this place from giving you more rules of caution and good behaviour having design'd another, wherein I intend a more copious relation.

Advice to the Female younger sort:

INcline not to sloth, and love not to laze in bed, but rise early; having drest your self with decency and cleanliness, prostrate your self in all humility upon your bended knees before God Almighty, beseeching his Infinite Majesty to forgive you whatever sins you have committed in deed, word or thought; begging protection from the sin and evil of that day, and his holy assistance in the prosecution of good all the days of your life. Having said your Prayers, then on your knees ask your Parents Blessing; and what they shall appoint for your Breakfast, do you by no means dislike or grumble at; waste not too much time in eating thereof, but hasten to School, having first taken your leave of your Parents with all reverence. Do not loyter by the way; or play the truant; abuse none whom you meet, but be courteous and mannerly to all who speak with you[.] Leave not any thing behind which you ought to carry with you, not only things you Learn in or by, but also Gloves, Pocket-Handkerchiefs; and have a special care of any thing that may mischief you by the way.

When you come to School, salute your Mistress in a reverent manner, and be sure to mind what she injoyns you to do or observe. You cannot but live well if you conform to what you hear. Be not offended if your Governess advise you rather what is most fitting than what is most pleasing; for such is the property of a good Instructress. And these are to be entertained with such indeared respect, as their speeches (be they never so tart) should not incense you; nor their reproofs by [*recte* be] they never so free distaste you; having done this, salute civilly your School-fellows, and then apply your self to your book, work, writing, or what-ever else you are to learn.

Show not your ill-breeding and want of manners, by eating in the School, especially before your Mistress.

Mind what you are about, and neglect not what you are to do, by vain pratling in the School: make no noise, that you may neither disturb your Mistress, or School-fellows.

When you are called to read, come reverently to your Mistress, or any whom she appoints; avoid reading with a tone, huddle not over your lesson, but strive to understand what you read, and read so plainly, distinctly, and deliberately, that others may understand; if you are doubtful of a word, carefully spell it, and mistake not one word for another; when you have done, return, shewing your reverence to your place. Whatever work you take in hand, do it cleanly and well, though you are the longer about it; and have a care of wasting or losing any thing that appertains thereunto. Sit upright at your work, and do not lean or lol: and forbear to carry Children in your arms out of a wanton humour; for these whilst you are so young, may incline your body to crookedness. If you write, be careful you do not blot your paper; take pains in the true forming or cutting your letters, and endeavour to write true and well after your copy. Preserve your Pens, spill not your Ink, nor slurt it on your own or others clothes, and keep your fingers from being polluted therewith.

Returning from School, make haste home, not gaping on every idle object you meet with by the way. Coming into the house, apply your self immediately to your Parents; and having saluted them according to your duty, acquaint them with what proficiency you have made in your learning that day; be not absent when Dinner is on the Table, but present when Grace is said, and sit not down before you have done your obeisance to your Parents, and the company then present. Keep your Clothes from greasing, by pinning or keeping your napkin tite about you; and receive what is given you, thankfully. Be not talkative at Table, nay, nor do not speak, unless you are askt a question. Eat not your meat greedily, nor fill your mouth too full; and empty your mouth before you drink; and avoid smacking in your eating. Grease not your fingers as those that are slovenly, up to the knuckles. You will show your self too saucy by calling for sawce or any dainty thing. Forbear putting both hands to your mouth at once; nor gnaw your meat, but cut it handsomely, and eat sparingly. Let your nose & hands be always kept clean. When you have dined or sup, rise from the table, and carry your trencher or plate with you, doing your obeisance to the company; and then attend in the room till the rest rise.
In the intervals of School-time, let your recreation be pleasant and civill, not rude and boisterous.
Sit not before your betters, unless you are so desired, and unless you are at meat, working, or writing.

Be no make-bate between your Parents and their Servants; tell not a lye in any case, nor mince it into a plausible excuse to save you from the hand of correction.

Going to bed, make no noise that may disturb any of the Family, but more especially your Parents; and before you betake your self to rest, commit your self into the hands of the Almighty; desiring his infinite Majesty not only to watch over you in the night, but preserve you for, and assist you in the duties of the ensuing day.

If the Poor beg at your Father's door, though you cannot your self supply his necessities, yet you may do it by perswading your Father or Mother, which may be the sooner induced to it by observing your early and forward inclination to Charity.

Get that Catechism the Government has made choice of for you, by heart; by the practice of which you will be enabled to perform your duty to God and man.

Behave your self in the Church reverently, giving an awful regard to what sacred truths the Minister shall deliver for your future observation and practice; and do not proclaim publickly to the whole Congregation your levity and vanity by laughing, talking, pointing with your finger, and nodding, or your careless contempt of Gods word by drowsiness or sleeping.

Do not despise the aged, but rather honour them for their antiquity; and indeed you have but little reason to contemn old people, if you consider this, that you will be old if God shall think fit to continue your days to the length of theirs, and therefore would not be so serv'd your self.

God inable you to observe and practice what I have here already laid down, and give you yielding hearts to the exercise of what shall hereafter follow, to the glory of God, the un-speakable comfort of your Friends, & eternal salvation of your immortal Souls.

Thus I have given you general instructions as to your learn-ing and deportment: Give me now leave to insist in particular on the duty you owe your Parents.

The duty of Children to their Parents.

THE duties of a Child (Male or Female) to Parents, may be branch'd out into these particulars; Reverence, Love, Obedience, (especially in Marriage) assisting them in their wants, nay all these considered as due debt to the worst of Parents.

You ought in the first place to behave your self towards them with reverence, respect, humility, and observance; and although their infirmities may tempt you into a contempt of them, yet you must not despise them in your behaviour, nor let your heart entertain an undervaluing thought. What infirmities they have, you must endeavour to cover and conceal, like *Shem* and *Japhet*, who whilst cursed *Cham* endeavoured to disclose the nakedness of their Father to publick view, they privately covered from the sight of others, that which they debarr'd their own eyes to look upon. It is a great fault in our days, and too frequently practised, for youth not only to deride the imperfections of their Parents, but forge and pretend more than they have, that their counsel and correction may seem rather the effect of weakness, than good judgment in the punishing their Childrens errors. They think they then best express their wit, when they can most flout and abuse grave Counsel. Let such, if they will not practise the exhortations, yet remember the threatnings of the wisest of men, *Prov.* 30, 17. *The eye that mocketh his Father, and despiseth to obey his Mother, the Ravens of the Valley shall pick it out, and the young Eagles shall eat it.*

Thus as your behaviour ought to be respectful to them, so ought you to shew them all the demonstrations of love imaginable, striving to do them all the good you can, and shunning all the occasions of their disquiet. This you are obliged unto by common gratitude; for they were not only the instruments of bringing you into the world, but of sustaining and supporting you afterwards; if you could but rightly weigh the fears and cares that are required in the bringing up a Child, you would judg your love to be but a moderate return in compensation thereof.

This love is to be exprest several ways: First, in all kindness of behaviour, carrying your self not only with awe and respect, but with kindness and affection, which will encourage you to do those things they affect, and make you avoid what may grieve and afflict them.

Secondly, This love is to be exprest in praying for them. The debt a Child owes her Parents is so great, that she can never make satisfaction unless she call God to her aid and assistance, by beseeching him to multiply his blessings on them. Do not for any temporal benefit, or to be freed from the severity of thy Parents, wish their death. God in the Old Testament hath denounced death and destruction to the Curser of his Parents and therefore certainly will not let thy ill wishes towards them go unpunished; certainly they who watch for the death of their Parents, may untimely meet with their own.

The third duty we owe them is Obedience; this is not only contained in the fifth Commandment, but injoined in many other places of Scripture. This obedience extends no farther than to lawful things; otherwise it is disobedience, and offends against a higher duty, even that you owe to God your Heavenly Father. How little this duty is regarded, daily experience makes evident; the careful Mother having her child no longer under her command, than under the rod.

Wherefore think not, though grown up to Womans estate, that you are freed from obedience; and let not your motive thereunto be out of worldly prudence, fearing to displease your Parents, lest they should diminish your intended portion, and so be a loser thereby; but let your obedience be grounded upon conscience of duty.

But of all the acts of Disobedience, that of Marrying against the consent of Parents is the highest. Children are so much the Goods and Chattels of a Parent, that they cannot without a kind of theft give themselves away without the allowance of those that have the right in them; and therefore we see under the Law, the Maid that had made any Vow, was not suffer'd to perform it without the consent of the Parent, *Number*. 30. 5. The right of the Parent was thought of force enough to cancel and make void the obligation even of a Vow; and therefore surely it ought to be so much considered by us to keep us from making any such whereby that right is infringed.

A fourth duty is, To minister to, and assist your Parents in what-ever necessities or infirmities God Almighty shall think fit to inflict upon them. It may be thy Parent is weak or decay'd in understanding, supply his or her wants according to thy ability, since in thy infancy thou didst receive the same benefits from them. When an infant, you had neither strength to support, nor understanding to guide your self, but was supply'd with both by your indulgent Parents; wherefore common gratitude, when either of these becomes their case, obligeth you to return the same offices back again to them.

And as for the relieving their Poverty, there is the same obligation with the former, it being but just to sustain those who had maintain'd thee.

How then shall those answer it, who will not part with or circumscribe their own excesses and superfluities for the relief of such to whom they owe their being and well-being? and worse it will be with those who out of pride deny their Parents, being themselves exalted, fearing lest the lowness of their condition should betray the meanness of their birth.

Lastly, that I may conclude this Discourse, assure your self, That no unkindness, fault, or poverty of a Parent, can excuse or acquit a child from this duty. Although the gratitude due to a kind Parent be a forcible motive to make the child pay his duty; yet though our Parent were ever so unnatural, yet still we are to perform our duty, though none of that tye of gratitude lie on us.

Take this for all, Honour and obey thy natural Parents in what condition soever; for if they cannot give the[e] riches, yet thy Heavenly Father hath promised thee length of days.

*Of a young Gentlewomans deportment to her Governess and
    Servants in the Family.*

IF your Parents have committed you to the care and tuition of a Governess in the house with you, think with yourself, that this person whom I must now call my Governess, is one whom my Father and Mother have elected and entertain'd for my education, to lessen their own trouble, but not their tender care of me. Therefore if I obey her not in all things requisite, I transgress the commands of my loving Parents, and displease God in abusing their kindness.

Next, consider within your self, that this person who is constituted the guide of my actions, is such a one as they are confident either in their own judgments; or those who have recommended her, to be fit in all points to perform this charge committed to her; therefore in obedience to them I must and will obey her, and follow those good examples and precepts she shall lay down for my better information.

If she seem somewhat harsh, reserv'd, & abridgeth your freedom, yet let not your green years be too forward in condemning her, nor let not the ill counsel of inferior servants perswade you against her; lest by so doing you betray your want of reason and good nature, and detract from your parents worthy care for you.

If you have just cause of complaint, yet speak not maliciously against her, but truly and opportunely impart your grief; by this means she will be either removed from you, or regulated by their commands. Be sure therefore that your complaints be just, lest you should have one in her stead who may more justly deserve your censure, and so make your self unhappy by your Parents fears of having a child that is refractory. Besides, think thus with your self, that too often complaining makes dull and careless the Auditor; and instead of extracting compassion, it creates a jealousie of an ill disposition.

If your Governess be a Woman in years, honour her the more; if young, you may promise your self more freedom with her; yet if I may advise, I would not have a person too young to have such a charge, for they will have sufficient to do to govern themselves, therefore the more unfit to govern others; besides youth will be the more easily induced to submit rather to their Elders than their Equals.

What I now declare, is the fruit of experience, having had too great a charge in this nature when I was very young; and do know how defective I was then in my duty, since I became a Mother of Children, having now more tenderness to youth; and can speak it knowingly, that a mild moderate way is to be preferred before rigor and harshness, and that correction of words is bet[t]er than that of blows.

Give me leave, Gentlewomen, to wish you a good Governess, not such a one as I have been, but as I could or would be now. I can now with a greater sense look back upon my faults, than I could discern them when first committed: Thus much to your Governess. Now to your Maid who is to dress you.

Be not peevish or froward to her, but sweetly accept her endeavours, and gently admonish her of her neglects or errors; if she be good-natur'd and willing to please, this carriage will oblige and command a constant diligence from her; otherwise you will cause her to serve you only for her own ends, and with an eye-service; and whilst you are making a wry face in the Glass, she will make another behind your back.

Be courteous to all the Servants belonging to your Parents, but not over-familiar with any of them, lest they grow rude and saucy with you; and indeed too much familiarity is not good with any, for contempt is commonly the product thereof.

If you can do any Servant good in any thing, either in mitigating your Parents anger towards them, or presenting their humble petition for them be not slack in so doing, for by this means you will purchase to your self both love and honour.

If any poor body sue to you to beg in their names that which is not unfit for them to ask, do not deny them, and God will not deny you your request; Do good to all, and turn not your face away from the indigent, but let your charity extend to their relief and succour.

Be courteous to all people inferior to your quality; but in such a way, that they may know you understand your self, and this will be a sweet kind of commanding reverence from them, and will give you the character of a good and humble spirit; assure your self it is better to be good than great. Majesty mixt with modesty and humility forcibly commands the service of all; but pride and imperiousness, though in a great person, breeds scorn and contempt in the heart and tongue even of the meanest Peasant. If God hath blest you with birth and fortune above others, be sure your virtue shine with greater luster than others.

Despise not those who have not so great a portion of wit and wealth as you possess; but think with your self, to whom the Lord gives much, he requires much from. As God made nothing in vain, so he gives nothing in vain. That person is not to be trusted, who doth not endeavour to improve what he is intrusted withal. If you have wisdom, boast not thereof, but give God thanks and use it to his glory and your own comfort.

What qualifications best become and are most suitable to a Gentlewoman.

I Have already endeavoured to prove, that though Nature hath differ'd mankind into Sexes, yet she never intended any great difference in the Intellect. This will evidently appear not only from those many arguments learned *Cornelius Agrippa* hath laid down in a particular Treatise for the Vindication of the excellency of the Female-Sex, but likewise from the many learned and incomparable Writings of famous Women, ancient and modern, particularly *Anna Comnena* who wrote the Eastern History in *Greek*, a large Folio. Nor can we without great ingratitude forget the memory of that most ingenious *Dutch* Lady *Anna Maria Schurman*, who was so much admired by the greatest Scholars in *Europe* for her unparallel'd, natural and acquired parts, that there were very few (as the great *Salmasius*, &c.) who did not frequently correspond with her by Letters. Her *Opuscula* or smaller works are now extant, printed in *Holland* in *Latin*, *Greek*, and *Hebrew*, in which there is a small tract, proving that a Womans capacity is no way inferior to mans in the reception of any sort of learning; and therefore exhorts all Parents who are not much necessitated, not to let their Children spin away their precious time, or pore on a Sampler, till they have prickt out the date of their life; but rather instruct them in the principles of those learned Tongues, whereby they may at pleasure pick-lock the Treasuries of Knowledg contained in those Languages, and adapt them for the conversation and discourse of most Nations.

I need not go out of our native Country to produce you examples enough of our own Sex for your imitation and incouragement in treading the paths of learning. I shall forbear to speak of the incomparable worth and pregnant parts of some Gentlewomen lately deceased as Mrs. *Philips* the ingenious Translatress of *Pompey, &c.* since what is extant of hers or her Contemporaries will more at large express their matchless merit; nor shall I eulogize or praise the living, nominating any person, lest I be thought one partially addicted to flattery: Yet give me leave to say, I could instance not a few, who (to the glory of our Sex, and the place of their Nativity if occasion modestly required) would not blush to answer a Capricious Virtuoso in three of the most useful Tongues spoken or understood, that is *Latin*, *French*, and *Italian*.

I desire not to hyperbolize; it is probable they may not be so expert in the anatomizing an insect or the discovery of some monstrous production, as these Academical Wits are; yet for ought I know, may find out many monstrosities in their brain, whilst they are subtilly plumming the depth of their self-admired understanding.

Now since it may hence appear, Ladies, that you have no Pygmean Souls, but as capable of Gygantick growth as of your Male opponents; apply your self to your Grammar by time, and let your endeavours be indefatigable, and not to be tired in apprehending the first principles of the *Latin* tongue. I shall forbear to give you rules for attaining the perfect knowledg thereof, but leave you to that method your Tutor or skilful Governess shall propound for your observation.

I need not tell you the vast advantages that will accrue hereby, your own experience will better inform you hereafter. However, I shall hint some, as first, your understanding the *Latin* tongue will inable you to write and speak true and good *English*; next it will accommodate you with an eloquent stile in speaking, and afford you matter for any discourse: lastly, you will be freed from the fear of rencountring such who make it their business to ransack a new world of words to find out what are long and obscure; not regarding how insignificant, if they carry a ratling sound with them. Thus these Fops of Rhetorick, spawns of non-intelligency, will venture the spraining of their tongues, and splay-footing their own mouths, if they can but cramp a young Gentlewomans intellect.

Our *English* tongue is of late very much refined, by borrowing many words from the *Latin*, only altering the termination, these you will never perfectly understand without the knowledg of the *Latin*, but rather misapply or displace them to your great discredit, although you should consult the *English Interpreters* that were ever extant.

And as our Mother-tongue hath finished her expressions with the *Roman* dialect; so to make them the more spruce and complacent, she hath borrowed some choice words from other Nations, more especially the neighbouring *French*, whose tongue you must in no sort be ignorant of, if you intend to speak with the air of the Court, or like the quaint Oratresses of the Court-air.

It is no small benefit which will accrue to you by learning the *Italian*; for by reason of our Gentries travelling into foreign parts, occasioned by our late unhappy and inhumane home-bred distractions, these two Languages are generally spoken in *England*; insomuch that a Court-Lady will not be induced to esteem a friend, or entertain a Servant who cannot speak one of them at least: and that you may not despair of a competent knowledg of either, or both, without going into those Coun[t]ries where they are naturally spoken, know there are many excellent Masters who teach here in *London* those Languages; but more especially that sober and learned natural *Italian* Seignior *Torriano*; and that unimitable Master of the *French* Tongue, Monsieur *Mauger*; both which have publisht their Grammars; the first a large and useful *Italian* Dictionary also. Both these Countrys have been happy, and may be justly proud in pro-ducing so many learned and ingenious men; so many, should I nominate them with their deserved Encomiums, this small Treatise would swell into Volumes; I shall therefore pass them over, but would not have you their Writings, where you shall find plenty of every thing, which shall either tickle your fancy, or furnish your understanding. Having thus adapted you for conversation, let me next show you your deportment therein.

Of a Gentlewomans civil Behaviour to all sorts of people in all places.

A Painter of old being about a draught of a most absolute beauty, propounded for the accomplishment thereof half a dozen of the most exquisite and wonderful fair Maidens he could find, that he might steal from each those charms and features which he thought were most powerful; but I will assure you a greater assistance is required in the framing and fashioning of a Woman, whose behaviour should be such as to please in all companies. Whatsoever Nature can afford, or good manners inform, come short of this purpose. In this subject the fairest Ornaments are most necessary; among which what I have already exprest, are highly to be prized, which with the aggregation of all the best qualities can be desired, are the proper things, which as in their Center must terminate in conversation.

The first things I judg most necessary, and do wish, with *Socrates*, were in you Ladies, as he desired in his Pupils, are *Discretion*, *Silence* and *Modesty*. But this is too general; wherefore since conversation (after the milk) is the first and chiefest thing, both animal as well as rational creatures do most desire and delight in, I shall first advise, as to choice of company; next, your carriage therein, both in gesture, look, speech and habit.

No wonder all Mankind is so generally inclined to conversation, since Life without Society is more insupportable than Death; it is discourse makes us pass over our tedious hours and days with delight. What a Desart would this world seem without company! And how dangerous would it prove were we not cautious in our election! For example is more forcible than precept; thus by ill company you may gain a bad custom, which all good instructions shall never root out. But should you be so prudent as not to follow their evil example; yet by associating your self, you will inevitably contract a suspition of being as bad as they; this made the Philosopher say, *Shew me thy Companion, and I will tell thee what thou art.*

Be not easily induc'd to enter into discourse with strangers, for nothing argueth levity and indiscretion more than that. Consort your self with your betters as near as you can, yet do not despise your equals, but in a most especial manner avoid all familiarity with your inferiors; if Female, in a little time they will thereby be drawn to slight you; if Male, they will be incouraged to attack your honour unlawfully, or subtilly insinuate themselves into affection, whereby though you are as high in fortune, as honourable in birth, you may stoop to so low a contract, that forgetting your self by the incessant importunities of their over-blown desires, you are overcome, & so become a grief to your friends, a shame to your selves, and a lamentable spectacle of reproach and sorrow to that worthy Family, from whence you had your Original.

Affect not the vanity of some, in being seen in publick too frequently. Thus many excellent Ladies have exposed themselves to the mercy of the Tempter, who otherwise had stood impregnable in the defence of their Chastities. You think, it may be, and intend no harm in your Promenades or walks; but by so doing, you give too often occasion for licentious Amorists to meet with you, and may thereby be perswaded to throw off the vail of circumspection, to give attention to some wanton smutty story. Consult not too much with youthful blood and beauty, lest they prove too dangerous enemies to be your Privy-Councellors.

Be not guilty of the unpardonable fault of some, who never think they do better than when they speak most; uttering an Ocean of words, without one drop of reason; talking much, expressing little: Much like that Woman Dr. *Heylin* unhappily met withal, in his younger years, with whom he was constrained to travel a long Journey in a Coach: So indiscreetly reserved she was at first meeting, that tendring his devoir of a salute, (as it is customary) she would not admit thereof; so speechless withal at first, as if a vow'd resolution had tied up her tongue to the strict observance of an everlasting silence; but the next day, she so far presumed on the slenderness of the acquaintance, that, though she was so silent before, she then opened upon their setting forward; and the continual click of her tongue never ceast till the Sun was set; which the motion of her tongue, and the Doctor's watch, kept exact time for eleven hours; and notwithstanding her seeming modesty in refusing a kiss, did now voluntarily prompt him to a close imbrace.

As I would not advise you to be over-reserv'd, so give not too loose reins to liberty, making pleasure your vocation, as if you were created for no other end than to dedicate the first-fruits of the morning to your Looking-glass, and the remainder thereof to the Exchange, or Play-house. Many of our Sex are to blame, who have no sooner ting'd their faces artificially, than some Attendant is dispatcht to know what Plays are to be acted that day; my Lady approveth of one which she is resolved to see, that she may be seen; being in the Pit or Box, she minds not how little she observeth in it, as how much to be observed at it. If the novelty or goodness of the Play invite them not, then what Lady Fashion-monger? Or what Lord Beauty-hunter?

Shun all affectation in your behaviour; for Vertue admits of no such thing in her gesture or habit, but that which is proper, and not enforced; native or decent, and not what is apishly introduced. Therefore since nothing better befits you than what is your own, make known by your dress, how much you hate formality. To this end play not the Hypocrite with your

Creator, in pretending to go to Church to serve him, whereas it is to serve your selves in the imitation of some new fashion. That which becometh another well, may ill become you. You deserve in your preposterous imitation, suitable correction with the Ass in the Fable, who seeing the Spaniel fawningly to leap on his Master, thought that the like posture would alike become and oblige him; which he adventuring to put in practice, alarm'd the whole Family, & was soundly beaten for his unadvised folly. Affectation cannot be conceal'd, and the indecency of your deportment will quickly be discovered in publick Societies; wherefore behave your self so discreetly abroad, that you may confer no less a benefit on such as see your behaviour, than you profit such as shall observe your carriage at home: Express in publick such a well-becoming Garb, that every action may deserve the applause & imitation of all that are in your company. Let your conceits be nimble and ready, and not temper'd or mixt with lightness; let your jests be innocent and seasonable, without the least capriciousness; let your discourse be free without niceness; your whole carriage delightful, and agreeable, and flowing with a seeming carelessness. Thus much in general, let me now come to particulars.

Of the Gait or Gesture.

IT is an easie matter to gather the disposition of our heart, by the dimension of our Gait. A light carriage most commonly discovers a loose inclination; as jetting and strutting, shew haughtiness and self-conceit. Were your bodies transparent, you could not more perspicuously display your levity than by wanton Gesticulations.

Decency when she seeth Women, whose modesty should be the Ornament of their beauty, demean themselves in the streets, or elswhere, more like an Actoress, than Virtu's Imitatress; she endeavours to reclaim them, by bidding them look back to preceding times, & there they shall find Women (though Pagans) highly censured, for that their outward carriage only made them suspected. A Vail (no Vizard-mask) covered their face, modesty measured each step, and so circumspect were they in general of their carriage, lest they should become a scandal or blemish to their Sex.

Their repair to their (prophane) Temples was decent, without any loose or light gesture; and having entred them, constant and setled was their behaviour. Quick was their pace in the dispatch of œconomick or houshold-affairs, but slow in their Epicurean visits, or extravagent Gossipings. How much more should you in these purer Christian times affect that most which most adorns and beautifieth! Eye your feet those bases of frailty, how they who so proudly exalt themselves on the surface of the Earth, are but Earth, and are the daily Porters which carry their earthly frame nearer its Earth.

With what apish gestures some walk, to discover their lightness; others like *Colosso's* discovering their ambition and haughtiness? How punctually these, as if they were Puppets, who are beholding for their motion to some secret Artifice? These unstaid dimentions, argue unsetled dispositions. Such as these, discretion cannot prize, nor sound judgment praise. Vulgar opinion, whose applause seldom receives life from desert, may admire what is new; but discretion only that which is neat. Having thus spoken what is requisite in Gesture, I shall next treat how the Eye ought to be governed.

Of the Government of the Eye.

AS prudence is the eye of the Soul, so Discretion is the apple of that Eye but as for the natural Eyes, they are the Casements of the Soul, the Windows of Reason: As they are the inlets of Understanding, so they are the outlets or discoverers of many inward corruptions. A wanton Eye is the truest evidence of a wandring and distracted mind. As by them you ought not to betray to others view, your imperfections within; so be not betray'd by their means, by vain objects without: This made the Princely Prophet pray so earnestly, *Lord turn away my eyes from vanity.* And hence appears our misery, that those eyes which should be the Cisterns of sorrow, Limbecks of contrition, should become the lodges of lust, and portals of our perdition. That those which were given us for our Assistants, should become our Assassinates.

An unclean Eye, is the messenger of an unclean Heart; wherefore confine the one, and it will be a means to rectifie the other. There are many Objects a wandring Eye finds out, whereon to vent the disposition of her corrupt heart.

The ambitious Eye makes Honour her object, wherewith she torments her self, both in aspiring to what she cannot enjoy; as likewise, in seeing another enjoy that whereto her self did aspire. The covetous makes Wealth her object; which she obtains with toil, enjoys with fear, forgoes with grief; for being got, they load her; lov'd they soil her; lost, they gall her. The envious makes her Neighbours flourishing condition her object; she cannot but look on it; looking, pine and repine at it; and by repining, with envy, murders her quiet and contentment. The loose or lascivious makes Beauty her object; and with a leering look, or wanton glance, while she throweth out her lure to catch others, she becomes catcht her self.

Gentlewomen, I am not insensible, that you frequent places of eminency for resort, which cannot but offer to your view variety of pleasing Objects. Nay, there where nothing but chast thoughts, staid looks, and modest desires, should harbour, are too commonly loose thought, light looks, and licentious desires in especial honour. The means to prevent this malady, which like a spreading Canker disperseth it self in all Societies, is to abate your esteem for any earthly Object. Do you admire the comeliness of any Creature? remove your Eye from thence, and bestow it on the contemplation of the superexcellency of your Creator.

Put a check to the stragling disposition of your eyes, lest *Dinah*-like, by straying abroad you are in danger of ravishing. Now to preserve purity of heart, you must observe a vigilancy over every sense; where, if the Eye which is the light of the body be not well disposed, the rest of the Senses cannot chuse but be much darkned. Be assured, there is no one sense that more distempers the harmony of the mind, nor prospect of the Soul, than this window of the body. It may be said to open ever to the Raven, but seldom to the Dove. Roving affections, it easily conveys to the heart; but Dove-like innocence, it rarely retains in the breast. The very frame of your eyes may sufficiently inform you how to govern and guide them. For it is observed by the most curious Oculists that whereas all irrational Creatures have but four Muscles to turn their Eyes round about;

Man alone hath a fifth to draw his Eyes up to Heaven. Do not then depress your Eyes, as if Earth were the Center of their happiness, but on Heaven the Haven of their bliss after Earth. To conclude, so order and dispose your looks, that censure may not tax them with lightness, nor an amorous glance impeach you of wantonness. Send not forth a tempting Eye to take another; nor entertain a tempting look darting from another. Take not, nor be taken. To become a prey to others, will enslave you, to make a prey of others will transport you. Look then upward, where the more you look, you shall like; the longer you live, you shall love. From the management of the Eyes let us next proceed to Speech.

Of Speech and Complement.

THE Eye entertains it self not with more Objects than the Invention furnisheth the Tongue with Subjects; and as without Speech, no Society can subsist; so by it we express what we are; as Vessels discover themselves best by the sound. Let Discretion make Opportunity her Anvil, whereon to fashion a seasonable Discourse; otherwise, though you speak much, you discourse little.

It is true (Ladies) your tongues are held your defensive armour, but you never detract more from your honour than when you give too much liberty to that slippery glib member. That Ivory guard or garrison, which impales your tongue, doth caution and instruct you, to put a restraint on your Speech. In much talk you must of necessity commit much error, as least it leaves some tincture of vain-glory, which proclaims the proud heart from whence it proceeded, or some taste of scurrility, which displays the wanton heart from whence it streamed.

A well-disposed mind will not deliver any thing till it hath rightly conceived; but its expressions are always prepared by a well-season'd deliberation. Think not I would have you altogether silent (Ladies) in company, for that is a misbecoming error on the other side; but I would have you when you do speak, to do it knowingly and opportunely.

A saying of a Philosopher will not be unworthy of your commemoration, who seeing a silent guest at a publick Feast, used these words, *If thou beest wise, thou art a fool; if a fool, thou art wise in holding thy peace.* For as propriety of Speech affords no less profit than delight to the Hearer, so it argues discretion in the Speaker.

By the way, let me advise you never to tye your self so strictly to elegancy, or ornament; as by outward trimming, the internal worth of right understanding should be altogether forgotten, and so your expressions savour of some absurd impertinency. This were to prefer the rind before the pith, and the sound of words before solid reason.

That excellent precept of *Ecclesiasticus*, though it was spoken in general yet I know not to whom it is more particularly useful than to young Women. Thou that art young, speak, if need be, and yet scarcely when thou art twice asked. *Comprehend much in few words; in many; be as one that is ignorant; be as one that understandeth, and yet hold thy tongue.*

Volubility of tongue in these, argues either rudeness of breeding, or boldness of expression. Gentlewomen, it will best become ye, whose generous education hath estranged ye from the first, and whose modest disposition hath weaned ye from the last, in publick Society to observe, rather than discourse; especially among elderly Matrons to whom you owe a civil reverence, and therefore ought to tip your tongue with silence.

Silence in a Woman is a moving-rhetorick, winning most, when in words it woeth least. If opportunity give your Sex argument of discourse, let it neither taste of affectation, for that were servile; nor touch upon any wanton relation, for that were uncivil; nor any thing above the Sphere of your proper concern, for that were unequal. This will make your Discourse generally acceptable, and free you from prejudicate censure.

Choice and general Rules for a Gentlewomans observation in Conversation with Company.

BEfore I shall direct you in a method for civil converse in Society, it will not be improper to give you an account of Civility, and in what it consists; next, the definition, circumstances, and several kinds thereof; lastly, the difference of things decent, and undecent according to custom.

Civility, or gentle plausibility, of which I intend to give you information; is in my slender judgment nothing else but the modesty and handsome decorum, to be observed by every one according to his or her condition; attended with a bonne grace, and a neat becoming air. It lyeth not in my power to lay you down rules and precepts for the procuring this charming air, and winning agreeableness. Nature hath reserved this to her self, and will not bestow this inexpressible boon, but to her choicest favourites, and therefore I do not see how Art with her utmost skill can imitate it to any purpose.

I confess this very much engageth the Eye, and sometimes doth very subtilly steal into the affections; but we rest too much on a trifle, if we do not endeavour to make our selves more grateful to the eye of Reason. It is not barely the outward ornamental dress, or becoming address which is the true principle and form of a compleat Gentlewoman; there is something, more required, more substantial and solid, which must discover the disposition of her Soul, rather than the gesticulations of her Body. Were it not for this, alas what would become of a great many to whom Nature hath proved an unkind Stepmother, denying them not only convenient use of members, but hath thrown on them deformity of parts; these Corporal incommodities would make them pass for Monsters, did not the excellency of their Souls compensate those irreparable defects; their minds being well cultivated and polite, their actions may be as pleasing as those of the handsomest; that Lady that is so unfortunate in the one, and so happy in the other, may say with the Poet:

Si mihi diffilis formam Natura negavit,
Ingenio forme damna rependo meæ.

In English thus;

If Nature hath deni'd me what is fit,
The want of Beauty I repay with Wit.

But whether you are afflicted with any natural or accidental deformity, or not, you can never be truly accomplisht till you apply your self to the Rule of Civility, which is nothing but a certain Modesty or *Pudor* required in all your actions: This is the Virtue I shall labour to describe, which description I hope will be sufficient to direct you towards the acquisition of that agreeable deportment, which hath the power to conciliate and procure the applause & affection of all sorts of people.

The definition of Civility may be thus understood; it is a Science for the right understanding our selves, and true instructing how to dispose all our words and actions in their proper and due places.

There are four circumstances which attend Civility; without which, according to its Rules, nothing can be done exactly.

First, Ladies, you must consult your years, and so accordingly behave your self to your age and condition.

Next, Preserve all due respect to the quality of the Person you converse withal.

Thirdly, Consider well the time. And, lastly, the place where you are.

These circumstances relating to the knowledg of our selves, and all persons in all conditions, having respect to time and place, are of such great consequence, and necessary import, that if you are deficient in any of these, all your actions (how well soever intended) are the rags of imperfection and deformity. I shall find it somewhat difficult to prescribe the exact rules of Civility, so as to render them compliable with all times, places and persons, by reason of variety of Customs: You may fall accidentally into the society of some exotick and forreign person of quality; and what may seem civil and decent in you, may seem undecent and ridiculous to another Nation. Nay, should you observe and practise in your behaviour what hath been applauded for useful & profitable, and commended to posterity for a Gentlewomans laudable imitation, may decline or grow altogether contemptible in our critical and curious Age. In short, nothing is so intrinsically decorous, but the experience or capricio of a phantastical Lady will alter or explode. By reason of this variety, I think it altogether requisite to treat of it as it stands at this time in reputation among such who call themselves Christians, and accordingly reduce these Notions into practice.

This modesty or Civility we speak of, take it according to its truest acceptation, is little else but Humility; which being well practis'd by Persons of Quality, is sufficient to stamp an everlasting impress on them of Virtue and Civility. And this Humility consists not only in a moderate and submiss opinion of our selves, but in preferring the satisfaction and commodity of other persons before our own; and that so ingeniously, first, by not provoking or disobliging any one; to be of this dispo- sition, is to be not only esteemed modest, but good-natur'd; the benefit that will redound to you hereby, may incite and en- courage you to the practice of this shining-Virtue: for as there is nothing will render any one more insuportable, and lessen estimation among all, than Insolence and Vanity, so nothing recommends more strongly to the good opinion and affection of all, than affability and submission.

This virtue of Humility, above all others, hath this great priviledg in extraordinary eminence. I have known some, who having been endued with a more than an ordinary measure hereof, have been so far from being accused for their formal indecencies, and other errors, which otherwise might have been objected to their disparagement, that every one endeavoured to excuse them. I have known, on the other side, a proud and an imperious carriage (though the person was adorned with much breeding, and beautified with all the usual ornaments of Art, yet) was beloved by few, because displeasing to most and hardly welcome to any. Modesty therefore is the effect of humility, as Civility and the gratefulness of our actions is the effect of Modesty. To conclude this Chapter, I shall add the difference or discrimination between things civil and uncivil, convenient and inconvenient, decent and undecent.

For the better understanding hereof, a good natural judgment is required in a Gentlewoman for the perception and discerning the various qualities of things; for want of this she may many times fall into a mistake, and commit gross absurdities.

In the next place, it is necessary that you take an exact observation of what is own'd and establisht for civil or uncivil, in the place wherein you are.

Lastly, You must have a special regard, not to confound Familiarity with Civility. To persons of Quality in a higher rank than your own, be very attentive to what they say, lest you put them to the trouble of speaking things twice. Interrupt them not whilst they are speaking, but patiently expect till they have done. Have a special care how you contradict them; but if finding them in an error, and necessity obligeth you to inform them of the truth, first beg your excuse; but if they persist therein, contend not, but refer your further discourse till another opportunity.

When it comes to your turn to speak to intelligent Ladies, entertain them not with things you understand but imperfectly. If you find the company more facetious and witty then your self, leave the discourse to time, and be silent, contenting your self to be an attentive hearer: if you will run the hazard, be smart and pithy, comprehending much in few words; and be not the vain Imitatrix of those who affect to have the whole talk; and when their mouths are once open, can never shut them again. If you are obliged to Complement any great person, do it as briefly as possible; and return your Answers rather in Court-ships, than in any Prolix Discourse. Avoid especially that rudeness that is too frequently practised among some, who think they are never heard, unless they come up so close to the face, as to run against your nose; in that case you are to pray heartily their breath be sweet, or you faint irrecoverably.

Let not your Visits be too long; and when you think it convenient to retreat, and that Lady you Visited will do you the honour to accompany you out of the Chamber, do not seem to oppose it in the least; that would imply she understood not what she went about; but you are only to testifie by some little formality how undeserving you are of that great honour.

When you enter into a Room by way of Visit, avoid the indiscretion and vanity of a bold entrance without Ceremony, but do it quietly and civilly. And when you come near the person you would salute, make your Complement, and render your Devoir modestly, and with some gravity, shunning all bawling noise or obstreprousness.

The Ladies which do you the civility of rising when you come in, do not displace, by assuming any of their Chairs; but make choice of another seat; observing still, not to sit down till they are most in their places: it being a great indecorum to seat your self in that case, whilst any person which gave you that respect continues in a standing posture.

It is an intollerable incivility to enquire what they were talking about; or if you see any two or more Discoursing or Dialoguing together, to interrupt them by hastily asking what they said last.

If you are in a mixt company, and you are qualified with those Languages (the knowledg whereof I have advised you to prosecute), speak as little as you can: But be sure you do not hold a Discourse in that Language the rest do not understand.

It is not civil to whisper in Company, and much less to laugh when you have done. The generality of Gentlewomen are suspicious, and somewhat conscious, and are apt to surmize what was never intended, and to apply to themselves what was meant of another; by which means they have conceived so great a displeasure, as never to be eradicated or removed.

I need not put you in mind of those Documents you learned every day when you were Children; that is, when ever you answer negatively or affirmatively, to give always the Titles of *Sir*, *Madam*, or *my Lord*. It is very unhandsome, when you contradict a person of Quality, to answer him with, *It is not so*; if you are necessitated thereunto, do it by Circumlocution, as *I beg your Honour's pardon*: *Madam, I beseech your Ladiship to excuse my presumption if I say You mistake*, &c. If any discourse you Complementally, and run out into some extravagant expressions in commendation of your person; it is a breach of civility if you should say, Pray forbear your jeers, my back is broad enough to bear your flouts; but say, You strangely surprize me, Sir; or, I am confident, Sir, what you now express, is rather to shew your wit and ingenuity, than to declare any thing worth a taking notice of in me. If your love and respect to a Ladies person obligeth you to reprove a fault in her, do not say, *Madam, you acted the part of a mad Woman, in doing such a thing;* but, *had such a thing been left undone, you had neither disobliged your self or friends.*

Take special care of speaking imperiously to your Superiors, but rather do it in some indefinite manner; as instead of saying, *Come, you must do, go, &c.* say, *Come, Madam, if you think it convenient*; or, *if it stand with your Ladiships pleasure, we will go to such a place, or do such a thing*; *in my opinion such a thing is requisite to be done, if it suits, Madam, with your approbation.*

As it is a great argument of indiscretion in a Gentlewoman that would be thought prudent and wise, to talk much in praise of her Relations in the presence of Persons of Honour; so it is very unhandsome to seem affected or over-much pleased in hearing others speaking largely in their commendations.

There is a certain ambitious vanity that possesseth the minds of some of the younger sort, who being Nobly extracted, think they add to the honour of their Parents, when having occasion to speak of them in honourable company, they never mention them without their titles of Honour (though we ought always to speak of them with respect), as My Lord my Father; My Lady my Mother: In my opinion every jot as ridiculous, as for young Gentlewomen of twelve years old to call them Dad and Mam. Avoid, as a thing very improper, to send Commendations or Messages to any person by your Superior; you may make choice of your equal for that purpose, but chuse rather your inferior.

In relating a story, do not trouble your Auditors with the vain repetition of, *Do you understand me*, *mark ye*, or *observe me*; and do not accustom your self to the empty tautologies of *said he*, and *said she*.

Be backward in discourse of minding any one of any thing which may renew their grief, or perplex and trouble their spirit.

Carelesly to nod, gape, or go away whilst one is speaking, is both an act of incivility and stupidity; to laugh, or express any Tom-boy trick, is as bad or worse; be careful therefore you do not pat or toy with her that sits near you; nor do not that childish or foolish thing which may provoke laughter; lest the company, being indisposed for such idle diversions, take distaste at you, and look upon you as the subject of their scorn.

It is very ungentle and indiscreet, to peep over any Ladies shoulder when she is either writing or reading; or to cast your eye seriously on any ones papers lying in your way.

Let it be your principal care, of not intruding upon persons in private discourse, which will be discovered either by their retirement, their whispering, or by changing their discourse upon your approach: Having observed either of these signs, make it your business to withdraw, lest you incur the censure of indiscretion.

If the person you visit be sick, and in bed, let not your stay be long: for sick persons are unquiet; and being tyed up to Physick, and controul'd by its operations, you may offend them by their being offensive to you: you must remember likewise to speak low; and urge him not to answer as little as you can.

In company it is ill-becoming to break out into loud and violent laughter, upon any occasion whatever; but worse by far, to laugh always without occasion.

Rules to be observed in walking with Persons of Honour; and how you ought to behave your self in congratulating and condoling them.

If you walk in a Gallery, Chamber, or Garden, be sure to keep the left hand; and without affectation or trouble to the Lady, recover that side every turn. If you make up the third in your walk, the middle is the most honourable place, and belongs to the best in the company; the right hand is next, and the left in the lowest estimation. If the Lady with whom you walk, hath a desire to sit down, to the intent she may repose her self; if you pretend any difference between persons, it would be very ridiculous and slighting to leave her to her rest, whilst you continue walking on.

If you understand a person for whom you have any difference or respect, meets with a subject or occasion of rejoycing or sorrowing; Civility requires you so to conform your self that this Lady may be fully perswaded of your affection, and how much you are concerned in all her affairs; and as your Countenances, so ought your Habit testifie the sentiment of your heart, as well as words and actions. How preposterous would it appear to the meanest capacity, for any out of a ridiculous nonconformity, who hearing of some joyful and successful accident which hath befaln some Noble Family of his or her acquaintance, repair thither with all the symptoms of sorrow and melancholy in the Countenance; and on the contrary, if it be in mourning, or under any eminent affliction, to express all the signs of joy and satisfaction?

And now since I have toucht on Clothes? I think this a fit place to give you an account of what kind of Habit is most necessary for a civil, sober, and modest conversation.

Of Habit, and the neatness and property thereof. Of Fashions, and their ridiculous apish imitation.

THE neatness and property of your Clothes, may be said to shew a great part of your breeding. Property, I call a certain suitableness and convenience, betwixt the Clothes and the

Person; as Civility is the framing and adapting our actions to the satisfaction of other People. And indeed the suitableness and comeliness of your Habit, makes the greatest discovery of your virtue and discretion; for it must consequently follow, that a ridiculous Garb is the most certain indicium of a foolish person.

Now if you desire to be exact, you ought to proportion your Clothes to your shape, condition, and age; and not to run into excesses, stimulated thereunto by too much exactness, or an overvalu'd conceit. And indeed it is a great fault in our Sex, being very much inclin'd to pride it in sin with what our merciful Creator bestow'd upon us to cover our shame. The fruit of a Tree made Woman first to sin, and the leaves thereof made her first covering.

How careful ought you to be in your Habit, since by it your modesty is best expressed, your dispositions best discovered? As none can probably imagin such to have modest minds, who have immodest eyes; so a Maid cannot be accounted modest whose attire openly proclaims arguments to the contrary. It matters not whether the quality of your Habits be Silken or Woollen, so they be civil and not wanton.

Pardon me, I am not of that Cynical and morose temper of some, who affirm all gorgeous apparel is the attire of sin; but if it be a sin, I am perswaded the quality of the person extenuates the quality thereof: For I read, that noble and eminent persons were in all times admitted to wear them, and to be distinguished by them; neither indeed is the sumptuousness of the Habit so reprehensible, as the phantastickness in respect of form and fashion, which of late hath been so much affected, that all fashion is in a manner exiled.

I shall not trouble myself with what the glittering *Bona Robas* of our times think, but I am confident it is Civility which adds most grace, Decency which expresseth best state, and Comeliness in attire, which procures most love. These misconceived ornaments are meer deformities to virtuous minds. Foreign fashions are no baits to catch them; nor phantastick, rather phanatick dressings, to delude them. Decency is their choicest livery, which sets them forth above others gaudy pageantry.

Those whose erected thoughts sphere them in an higher Orb than this Circle of frailty; those whose spotless affections have devoted their best services to goodness, and made modesty the exact mold of all their actions, will not easily be induced to stoop to such worthless brain sick lures.

Now such of you whose generous descent as it claims precedence of others, so should your vertuous demeanor in these four things which I have already spoken of, *viz.* Gesture, Look, Speech, and Habit, improve your esteem above others. In Gesture, by appearing humbly where ever you are; in Look, by disposing it demurely; in Speech, by delivering it moderately; in Habit, by attiring your self modestly.

Frown not on me, Ladies, that I seem to be thus severe in reproving the excess of Apparel; yet I do not deny, there is a kind of priviledg in youth for wearing fashionable Clothes, Jewels and Diamonds, which Nature (who doth nothing in vain) hath provided; and whatsoever some maliciously may whisper to the contrary; the use of Apparel is to dignifie the Wearer, and add more beauty to the Creature, provided the Apparel be not above the dignity of her that weareth it, nor doth exceed the Arithmetick of her Revenues.

But whilst I seem to give you (young Gentlewomen) some allowance of liberty in your Clothing; for indeed it is impossible there should be youth without some vanity; yet I know not how to excuse the vain custom now so much in fashion, to deform the face with black Patches, under a pretence to make it appear more beautiful. It is a riddle to me, that a blemish should appear a grace, a deformity be esteemed a beauty: I am confident were any of them born with those half-Moons, Stars, Coach and Horses, and such like trumpery, by which a Lady becomes a stranger to her self, as well as others, she would give more money to be freed from them, than a seven years costly expence, in following the fashion, would amount to.

It must not be denied but that the indulgence of Nature hath left a greater liberty to Women, than unto Men, in point of curiosity in Apparel. A priviledg which men ought not to envy them, because whatever imbellishment she bestows on her own beauty, is to be supposed an effect of that great love she would shew to man, by endeavouring and studying how to shew her self most complaisant, grateful, and acceptable to man. And yet Nature hath limited this priviledg of Women with strict Laws. The dictate of this natural Law, is, That no Woman use any Habit or form of attire but that which contributeth to her truest beauty. For since the Fall of their first Parent hath subjected them to the necessity of apparel, they must ever remember to wear it as an ornament of decency, and not of vanity. But if we shall examine the present fashions by the standard of this rule, we shall find, to the amazement of sober thoughts, a new-born Law of Custom to have defaced the reverend old Law of Nature.

I cannot imagine whence our Ladies borrowed that monstrous and prodigious custom of patching their faces; if they did borrow it from the *French*, they did ill to imitate such, who it may be made use of the fashion out of pure necessity, and not novelty; having *French*-pimples, they needed a *French*-plaister. Meer need taught us at first to build Houses, and wear Clothes, which afterwards were used for Ornament: Who then can tax their witty-pride (although justly we may the imitation of the *English* Gentry therein) which could so cunningly turn botches into beauty, and make ugliness handsome? I know not but that the fashion of wearing Farthingals of old, were politickly invented to hide the shame of great Bellies unlawfully puft up; and of late the large-topt stockings with supporters to bear them up, were a good excuse for some hot Gallants, in that they stradled so much when they walkt the streets; whereas, poor Gentlemen, they could do no otherwise.

I have read, that the *Indians* did accustom themselves to paint the volume of their bodies all over with Apes, Monkies, and other Beasts. I know not whether our Ladies have endeavoured to epitomize their Works, and abridg them into the narrow compass of the Title-page of their own faces. But sure I am, that they are much beholding to the ingenious Artist, whose skilful hand much exceeded his who writ the Ten Commandments and *Pater-noster* (to be legibly read) within the compass of a penny. Such a one is able to vie with Wonder it self, since he can pass a Camel through the eye of a *Spanish* Needle without a Miracle; and contract a Coach and Horses into the narrow dimension of four Gnats.

By the impertinent pains of this curious Face-spoiling-mender, the Exchanges (for now we have three great *Arsenals* of choice Vanities) are furnished with a daily supply and variety of Beauty-spots (with many other things, whose names are only known to the Inventer and Buyer); and these Patches are cut out into little Moons, Suns, Stars, Castles, Birds, Beasts, and Fishes of all sorts, so that their Faces may be properly termed a Landskip of living Creatures. The vanity and pride of these

Gentlewomen hath in a manner abstracted *Noah*'s Ark, and exprest a Compendium of the Creation in their Front and Cheeks. Add to this the gallantry of their Garb, with all the Ornamental appurtenances which rackt Invention can discover, and then you will say, there wanted nothing except it be that which a *Roman* Writer said was wanting to the accomplishments of *Poppæa Sabina* (Mistris to bloody *Nero*), *That she was defective in nothing but a vertuous mind.*

Mediocrity in most things is the best rule for your observation: As in mode and fashion you are to avoid profusion, so you are to shun singularity: The one, as well as the other, will render you ridiculous. I would not advise you to be obstinate, and altogether oppose the torrent of the fashion then in being: for example, should you now wear a Farthingal, or narrow-brim'd Hat with a long crown, and a strutting Ruff (it is not long since such things were in fashion), a Jack-pudding could not attract more Boys after him, than would follow you. Or should you always keep in one fashion, you would be laught at for our singularity, almost as much as others for their profuseness.

To avoid this incommodious extravagancy, incline somewhat to the Mode of the Court, (which is the source and foundation of fashions); but let the example of the most sober, moderate, and modest, be the pattern for your imitation.

Those who are too remote in the Country, or hindred by any other impediment to resort to Court, let them acquaint themselves (if they can) with some prudent person who is frequently there, and by her pattern and direction order your Habit with reference, as near as may be, to your quality, age, and estate. Your own wit and ingenuity may so contrive your Clothes, as to retrench a great part of the luxury of a fashion, and reduce it to suit with your convenience, modesty, and Christian deportment.

I have already declared, your Habits ought to be adapted to your conditions; it is easie to judg of the truth of this Rule, if you consider how preposterous you would appear (being nobly born) drest in the Habit of a Dairy-maid, or for a Scullion to be array'd in the dress of a Ladies daughter; this would be looked on as no other than a Masquerade, or a Christmass Mumming. As it is very unfit to suit your selves unsuitably to your condition, so 'tis likewise as to your age. For an old Woman to habit her self as youthfully as a Gentlewoman of fifteen, is as improper as to sing a wanton song at a Funeral. For a young

Woman to clothe her self in the Habit of a grave and aged Matron is as preposterous as to weep and mourn at a merry Gossiping.

Proportion therefore your Clothes to your bodies, and let them be proper for your persons. I could not forbear to laugh heartily, when heretofore I saw a little man lost in a great Band; nor can I now abstain from laughter, when I see a man of small stature with a monstrous broad brim'd Hat; I have often thought the Hat hath walkt alone, and that the narrow Breeches and short Coat shrunk, for fear of the Hats greatness, into an exact fitness for an overgrown Monky or Baboon.

Agreeableness therefore ought to be exact, and adequate both to age, person, and condition, avoiding extremities on both sides, being neither too much out, nor in the fashions.

Now lest I have been too rigid concerning Apparel, and so have justly incur'd the displeasure of some Ladies I am ever bound to respect for those singular favours they have from time to time confer'd on their poor Servant; I shall endeavour to make them amends for it, without wronging my Conscience, in this ensuing Chapter.

Of New Fashions.

MAN at first was left at liberty to be his own Taylor, and had the whole World to furnish him with all sorts of Materials, both for Stuff and trimming, and so made his Clothes as he thought fit and convenient.

Hence it is apparent that he was the first fashion inventer; some of his posterity imitated him, and others them, and we others; since then fashions seem to be left at liberty, I think no wise man should reprehend them, unless inconvenient and ridiculous.

If Womens palats are not confinable to one sort of meat, why should their fancies to one particular mode? Nature is the Mistress of Variety; shall we then be so ingrateful to her various kindnesses as to rest in the enjoyment of one Individual? She made all things for strength, use and ornament; and shall we be so slothful and negligent, as not to contemplate their worth, and applaud them in our due use?

It is true, we never heard any thing of Apparel till sin sent man in an errand to seek for it; at first it was chosen for a covering for our first Parents shame; but their progeny beside that, have since found a decency therein. And certainly good Clothes are not displeasing to Heaven; had they been so, God would never have commanded the Garments of his High-Priests to be glorious and beautiful; not only to be rich in the outward Materials, but richly wrought with the best eye-pleasing colours, and refulgent with precious Stones and Jewels.

The Peacocks starry train we cannot look on, but we must incline to admiration; and that the glory thereof may not be useless, Nature hath given that Bird an excellent art to spread it to the best advantage.

I may be bold to say, you sin more in the sordidness of your Apparel, than in its splendour; and you will not lose in your reputations, by being cloth'd a little above your rank, rather than altogether beneath it. A Jeweller when he would enhance the price of his Commodity, sets his precious Stones to the best advantage; and the richer they are, the greater is his endeavour and care to grace them in the luster. Its true, a Diamond will sparkle in the dark, and glitter, though unpolisht or ill set; yet we think the excellency of the cut, or water, can never cast abroad its rays too much.

Let me ask the gravest and most prudent Matron living, Whether it be not only convenient, but necessary, that as occasion shall require, young Gentlewomen should be finer than ordinary, as upon their adddresses and visitings of persons of Quality, on days of publick feasting and joy, and on solemn and sacred meetings? *Socrates*, though a serious and sour Philosopher, being askt the question, *Why one day he was so unusual fine and brave?* answered, *That he might appear handsome to the handsome.* We ought in our Clothes to conform our selves to those with whom we do converse.

Besides, we commonly guess at the fatness and goodness of the soil, by the grass which we see upon the ground. Since most then judg by outward apparencies, it is requisite to provide for a good estimation, even from externals.

I have heard of some profuse Gallants, who having spent all their money, yet prudently and for credit, have kept good Clothes to their back, otherwise they might have hoop'd for a Dinner, and look'd for a Lodging.

If there were not a due respect to be had, according to rank and quality, what use would there be of Scarlet, Velvet, Cloth of Tissue, Silk, Satten, Jewels, and precious Stones of all sorts? They would be accounted superfluous, and rather burdens than benefits to the world.

This is a maxim undeniable, *That Nature doth nothing in vain.* Certainly then she had never produced such multiplicity and quantity of excellent and inestimable things, but for our use and ornament: Yet withal remember the saying of *Demonax*, who feeing a Gallant brave it in the fashion, and insult with his Feather, whispered these words in his ear, *The Silk and fine Clothes you boast of, were spun by a worm, and worn by a Beast, before they came on your back, and yet the Worm continues still a Worm, and a Beast a Beast; and the Bird in whose tayl was the Feather you wear, is a Fowl still.* There are some persons whose Gallantry of Apparel can never hide the fool from them, whilst others do grace and are graced by every thing they wear. Yet still we must conclude, that comely Apparel is to be prefer'd before what is costly or conceited.

Some choice Observations for a Gentlewomans Behaviour at Table.

Gentlewomen, the first thing you are to observe, is to keep your body strait in the Chair, and do not lean your Elbows on the Table. Discover not by any ravenous gesture your angry appetite; nor fix your eyes too greedily on the meat before you, as if you would devour more that way than your throat can swallow, or your stomach digest.

If you are invited abroad, presume not on the principal place at the Table, and seem to be perswaded with some difficulty to be seated, where your Inviter hath chosen in his opinion the most convenient place for you. Being a Guest, let not your hand be first in the Dish; and though the Mistress of the Feast may out of a Complement desire you to carve, yet beg her excuse, though you are better able to do it than her self.

In carving at your own Table, distribute the best pieces first, and it will appear very comely and decent to use a Fork; if so, touch no piece of meat without it.

I have been invited to Dinner, where I have seen the good Gentlewoman of the House sweat more in cutting up of a Fowl, than the Cook-maid in roasting it; and when she had soundly beliquor'd her joints, hath suckt her knuckles, and to work with them again in the Dish; at the sight whereof my belly hath been three quarters full, before I had swallowed one bit. Wherefore avoid clapping your fingers in your mouth and lick them, although you have burnt them with carving. Take these more especial Rules, according to the newest and best mode for Carving.

If Chicken-broth be the first dish, and you would help your principal Guest with a part of the Chicken, the best piece is the breast; the wings and legs are the next; and of them, the general opinion of most is, That in all boil'd Fowl the legs are look'd on as chief.

As to all roasted Fowl, those which are curious in the indulging their pallats, do generally agree, that flying Wild-fowl are much tenderer than Tame-fowl, and quicker of concoction; such as scratch the Earth, and seldom use the Wing, the Legs are to be preferr'd before any other part; the wings and breasts of wild-fowl are best.

The ordinary way of cutting-up a roast-fowl, is by dividing the four principal members, beginning first with the legs; and be not tedious in hitting the joynts, which you may avoid by well considering with your eye where they lye, before you exercise your knife.

The best piece to carve to the best in the company, of the larger sort of Fowl, as Capons, Turkies, Geese, Duck, and Mallard, Pheasant, Dottril, Cock of the Wood, &c. is the piece on the breast, observing always to cut it long-ways towards the rump. But do not cut your Oranges long-ways, but cross.

Since in Butchers-meat there are few ignorant of the best pieces, it will be to little purpose to give you an account of them in this place; for my design is to treat of that which is not commonly known: However, without deviating from my intention, take these remarks which follow.

In boiled or roasted Beef, that which is interlin'd or interlarded with fat, is most to be esteemed; and the short ribs being most sweet and tender, is to be preferred before any other.

Cut a Loin of Veal in the middle, and present the Nut or Kidney as the best part in the whole Joint. Thrust your knife into a Leg of Mutton a considerable depth, above the handle, to let out the gravy; and begin to cut on the inside, as if you intended to split it; in the joint on the other side, is a little bone fit to be presented, and in great estimation among the Curious.

I heard of a Gentleman coming from hunting, and falling into a friend's house, complained he was extreamly hungry; the Mistris thereof replied, That she was very sorry she had nothing to accommodate him with but a cold Leg of Mutton. His appetite being very sharp, made him commend that Joint beyond any other; whereupon it was brought: But finding that choice bone remaining still untoucht, refused to eat a bit: Being demanded the reason, Madam, said he, the sharpness of my Stomach shall never make me feed uncleanly; for I am confident they must be Bores and Clowns that first handled this leg of Mutton, or else their breeding would have taught them not to have left untoucht the choicest bit in the whole joint. I cannot but applaud the jest, but I must condemn the rudeness of the Gentleman.

A Shoulder of Mutton is to be cut semicircularly, between the handle and the flap; the Pope's eye (as it is commonly called) is a choice bit both in Leg and Shoulder.

In a roasted Pig, the dainty most approve the ears and divided Jaws, the neck and middle-piece, by reason of the crackling. In Hares, Leverets, and Rabbets, the most esteemed (called the Hunts-mans piece) is by the sides of the tail; and next to that, is the back, legs, and wings, improperly so termed.

Some who esteem themselves the *Virtuosi* for rarity of diet and choice provision, esteem (in Fish) the head, and what is near about it, to be the best: I must acknowledg it in a Cods-head, with the various appurtenances, drest *secundum artem*, sparing no cost; such a dish in *Old* and *New Fish street*, hath made many a Gallant's pocket bleed freely. As also, I approve it in a Salmon or Sturgeon, the Jowles of both being the best of the Fish; likewise in Pike or Carp, where note, the tongue of this last-named is an excellent morsel; but in other Fish you must excuse the weakness of my knowledg. In Fish that have but one long bone running down the back (as the Sole), the middle is to be carved without dispute; there is none so unacquainted with fare, to contradict it.

If Fish be in paste, it is proper enough to touch it with your knife; if otherwise, with your fork and spoon, laying it handsomly on a plate with sauce, and so present it. But should there be Olives on the board, use your spoon, and not your fork, lest you become the laughter of the whole Table.

All sorts of Tarts, wet-Sweat-meats, and Cake, being cut first in the dish wherein they were served to the Table, are to be taken up at the point of your knives, laid dextrously on a plate, and so presented: and whatever you carve and present, let it be on a clean plate; but by no means on the point of your knife, or fork, nor with your spoon. If any one carves to you, refuse it not, though you dislike it.

Where you see variety at a Table, ask not to be helpt to any dainty; and if you are offered the choice of several dishes, chuse not the best; you may answer, *Madam, I am indifferent, your Ladiships choice shall be mine*.

Be not nice nor curious at the Table, for that is undecent; and do not mump it, mince it, nor bridle the head, as if you either disliked the meat, or the company. If you have a stomach, eat not voraciously; nor too sparingly, like an old-fashion'd Gentlewoman I have heard of, who because she would seem (being invited to a Feast) to be a slender eater, fed heartily at home (before she went) on a piece of powder'd-beef and cabbage; by chance a steak thereof fell on her Ruff, and not perceiving it, went so where she was invited; being observed to eat little or nothing, a Gentlewoman askt her why she did not eat; Indeed, Madam, said she, I did eat (before I came forth) a whole pestle of a Lark to my Breakfast, and that I think hath deprived me of my appetite. The witty Gentlewoman presently replied, I am easily induced to believe you fed on that Bird, for on your Ruff I see you have brought a feather of him with you. Thus your nicety may be discovered by means you dream not of, and thereby make your self the subject of publick laughter.

On the other side, do not bawl out aloud for any thing you want; as, I would have some of that; I like not this; I hate Onions; Give me no Pepper: But whisper softly to one, that he or she may without noise supply your wants.

If you be carved with any thing (as I said before) which you do not like, conceal (as much as in you lieth) your repugnancies, and receive it however: And though your disgust many times is invincible, and it would be insufferable tyranny to require you should eat what your Stomach nauseats, yet it will shew your civility to accept it, though you let it lye on your plate, pretending to eat, till you meet with a fit opportunity of changing your plate, without any palpable discovery of your disgust.

If you are left to your own liberty, with the rest, to carve to your self, let not your hand be in the dish first, but give way to others; and be sure to carve on that side of the dish only which is next you, not overcharging your plate, but laying thereon a little at a time. What you take, as near as you can let it be at once; it is not civil to be twice in one dish, and much worse to eat out of it piece by piece; and do not (for it savours of rudeness) reach your arms over other dishes to come at that you like better. Wipe your spoon every time you put it into the dish, otherwise you may offend some squeamish stomacks. Eat not so fast, though very hungry, as by gormandizing you are ready to choak your selves. Close your lips when you eat; talk not when you have meat in your mouth; and do not smack like a Pig, nor make any other noise which shall prove ungrateful to the company. If your pottage be so hot your mouth cannot endure it, have patience till it be of a fit coolness; for it is very unseemly to blow it in your spoon, or otherwise.

Do not venture to eat Spoon-meat so hot, that the tears stand in your eyes, or that thereby you betray your intolerable greediness, by beraying the room, besides your great discomposure for a while afterwards. Do not bite your bread, but cut or break what you are about to eat; and keep not your knife always in your hand, for that is as unseemly as a Gentlewoman who pretended to have as little a stomach as she had a mouth, and therefore would not swallow her Pease by spoonfuls, but took them one by one, and cut them in two before she would eat them.

Fill not your mouth so full, that your cheeks shall swell like a pair of *Scotch*-bag-pipes; neither cut your meat into too big pieces.

Gnaw no bones with your Teeth, nor suck them to come at the marrow: Be cautious, and not over-forward in dipping or sopping in the dish; and have a care of letting fall any thing you are about to eat, between the plate and your mouth.

It is very uncivil to criticize or find fault with any dish of meat or sauce during the repast, or more especially at another's Table; or to ask what such a Joint or such a Fowl cost; or to trouble your self and others with perpetual discourses of Bills of Fare, that being a sure sign of a foolish Epicure.

It is very uncomely to drink so large a draught, that your breath is almost gone, and are forced to blow strongly to recover your self: nor let it go down too hastily, lest it force you to an extream cough, or bring it up again, which would be a great rudeness to nauseate the whole Table; and this throwing down your liquor as into a Funnel, would be an action fitter for a Juggler than a Gentlewoman. If you sit next a Person of Honour, it will behove you, not to receive your drink on that side; for those who are accurately bred, receive it generally on the other.

It is uncivil to rub your teeth in company, or to pick them at or after meals, with your knife; or otherwise; for it is a thing both indecent and distastful.

Thus much I have laid down for your observation in general; wherein I am defective as to particulars, let your own prudence, discretion, and curious observation supply.

Rules for a Gentlewomans behaviour at a Ball.

Ladies, it is presumed you know the grounds of Dancing, else your resort to a Ball amongst well-accomplisht Gentlewomen, would not only be improper but very much hazard your repute and good esteem among them; and as you can dance, so I would have you understand the rules and formalities of dancing, which are practised in that place.

If you are skilful in this faculty, be not difficultly perswaded to make a demonstration of your art. A fault is found in many of whom if you request a Dance or Song, they will be deaf to all your importunities; but may be when you are out of humour, and have left them to their own liberty, will dance so long till they have tired themselves and the Spectators; and Sing till they have neither voice, nor their Auditors ears.

I say, if you have skill, be not over-conceited thereof, lest it lead you into the error of engaging in some Dance you do not understand; or but imperfectly.

If you are perswaded to Dance, and though you alledg a great many Apologies to the contrary, yet when you find your self obliged thereunto, by no means refuse. For it is much better to expose your self to some little disorder in being complacent, than be suspected of pride.

Rules to be observed by a Gentlewoman in Vocal and Instrumental Musick.

Do not discover upon every slight occasion you can sing or play upon any Instrument of Musick; but if it be known to any particular friend in company, whom you have a special respect for, and he or she perswade you to sing, excuse your self as modestly as you may; but if your friends persist, satisfie their desires, and therein you will express no part of ill breeding: your prompt and ready compliance thereunto shall serve you against censure; whereas, a refractory resistance favours of one that makes a livelyhood of the profession, and must expect to have but small doings, if there be no better recommendation than that distastful kind of morosity.

Use not your self to hemming or hauking, a foolish custom of some, endeavoring to clear their throat thereby; nor be not too long in tuning your Instrument.

Having commenced your Harmony, do not stop in the middle thereof to beg attention, and consequently applause to this trill, or that cadence, but continue without interruption what you have begun, and make an end so as not to be tedious, but leave the Company an appetite: As you would desire silence from others being thus applied, be you attentive, and not talkative when others are exercising their harmonious voices.

Let the Songs you make choice of be modest, yet witty, and ingenious; and because there are so many, which though they may please the ear, yet may corrupt good manners; let me give you this caution to have a care.

Of wanton Songs, and idle Ballads.

Let your prudence renounce a little pleasure for a great deal of danger. To take delight in an idle vain Song without staining your self with the obscenity of it, is a thing in my mind almost impossible; for wickedness enters insensibly by the ear into the Soul, and what care soever we take to guard and defend our selves, yet still it is a difficult task not to be tainted with the pleasing and alluring poyson thereof.

Physicians endeavour to perswade the wiser sort of men, as well as ignorant and credulous women, That a Mother fixing stedfastly her eye on a Picture, she will secretly convey the Complexion, or some other mark on the Infant; from hence we may be induced to believe, That the lascivious and wanton expressions contain'd in some Songs and Ballads may have the same effect in our imagination, and do most frequently leave behind them some foul impressions in our spirits.

The reading these wanton things do heat by little and little; it insensibly takes away the horrour and repugnancy you ought to have to evil; by this means you acquaint your self so thorowly with the image of Vice, that afterwards you fear it not though you meet with Vice it self.

Licentiousness is not bred in a moment, at one and the same instant; so the contagion of loose Songs seizeth by degrees on the heart; they may be said to work on the minds of youth as seed in the ground, it first appears only above the surface of the Earth, but every day afterwards adds to its growth till it be fit for the sickle.

Nay more, these Songs of wantonness will breed in you a more than fitting boldness, which will put you on the confidence of practising what you read or sing. Assure your self, if you admit of a familiarity with these things, your innocency will be in daily danger.

You may easily believe this to be truth, if you consider the multiplicity of vanity and trumpery which stuff these Ballads; how an amorous or rather foolishly-fond Virgin forsook Kindred and Country, to run after a stranger and her Lover. In another you find how craftily two Lovers had plotted their private meetings to prosecute their unlawful enjoyments; and the Letters that pass between for the continuation of their affection; which straight-ways makes the Reader up to the ears in Love. In the one is exprest the Constancy of two Fools one to the other; in the other, what trouble, what hazard, and what not, they run into, to ruin themselves, distract their Parents, and leave a stain on their own reputations, never to be washt out.

These are the things which contain cunning Lessons to learn the younger sort to sin more wittily; and therefore no judicious person can comprehend with what reason these dangerous Songs and Sonnets can be justified.

The *Lacedemonians* prohibited Plays, because Adulteries were exhibited; then why should such Pamphlets be permitted where such dishonest actions, lascivious examples, and extravagant passions are maintained? Shall it be said, that Christians have less love for Virtue than Infidels?

Ladies, accuse me not of too much severity, in endeavouring to take away this too much accustomed delight in singing wanton, though witty Sonnets: I say excuse me rather, since I aim at nothing more than your welfare. I know your inclinations, as you are young and youthful, tend rather to these things, than what is more serious; and are apt to read those Books which rather corrupt and deprave good manners than teach them.

Some may be so vain as to delight more in a Comedy than a Sermon, and had rather hear a Jack-pudding than a preacher: This made a sober Philosopher complain, he had fewer Scholars than such a one of meaner parts, and a greater Libertine; because there are more who haunt the School of Voluptuousness, than that of Virtue; and we love them better who flatter and make us merry, than those who tell us the truth, and the danger, if we follow not her precepts.

Wherefore I cannot allow of any sort of Poetry, though it be ever so ingenious, if Vice lurk therein to do you harm; and wheresoever you find Vice, let it be your intention and strong resolution to fight against it, and throw aside all those instruments and implements, which will but learn you to sin with the greater dexterity. This is one vanity the younger sort incline to, and there are a great many more which our Sex (and to their shame) are prone to follow, take a brief account of them.

Of the Vanities some young Ladies and Gentlewomen are too prone to prosecute.

I need not speak of the vanity of Gentlewomen in overmuch affecting bravery, since we find it thorowly ingrafted in most of them; so that we may as easily take off their skins from their bodies, as this vanity from their minds.

If this were to be observed only in some particular Court-Ladies, it were something excusable; but this is an innate humour, an original sin which Gentlewomen bring into the world with them; the tincture of which infirmity their Baptism washeth not off. From hence proceeds the *Babel* or confusion of Habits, insomuch that of late there is neither order observed, nor distinction; a Chamber-maid finified on a Festival or Holiday, may be taken for her Mistress, and a Citizens Wife mistaken for a Court-Lady.

Where shall we find any so regular as to follow the dictates of Modesty and Mediocrity, so that the most severe cannot blame their superfluities, nor the more favourable accuse their defects? A young Gentlewoman well accomplisht, is like a Star with five rays, Devotion, Modesty, Chastity, Discretion and Charity; such Women whose composition is made up of these, seem to have been moulded upon the Cœlestial Globes, by the hands of Cherubims; so excellent are their Virtues, and so sweet their deportments; they are in their Houses as the Sun in his proper Sphere: Should I attempt to represent their worth, I might sooner find poverty in the Center of all the rich Ore and precious stones of the Earth, than want of merit in this subject.

Were all our Sex of the same temper, by being inhabitants of this Earth, they would speedily convert it into a Heaven. But alas, too many there are who every day must be dressed up like Idols, as if they intended thereby to be worshipped. Their *Filles de Chambre* have more to do in attending their Beauties, than some have in fitting and rigging out a Navy. Their Glass with studied advantages takes up the whole morning, and the afternoon is spent in visits.

And indeed should a man come into some Ladies Chambers unacquainted with the Furniture that belong'd to them, and seeing them lie on the Table, having never seen such vanities before, would think them the coverings and utensils of some Creature of a monstrous and prodigious bulk, and that there was Mercery enough to furnish a little City, rather than the body of a little Lady. They may be fitly compared to some Birds I have seen, who though they have but little bodies, yet have abundance of Feathers. And though they seem to load themselves with variety of things, yet they do but seem to cover what they should disclose to none; and though they have but little flesh, they will show as much of it as they can. It was a true saying of one, and very applicable to this purpose; *I know not what may be reserved for the eyes of a chast Husband, when almost through all Markets where they go, the secret parts of his Wives body are exposed, as if they were ready to be delivered to the best bidders.*

Moreover, how dangerous is it for young Gentlewomen to affect a small Waste, thinking that the most exquisite proportion? Endeavouring by strait-lacing to be as slender in the middle as the Strand-May-pole is tall in its height. I am sure they are big enough to be wiser, who never think themselves finer, than when the Girl with her span can make a Girdle. I know Gentlewomen, that the inconveniences which attend this affectation, do not proceed altogether from you, or that you are in the fault, but your Mothers or Nurses: But did they know how speedily and wilfully they destroy you by girding your tender bodies, certainly they would prove kinder Mothers, than be your cruel Murderers. For by this means they reduce your bodies into such pinching-extremities, that it engenders a stinking breath; and by cloistering you up in a Steel or Whale-bone-prison, they open a door to Consumptions, with many other dangerous inconveniences, as crookedness: for Mothers striving to have their daughters bodies small in the middle, do pluck and draw their bones awry; for the ligatures of the back being very tender at that age, and soft and moist, with all the Muscles, do easily slip aside. Thus Nurses, whilst they too straitly do lace the breasts and sides of children on purpose to make them slender, do occasion the breast-bone to cast it self aside, whereby one shoulder doth become bigger and fuller than the other.

Though I would not have too great a restriction laid on your bodies, yet I would not have them by inconsiderate loosness run out into a deformed corpulency, like the Venetian-Ladies, who seldom lace themselves at all, accounting it an excellency in proportion to be round and full-bodied; and that they may attain that (meerly supposed) comeliness, if Nature incline them not to be somewhat gross or corpulent, they will use art, by counterfeiting that fulness of body, by the fulness of garments. Thus you see, that in all things (except Piety) Mediocrity, or the Golden-mean, is to be observed.

Of a young Gentlewoman's fit hours and times for their Recreation and Pleasure, and how to govern themselves therein.

THE chief thing that you ought to consider is how to govern and behave your selves in your Pastimes: Wisdom therein must be your guide; and the chief rule it can teach you, is To shun all pleasures which are vitious; and in the reception of thos which are lawful, exceed not the Rule, nor Moderation; which consists, first, in not giving offence, scandal, damage, or prejudice, to your associates or others: Next, that it be without injury to your health, reputation, or business. Lastly, Let your Recreation be with moderation.

You must by no means make pleasure your business, but by the enjoyment thereof return with more alacrity and chearfulness to your business. Young Ladies may use it, but not abuse it, which they never do more than in the excess thereof; for it softneth and weakeneth the vigour both of Soul and Body, it besotteth the best complexions, and banisheth the principal Vertues.

If pleasure be taken as it was at first provided, it will be taken without a sting; but if you exceed either in measure or manner, you pollute the purer stream, and drink your own destruction. The Heathen of old did put a check on Men and Women, forbidding them to let loose the reins to all the corrupt and mistaken pleasures of this life, much more should Christians forbear the inordinate enjoyment of them.

Above all, these pleasures are most to be commended, which in every respect are so lawful, that they leave in the Conscience no private check behind them to upbraid the sense for the unlawful using of them. He that plungeth himself into a puddle, doth but engage himself thereby to an after-washing, to purge that filth away he contracted by that imprudent action. Or would you be so mad to feed on that you are certain will make you sick in the eating? Almighty God would never have allowed you the desire of pleasure, nor the faculties to enjoy it, if he had not design'd that with decency you should use them. An action of this kind is but natural, and will not be unlawful unless it be found to run into excess attended with unlawful circumstances.

There is so much corruption adhering to the use of pleasure, by exceeding the measure, mistaking the manner, misplacing the time; that although Recreations be lawful in themselves, yet if they be circumstanced amiss, they are not expedient.

Recreations and pleasures are indisputably lawful, if you are not irregular in measure, manner, or time; had they been otherwise our most wise and merciful Creator would never have made them so distinct in their kinds, nor so many in their number. All the several tastes in food and fruit were intended to please the pallate, as well as satisfie the appetite. Of all the beautiful and pleasant fruits in Paradise there was but one only Tree excepted. From hence it may be concluded, Mankind may enjoy those delights which they have a well-grounded inclination unto, with this proviso, they abuse them not.

Before you do or act any thing, examine well the sequel; if that be clear the present enjoyment will be accompanied with content, otherwise it will end in repentance.

What Recreations and Pleasures are most fitting and proper for young Gentlewomen.

REcreations which are most proper and suitable to Ladies, may be rankt under four principal heads, Musick, Dancing, Limning and Reading. Of Dancing I have already lightly treated on in the directions for your deportment at Balls; however this I will say further of it, that though the *Romans* had no very great esteem for it as may appear by *Salusts* speaking of *Sempronia*, She danced better than became a virtuous Lady; yet the mode and humour of these times look upon it not only as a generous and becoming property, but look upon Gentility ill-bred if not thorowly acquainted therewith; and to speak the truth it is the best and readiest way to put the body into a graceful posture; behaviour must of necessity halt without it; and how will you blush when you come into a mixt society, where each person strives to shew her utmost art and skill in Dancing, and you for the want thereof must stand still and appear like one whose body was well framed but wanted motion, or a soul to actuate it.

In the next place, Musick is without doubt an excellent quality; the ancient Philosophers were of the opinion, that Souls were made of Harmony; and that that Man or woman could not be virtuously inclined who loved not Musick;

wherefore without it a Lady or Gentlewoman can hardly be said to be absolutely accomplished.

Limning is an excellent qualification for a Gentlewoman to exercise and please her fancy therein. There are many foreign Ladies that are excellent Artists herein; neither are there wanting Examples enough in his Majesty's three Kingdoms of such Gentlewomen, whose indefatigable industry in this laudable and ingenious Art, may run parallel with such as make it their profession.

Some may add Stage-plays as a proper recreation for Gentlewomen; as to that (provided they have the consent of Parents or Governess) I shall leave them to make use of their own liberty, as they shall think convenient.

I am not ignorant that Stage-plays have been much envy'd at, and not without just cause; yet most certain it is, that by a wise use, and a right application of many things we hear and see contain'd therein, we may meet with many excellent precepts for instruction, and sundry great Examples for caution, and such notable passages, which being well applied (as what may not be perverted) will confer no small profit to the cautious and judicious Hearers. *Edward* the Sixth the Reformer of the *English* Church, did so much approve of Plays, that he appointed a Courtier eminent for wit and fancy to be the chief Officer in supervising, ordering, and disposing what should be acted or represented before his Majesty; which Office at this time retains the name of Master of the Revels. Queen *Elizabeth*, that incomparable Virtuous Princess, was pleased to term Plays the harmless Spenders of time, and largely contributed to the maintenance of the Authors and Actors of them.

But if the moderate recourse of Gentlewomen to Plays may be excused, certainly the daily and constant frequenting them, is as much to be condemned.

There are an hundred divertisements harmless enough, which a young Lady may find out, suitable to her inclination; but give me leave to find out one for her which hath the attendance of profit as well as pleasure and that is Reading.

Mistake me not; I mean the reading of Books whose subjects are noble and honourable. There are some in these later days so *Stoical*, that they will not allow any Books to Womankind, but such as may teach them to read, and the Bible. The most severe of them do willingly permit young Gentlewomen to converse with wise and learned men; I know not then by what strange nicety they would keep them from reading their Works. There are a sort of Religious men in foreign parts, who do not debar the people from knowing there is a Bible; yet they prohibit them from looking into it.

I would fain ask these sowre *Stoicks* what can be desired for the ornament of the mind, which is not largely contain'd and exprest in Books? where Virtue is to be seen in all her lovely and glorious dresses, and Truth discovered in what manner soever it is desired. We may behold it in all its force, in the Philosophers; with all its purity in faithful Historians; with all its beauty and ornaments in golden-tongu'd Orators, and ingenious Poets.

In this pleasing variety (whatsoever your humour be) you may find matter for delectation and information. Reading is of most exquisite and requisite use, if for nothing but this that these dumb Teachers instruct impartially. Beauty, as well as Royalty, is constantly attended with more flatterers than true informers. To discover and acknowledg their faults, it is necessary that they sometimes learn of the dead what the living either dare not or are loth to tell them. Books are the true discoverers of the mind's imperfections, as a glass the faults of their face, herein shall they find Judges that cannot be corrupted with love or hate. The fair and the foul are both alike treated, having to do with such who have no other eyes but to put a difference between Virtue and Vice. In perswading you to read, I do not advise you should read all Books; advise with persons of understanding in your choice of Books; and fancy not their quantity but quality. For why should ye seek that in many which you may find in one? The Sun, whilst in our Hemisphere needs no other light but its own to illuminate the World. One Book may serve for a Library. The reading of few Books, is not to be less knowing, but to be the less troubled.

Of the guidance of a Ladies love and fancy.

I Suppose you, virtuous Ladies and Gentlewomen to whom I direct this Discourse, yet know, that though you are victoriously seated in the Fort of Honour, yet Beauty cannot be there planted, but it must be attempted. However I would have you so constantly gracious in your resolves, that though it be assaulted, it can not be soiled; attempted but never attainted.

How incident and prone our whole Sex is to love, especially when young, my blushes will acknowledg without the assistance of my tongue; now since our inclination so generally tend to love and fancy, and knowing withal how much the last good or evil of our whole lives depend thereno [*recte* thereon], give me leave to trace them in all or most part of their *Meanders*, wherein you will find such suitable instructions as will give you for the future safe and sound direction.

Fancy is an affection privily received in by the eye, and speedily convey'd to the heart; the eye is the Harbinger, but the heart is the Harbourer.

Look well before you like; love conceived at first sight seldom lasts long, therefore deliberate with your love, lest your love be misguided; for to love at first look makes an house of misrule.

Portion may wooe a Wordling, Proportion a youthful Wanton, but it is Vertue which wins the heart of Discretion; admit he have the one to purchase your esteem, and the other to maintain your Estate, yet his breast is not so transparent as to know the badness of his disposition; if you then take his humour on trust, it may prove so perverse and peevish, that your expected Heaven of bliss may be converted into an Haven of insupportable crosses. *Themistocles* being asked by a Noble-man, whether he had rather marry his Daughter to a vicious Rich man or an Honest poor man; return'd this answer, That he had rather have a man without money than money without a man. Whence it was that prudent *Portia* replied, being asked, When she would marry? then said she, When I find one that seeks me, and not mine.

There is no time requires more modesty from a young Gentlewoman, than in wooing-time; a shamefast red then best commends her, and is the most moving Orator that speaks in her behalf. Like *Venus* Silver-Dove she is ever brouzing on the Palm of Peace, while her Cheeks betray her love more than her tongue.

There is a pretty pleasing kind of wooing drawn from a conceived yet concealed fancy. Might they chuse, they would converse with them freely, consort with them friendly, and impart their truest thoughts fully, yet would they not have their bashful loves find discovery.

> *Phillis, to willows, like a cunning Flyer*
> *Flys, yet she fears her Shepherd should not spy her.*

Whatever you do be not induced to marry one you have either abhorrency or loathing to; for it is neither affluence of estate, potency of friends, nor highness of discent can allay the insufferable grief of a loathed bed. Wherefore (Gentlewomen) to the intent you may shew your selves discreetest in that, which requires your discretion most, discuss with your selves the parity of love and the quality of your Lover, ever reflecting on those best endowments which render him worthy or unworthy of your greatest estimation. A discreet eye will not be taken only with a proportionable body, or smooth countenance; it is not the rind but the mind that is her Loadstone.

Justina a *Roman* Maid, no less nobly descended than notably accomplished, exclaimed much against her too rigid fate in being married to one more rich than wise: And good reason had she, being untimely made by his groundless jealousie a sad tragick spectacle of misery. For the whiteness of her neck was an object which begot in him a slender argument of suspect, which he seconded with rash revenge.

Let deliberation then be the Scale wherein you may weigh love with an equal poize. There are many high consequent-circumstances which a discreet Woman will not only discourse, but discuss, before she enter into that hazardous though honourable state of Marriage.

Disparity in descent, fortunes, friends, do often beget a distraction in the mind. Disparity of years breeds dislike, obscurity of descent begets contempt, and inequality of fortunes discontent.

If you marry one very young, bear with his youth, till riper experience bring him to a better understanding. Let your usage be more easie than to wean him from what he affects by extremity. Youth will have his swinge; time will reclaim, and discretion will bring him home at last. So conform your self to him as to confirm your love in him, and undoubtedly this conjugal duty, mixt with affability, will compleatly conquer the moroseness of his temper. If he be old, let his age beget in you the greater reverence; his words shall be as so many aged and time-improved precepts to inform you; his actions as so many directions to guide you; his kind rebukes as so many friendly admonitions to reclaim you; his Bed you must so honour, as not to let an unchast thought defile it; his Counsel so keep, as not to trust it in any others breast; be a staff in his age to support him, and an hand upon all occasions to help him.

If he be rich, this shall not or must not make you proud; but let your desire be, that you both employ it to the best advantage. Communicate to the Needy, that your Wealth may make you truly happy. That is a miserable Wealth which starves the Owner. I have heard of one worth scores of thousands of pounds who bought billets not for fewel but luggage; not to burn them and so warm himself, but to carry them on a frosty morning up stairs and down, and so heat himself by that labouring exercise. Wherefore let me perswade you to enjoy your own, and so shun baseness; reserve a provident care for your own and so avoid profuseness.

Is your Husband fallen to poverty; let his poor condition make you rich; there is certainly no want, where there wants no content. It is a common saying, *That as Poverty goes in at one door Love goes out at the other*; and love without harbour falls into a cold and aguish distemper; let this never direct your thoughts, let your affection counterpoize all afflictions. No adversity should divide you from him, if your vowed faith hath individually tyed you to him.

Thus if you expostulate, your Christian constant resolves shall make you fortunate. If your fancy be on grounded deliberation, it will promise you such good success, as your Marriage-days shall never fear the bitter encounter of untimely repentance, nor the cureless anguish of an afflicted conscience.

Now as I would have you, Gentlewomen, to be slow in entertaining, so be most constant in retaining. Lovers or Favourites are not to be worn like Favers; now near your bosom, or about your wrist, and presently out of all request. Which to prevent,

entertain none so near your heart, whom you observe to harbour in his breast something that may deserve your hate.

Carefully avoid the acquaintance of Strangers, and neither
affect variety nor glory in the multiplicity of your Suitors. For
there is no greater argument of mutability and lightness. Constant you cannot be where you profess, if change you do affect.
Have a care; vows deliberately advised, and religiously grounded, are not to be slighted or dispensed with. Before any such
things are made, sift him, if you can find any bran in him; task
him, before you tye your self to take him. And when your desires
are drawn to this period, become so taken with the love of your
Choice, as to interpret all his actions in the best sense; this will
make one Soul rule two hearts and one heart dwell in two bodies.

Before you arrive to this honourable condition all wanton
fancy you must lay aside, for it will never promise you good
success since the effect cannot be good where the object is evil.
Wanton love hath a thousand devices to purchase a minutes
penitential pleasure. Her eye looks, and by that the sense of
her mind is averted; her ear hears, and by it the intention of
the heart is perverted; her smell breaths, and by it her good
thoughts are hindred; her mouth speaks, and by it others are
deceived; by touch, her heat of desire upon every small occasion is stirred: never did *Orlando* rage more for his *Angelica*
than these *Utopian* Lovers for their imaginary shadows.

These exorbitancies we must endeavour to remedy; and that
therein we may use the method of art, we must first remove the
cause, and the effect will follow. Let me then discover the
incendiaries of this disorderly passion, next the effects arising
from them, and lastly their cure or remedy.

The original grounds of this wanton fancy, or wandring
phrenzie, are included in these two lines.

Sloth, Words, Books, Eyes, Consorts, and luscious fare,
The lures of lust, and stains of honour are.

For the first, sententious *Seneca* saith, *He had rather be*
exposed to the utmost extremities Fortune can inflict on him, than
subject himself to Sloth and Sensuality. For it is this only which
maketh of Men, Women; of Women, Beasts; and of Beasts
Monsters.

Secondly, Words corrupt the Disposition; they set an edg or gloss on depraved liberty; making that member offend most, when it should be imployed in profiting most.

Thirdly, Books treating of light Subjects, are Nurseries of wantonness; remove them timely from you, if they ever had entertainment by you, lest like the Snake in the Fable, they annoy you.

Fourthly, Eyes are those windows by which death enters. *Eve* looked on the fruit before she coveted; coveting, she tasted; and tasting, she perished; place them then on those objects whose real beauty make, take them, and not on such vanities which miserably taint them.

Fifthly, Consorts are thieves of time, which will rob you of many precious opportunities. Chuse then such Consorts of whom you may have assured hope, that they will either better you or be better'd by you. Chuse such whom you may admire when you see and hear them; when you see their living Doctrine, and hear their wholsome instruction.

Lastly, Luscious fare is the fewel of inordinate desires, which you must abstain from, or be very temperate in, if you intend to have your understanding strengthned, virtue nourished, and a healthy bodily Constitution.

The next thing we are to insist upon, is the evil effects of this wanton fancy, many may be here inserted, might I not be taxed with prolixity, and terrifie the Reader with examples of too much horror and cruelty. But if you would understand them, our late *Italian* Stories will afford you variety, for the satisfaction of your curiosity; where indiscreet love closeth her doleful *Scene* with so miserable an *Exit*, as no Pencil can express any picture more to the life than an Historical line hath drawn out the web of their misfortunes.

Now to cure this desperate malady (though to you, Gentlewoman, I hope the cure is needless, being void of all such violent distempers) the best and most soveraign Receipt, is to fortifie the weakness of your Sex with strength of resolution. Be not too liberal in the bestowing your favours nor too familiar in publick converse.

Make a contract with your eyes not to wander abroad, lest they be catcht in coming home. Treat not of love too freely; play no waggish tricks with the blind boy; he hath a dangerous aim, though he hath no eyes; sport not with him that may hurt you; play not with him that would play on you. Your sports will turn to an ill jest, when you are wounded in earnest; let the Fly be your Emblem.

So long the foolish Fly plays with the flame,
Till her light wings are sindged in the same.

Be watchful; there are many snares which students in Loves mysteries have laid to entrap Female credulity: How many are there can tip their tongues with Rhetorical protestations, purposely to gull a believing creature, for the purchase of an unlawful pleasure; which no sooner obtained, than the person slighted and left alone to bemoan her irrecoverable lost honour? With more safety therefore ought you to suspect, than too rashly to affect; and be sure you check your wild fancy by time lest a remediless check attend your choice. Repentance comes too late at the Marriage-night.

And yet I cannot commend your extraordinary coolness in affection, slighting all, as if none were worthy of your choice. The extreams of these two indisposed fancies ought to be seasoned with an indifferent temper.

Now the difference betwixt a wise and a wild love is this; The one ever deliberates before it loves; and the other loves before it deliberates.

There are a sort of wild Girls who compute their riches by the quantity of their Suitors. I have heard of a couple of Maids of different tempers; who contending with one another, said the one, *I have such and such vertuous and wealthy relations. I but* (replied the other) *I have more Suitors than thou hast friends. More shameless you* (answered the other) *unless you mean to set up an house of entertainment.* Such an one as this, never cares for more than to be married, if she may but see that day, it accomplisheth her content, though she have but one Comical-day all her life: Yea, it is as well as can be expected from their hands, if they attain unto that stile without some apparent foil. Such as these I could wish, to prevent the worst, they were married betimes, lest they marry themselves before time,

To you then, kind-hearted Gentlewomen, am I to recommend some necessary cautions; the careful observation of which I hope will prevent that danger which threatens the goodness of your Sex and Natures. The Index of your hearts you carry in your eyes and tongues; for shame learn silence in the one, and secrecy in the other. Give not the power to an insulting Lover to triumph over your weakness; and which is worse, to work on the opportunity of your lightness. Rather dam up those portals which betray you to your enemy; and prevent his entry by your vigilancy. Keep home and straggle not, lest by gadding abroad you fall into *Dinah*'s danger and mishap. Let not a stray'd thought prove the Traytor to your Innocency. Check your roving fancy; and if it use resistance, curb it with greater restraint.

And now a word or two to you coy Ladies whom either coldness of nature hath benumb'd or coyness hath made subtil to dissemble it. You can look and like, and yet turn away your head from what you love most. No object of love can take you, till it overtake you.

You may be modest, and spare a great deal of this coyness; yet so conceal and smoothly palliate your love, as your Lover may not despair of obtaining it. Indifferent courtesies you may shew without lightness, and receive them too in lieu of thankfulness.

Have a special regard to your Honour, which is of an higher esteem than to be undervalued. Light occasions are often-times grounds of deep aspersions. Actions are to be seasoned with discretion, seconded by direction, strengthned with instruction, lest too much rashness bring the undertaker to destruction.

In the Labyrinth of this Life, many are our Cares, mighty are our Fears, strong our Assailants, weak our Assistance; and therefore we had need have the Brasen-wall within us, to fortifie us against these evil occurrents. The scene of your life is short; so live then that your noble actions may preserve your memory long. It was the advice of *Seneca* to his Friend, Never to do any thing without imagining a *Cato*, a *Scipio*, or some other worthy *Roman* was present. To second his advice (which may confer on your glorious actions eternal praise[)], set always before your eyes, as an imitable mirrour, some good Woman or other, before whom you may live, as if she eyed and continually viewed you. There is no scarcity of Examples of such famous Women, who though weak in Sex and condition, yet parallels to Men for Charity, Chastity, Piety, Purity, and vertuous Conversation. It will not be amiss here in this place to insert some few eminent patterns for your Imitation.

The Gentlewomans Mirrour, or Patterns for their imitation, of such famous Women who have been eminent in Piety and Learning.

Revisit those ancient Families of *Rome*, and you shall find those Matrons make a Pagan State seem Morally Christian. *Octavia*, *Portia*, *Cæcilia*, *Cornelia*, were such, who though dead, their actions will make their memories live perpetually: Nor were *Niostrata*, *Corvina* and *Sappho*, Women less famous for Learning, than the other for blameless-Living. Neither have our modern times less flourished with Feminine Worthies, as might be illustrated with several eminent instances, were there not already of them so many Panegyricks extant.

It is said of *Dorcas*, *She was full of good works and alms which she did*. Yea even the Coats and Garments which she made when living, were shown the Apostle as arguments of her industry, and memorials of her piety. Hence it was that Saint *Jerome* counselled the holy Virgin *Demetrias* to eschew idleness; exhorting her when she had finished her Devotion, she should work with her hands after the commendable example of *Dorcas*; so that by change of works the day might seem less tedious, and the assaults of the Devil less grievous. And know, that this *Demetrias* was not one whom poverty did enforce to such actions of necessity, but one honourably descended, richly endowed, powerfully friended.

Devout mention is made of zealous *Anna*, who made frequent recourse to the Temple. Of whom to her succeeding memory the Scripture recordeth, that after her tears devoutly shed, her prayers sincerely offer'd, her religious vows faithfully performed, she became fully satisfied: Thus sighing she sought, seeking she obtain'd, and obtaining she retained a grateful memory of what she received.

Queen *Esther*, with what fervency and zeal did she make Gods cause the progress of her course, desiring nothing more than how to effect it, which was seconded with a successful conclusion? Because begun, continued, and ended with devotion.

Neither was *Judith* backward in zeal; Faith armed her with resolution, and constancy strengthened her against all opposition: Prayer was her armour, and holy desires her sole attendants. *Nazianzen* reporteth of his Sister *Gorgonia*, that by reason of the incessancy of her prayers, her knees seemed to cleave to the Earth. *Gregory* relates, that his Aunt *Thrasilla* being dead, was found to have her Elbows as hard as horn, which became so by leaning to a Desk, at which she usually prayed. Such as these deserve your imitation, who prayed and obtain'd what they pray'd for, they liv'd and practic'd what they fought for; they dy'd and enjoy'd what they so long sighed for.

Should you consider what troops of furious and implacable enemies lie in Ambuscado for you; how many Soul-tempting *Syrens* are warbling notes of ruine to delude you; what fears within you, what foes without you, what furies all about you; you would not let one minute pass undedicated to some good employment.

The commendable and admired Chastity of *Penelope* must not be forgot, which suffer'd a daily siege; and her conquest was no less victorious than those Peers of *Greece*, who made *Troy* their triumph. Estimation was her highest prize. Suiters she got; yet amidst these was not her *Ulysses* forgot. Long absence had not estranged her affection; youthful consorts could not move in her thoughts the least distraction; neither could opportunity induce her to give way to any light action. Well might famous *Greece* then esteem her *Penelope* of more lasting fame than any Pyramid that ever she erected. Her unblemished esteem was of purer stuff than any Ivory Statue that could be reared.

Nor was *Rome* less beholden to her *Lucretia*, who set her honour at so high a price, that she held death too light to redeem such a prize.

> *Though force, fright, foes and furies gaz'd upon her,*
> *Those were no wounds but wonders to her honour.*

The presence of a Prince no less amorous than victorious, could not win her; though with him, price, prayer and power, did jointly woo her. Well deserved such two modest Matrons the choice embraces of two such heroick Champions, as might equal their constant loves with the tender of their dearest lives.

There were seven *Milesian* Virgins, who at such time as the *Gauls* raved and raged every-where, subjecting all to fire and faggot, deprived themselves of life, lest hostile force should deprive them of their honour. I have read of two Maidens living in *Leuctra*, a Town in *Bœotia*, who having in their Fathers absence hospitably entertained two young men, by whom made drunk with Wine, they were deflowred that very night; the next morning conceiving a mutual sorrow for their lost Virginity, became resolute Actors in their own bloody Tragedy.

We may draw nearer home, and instance this Maiden-constancy in one of our own. It was not long since there lived within the Walls of *London* a notable-spirited Girl, who notwithstanding she frequented places of publick concourse boldly, discoursed freely, expressed her self in all essays forwardly, yet so tender was she in the preservation of her honour, that being on a time highly courted by a spruce and finical Gallant, who was as much taken with the height of her spirit, wherewith she was endowed, as he preferred it before the beauty of an amorous face, wherewith she was not meanly enriched. She presently apprehending the loosness of his desires, seemingly condescended; so that the business might be so secretly managed, as no occasion of suspition may be probably grounded. In order hereunto a Coach is provided, all things prepared, the place appointed where they shall meet, which for more privacy must be the Country. Time and place they observed; but before she would admit him to her imbraces, she told him (calling him aside) that she would never consent to any such thing with any Man, unless she had first tried his valour in the field; and to that purpose she had furnished her self with a Sword, and therefore bid him draw; he smilingly refus'd, as thinking she was in jest, but seeing by her home-passes how earnestly she prosecuted his life, he was constrained to draw: But this *Virago*, which was metal to the back, disarm'd him in an instant, and had like to have made this a bloody combat, instead of an amorous conflict. Our amazed Gallant not knowing what to think, say, or do, was at last compell'd to beg his life of her; in granting which, she bestow'd on him plentifully her Kicks, advising him ever after to be more wary in the attempting a Maidens Honour.

Excellent was the answer of the *Lacedemonian* Wives, who being courted and tempted to lewd and immodest actions, made this reply, *Surely we should give way to this your request, but this you sue for, lies not in our power to grant; for when we were Maids, we were to be disposed of by our Parents; and now being Wives, by our Husbands.*

Lastly, (that I may avoid prolixity) what singular mirrors of vidual Continency and Matron-like modesty were, *Cornelia*, *Vetruria*, *Livia*, and *Salvina?* Now what may you suppose did these Pagan Ladies hold to be the absolute end whereto this tender care of their reputation aspired chiefly, and wherein it most cheerfully rested? It was not riches, for these they contemned, so their honour might be preserved: Certainly there was implanted in them an innate desire of moral goodness, mixed with an honest ambition, so to advance their esteem during life, that they might become Examples to others of a good moral life, and perpetuate their memories after death.

Your ambition, Gentlewomen, must mount more high, because your Conversation is most heavenly. It is immortality you aspire to, a lower orb cannot hold you; nothing else may confine you.

Of Marriage, and the duty of a Wife to her Husband.

MArriage is an holy and inviolable bond; if the choice on both sides be good and well-ordered, there is nothing in the World that is more beautiful, more comfortable. It is a sweet Society, full of trust and loyalty. It is a fellowship, not of hot distempered love, but endeared affection; for these two are as different as the inflamed fit of an high Feaver, from the natural heat of a sound and healthy body. Love in the first acceptation is a distemper, and no wonder then that Marriages succeed so ill, which have their original from such disordered amorous desires. This boiling affection is seldom worth any thing. There are these two Essentials in Marriage, Superiority and Inferiority. Undoubtedly the Husband hath power over the Wife, and the Wife ought to be subject to the Husband in all things. Although the Wife be more noble in her extraction, and more wealthy in portion, yet being once Married is inferior to her Husband in condition. Man, of human kind, was Gods first workmanship; Woman was made after Man, and of the same substance, to be subservient and assisting to him.

Though the power of an Husband in this Kingdom extends it self farther than it is commonly exercised, yet something more moderate than in foreign parts. Amongst the *Romans* the Husband had power to kill the Wife in four cases; Adultery, suborning of Children, counterfeiting false Keys, and drunkenness.

It is customary among the *Indians* (but I do not therefore approve of it as lawful) that when the Husband dies, the death of the Wife immediately follows. This is not only practiced by the publick Laws of the Country, but oftentimes with such ardent affection, that the Wives (for they allow Polygamy) will contend one amongst the other who shall first sleep with their departed Husband. Though this custom I cannot only reject as unreasonable, but cruel and horrible; so I cannot but applaud those Wives (as they are in duty bound) who affectionately and patiently content themselves to accompany their Husbands in all conditions, in adversity as well as prosperity.

Many Examples hereof we may find at home as well as abroad, though in these late depraved and corrupted times there are not so many as may justly be desired. *Lentulus* being exiled by a Decree of the *Roman* Senate into *Sicily*, his loving Wife *Sulpitia* sold all, and followed him thither. *Ipsicrates* follow'd her vanquished Husband and King *Mithridates* through-out all extremities, notwithstanding she was advantagiously perswaded to the contrary.

Theagena Wife to *Agathocles* shew'd admirable constancy in her Husbands greatest misery; shewing her self most his own; when he was relinquisht and forsaken of his own; closing her resolution with this noble conclusion, She had not only betaken her self to be his companion in prosperity, but in all fortunes which should befal him.

Conform your selves to this mirror, and it will reform in you many a dangerous error. Thus if you live, thus if you love, honour cannot chuse but accompany you living; much comfort attend you loving, and a virtuous memory embalm you dying.

The more particular duties of a Wife to an Husband, are first, to have a greater esteem for him than for any other person; and withal, to have a setled apprehension that he is wise and prudent. That Woman that will entertain mean and low thoughts of her Husband, will be easily induced to love another, whom she ought not to affect. On this good esteem depends a great part of the Wives obedience, who will be apt to run into extravagancies when she is once possessed of the weakness of her Husbands understanding: She is to give honour, respect, and reverence to her Husband; so have the wisest ever done, and those which do it not, betray their indiscretion; with reverence she is to express her obedience in all lawful things;

and apply and accommodate her self (as much as in her lies) to his humour and disposition.

You must be mindful of what you promised your Husband in Marriage; and the best demonstration thereof will be in your carriage; honour and obey, and love no mans company better than his.

Be quiet, pleasant, and peaceable with him, and be not angry, when he is so; but endeavour to pacifie him with sweet and winning expressions; & if casually you should provoke him to a passion, be not long ere you shew some regret, which may argue how much you are displeased with your self for so doing; nay bear his anger patiently, though without a cause.

Be careful to keep your house in good order, and let all things with decency be in readiness when he comes to his repast; let him not wait for his meals, lest by so staying his affairs be disorder'd or impeded. And let what-ever you provide be so neatly and cleanly drest, that his fare, though ordinary, may engage his appetite, and disingage his fancy from Taverns, which many are compell'd to make use of by reason of the continual and daily dissatisfactions they find at home.

Shew respect and kindness to what Friends he brings home with him, but more especially to his Relations; for by this means he will find your love to him by your respect to them; and they will be obliged to love you for your own as well as his sake.

Suffer not any to buz in your ears detracting stories of him, and abhor it in your Servants, for it is your duty to hide his faults and infirmities, and not detect them your self, or suffer them to be discovered. Take them for your greatest enemies who perswade you against your Husband; for without question they have some dangerous design in it. *Those whom God hath joined together, let no man put asunder*; Cursed then is that instrument which occasions their separation.

Breed up your Children in as much or more obedience to him than your self; and keep them in so much awe that they shew no rudeness before him, or make any noise to his disturbance. Make them shew him all awful regard, and keep them sweet, clean, and decent, that he may delight himself in them.

Let him see your love to him in your care for them; educating and bringing them up in the knowledg of Religion, with their Learning.

Be careful to manage what money he doth trust you with, to his and your own credit: abuse not the freedom you have of his purse, by being too lavish; and pinch not the Guts of your Family at home, that you may pamper yours abroad; or throw away that money in buying trifles, which shall evidence your vanity as well as luxury.

To govern an House is an excellent and profitable employment; there is nothing more beautiful than an Houshold well and peaceably governed; it is a profession that is not difficult; for she that is not capable of any thing else, may be capable of this.

The principal precepts that belong to the frugal ordering and disposing Houshold-affairs may be compremis'd under these heads.

First to buy and sell all things at the best times and seasons.

Secondly, to take an especial care that the goods in the house be not spoiled by negligence, of servants or otherwise.

Let me counsel you not only to avoid unnecessary or immoderate charges, but also with a little cost make a great shew; but above all suffer not your expence to exceed the receipt of your Husbands income. There is a Proverbial saying, *That the Masters eye maketh the Horse fat*; I am sure the active vigilance of a good and careful Wife is the ready way to enrich a bad Husband.

Of Womens behaviour to their Servants, and what is to be required of them in the house, or what thereunto appertains.

IF by a thorough inspection and experience you find you have a faithful Servant give her to understand you are not insensible thereof by your loving carriage, and kind acknowledgment of her fidelity, and frequently find out some occasions to give her some little encouragements to engage her continuance therein; do not dishearten her in her duty, by often finding fault where there is little or none committed, yet be not remiss in reproving where she doth amiss.

If you find you have a bad or unfaithful Servant (as now adays there are too many, more than ever) whom you cannot either by fair means or foul reclaim: Vex not nor fret at what you see is remediless, but first making her thoroughly sensible of her errors, give her fair warning to provide for her self, and convenient for your own affairs; and do not (as a great many much to blame) give too ill a character of her, which will raise you little benefit, although it may lay the basis of her utter ruin; but rather be silent if you cannot speak good, which course I should think was sufficient to work on the greatest stupidity for a future amendment. Though a bad Servant detain not the wages, nor any part that is justly due, *for the Labourer is worthy of his hire*.

Be not too passionate with your Servants; and look narrowly to them, that they waste or lavish nothing, lest thereby you impair your estate and so purchase the repute of a careless and indiscreet Woman.

If you find that they affect bravery too much, and presume to wear what misbecomes their present condition, rebuke them mildly into a moderation for their future advantage, and the credit of the Family wherein they are.

Let not the business of the House take them clearly off the service of God, but let them so relieve one the other in their duties, that they may be sometimes hearers of a good Sermon; and do not forget to make enquiry how they improve by what they hear at Church, and in your own house.

Let every Servant, Men and Women have their daily work appointed them, which must be duly executed, and taken account of, either by your self or some superior servant constituted by you for this purpose and let not your constant and painful care of your worldly affairs exclude your greatest concern, the things of Heaven, and therefore appoint certain hours, Morning and Evening for publick prayers for the Family, and let not any Servant be absent, unless some extraordinary occasion hinder.

As near as you can, keep one set and certain time with good orders observed for the Table, in which be free, yet frugal. Let there be a competent allowance for the Servants, that they may have no just cause to complain; nor so much superfluity as that they may entertain a sort of loose Gossips in corners, the very bane and spoil of Servants.

Invert not the course of Nature (as too many do of late) by converting day into night, and night into day; but keep good hours for your repose, that your Servants may be the better disposed for the next day's labour. Observe due times for washing and smoothing up the Linnen quickly, that it may not be thrown up and down and be mildewed and spoil'd, and so be fit for nothing but the wash again; and forget not to dearn or mend it every week that it may not run to tatters before it be half-worn; and do not suffer any Servant to be idle.

If you have a Dairy, see it be kept clean and neat. Let not the Corn in the Granary muste and spoil for want of skreening and turning.

Let your Servant see that your Beasts and Poultry be fatted in their due season; and that your Stable keep no more Horses than your own.

In the Brew-house, that the first Wort be not drunk up by idle people, and so the smallness of your Beer become a disparagement to your Family.

In the Bake-house, that your Dough which should be for the finest Bread at your Table, be not half consumed in making of Cakes. That there be always Bread enough for the Servants before hand, for it is a point of ill Huswifry to eat hot or very new Bread.

In the Kitchin, that there be no Necessaries wanting, nor no waste or spoil made, but that the Meat be salted, and spent in due time.

In the Parlour, let the Fire be made, and the Cloth laid in due time, that the Cook may have no excuse for the spoiling of his Meat.

In the Chambers, that every thing be kept cleanly; the Beds often turned, the Furniture often beaten in the Sun, and well brushed.

Every Saturday take an account of every Servants layings out; and once a Month an account of all the expences of the whole House.

In the Buttery and Cellars, that the Butler be careful of not making every idle fellow drunk that comes to the House, and so squander away without credit the Wine, Ale, and Beer.

Now because you will have frequent occasions for Banquets, in the entertaining of persons of Quality, I think it not unfit for a Gentlewoman to learn the art of Preserving and Candying, of which I shall, according to the Profession I make thereof, give you an ample account or instruction in some Chapters following. Frugality will perswade you to learn these excellent Arts, for in the constant use of the product thereof, you will have much for Sweetmeats, you will make much cheaper than you can buy them, and more commendable.

Other things you will meet withal worthy of your observation, of which this is no mean one, most requisite and in no wise dishonourable; that is, your understanding how to dress Meat as well as eat it that your Servants may be guided by you, and not you by them.

Gentlewomen, I will appeal to you as persons competent to judg whether the right understanding of these things be not altogether requisite and necessary; and as to your divertisements, none carries in it more profit than Cookery. Now to the intent I may be instrumental to the making up a compleat and accomplished Gentlewoman, give me leave here to set you down such *A-la-mode* instructions, as may perfectly inform you in every thing that belongs to the commendable art of cookery.

Terms for Carving all sorts of Meat at Table.

B Efore we shall treat of the body of Cookery, I think it fit by way of Prologue or Introduction, to acquaint you with those proper terms in Carving, which are used abroad and at home, by the curious students in the art of Carving; take them thus as follows.

In cutting up all manner of small Birds, it is proper to say, Thigh them; as thigh that Woodcock, thigh that Pidgeon; but as to others say, Mince that Plover, Wing that Quail, and Wing that Partridg, Allay that Pheasant, Untach that Curlew, Unjoint that Bittern, Disfigure that Peacock, Display that Crane, Dismember that Hern, Unbrace that Mallard, Frush that Chicken, Spoil that Hen, Sauce that Capon, Lift that Swan, Rear that Goose, Tire that Egg. As to the flesh of Beasts, Unlace that Coney, Break that Deer, and Leach that Brawn.

For Fish; Chine that Salmon, String that Lamprey, Splat that Pike, Sauce that Plaice, and Sauce that Tench, Splay that Bream, Side that Haddock, Tusk that Barbel, Culpon that Trout,

Transon that Eel, Tranch that Sturgeon, Tame that Crab, Barb that Lobster.

I F you will *Lift a Swan*, slit her right down in the middle of the Breast, and so clean through the back, from the neck to the rump, and so divide her equally in the middle without tearing the flesh from either part; having laid it in the Dish with the slit-sides downwards, let your sawce be Chaldron a-part in Sawcers.

You must *Rear* or *Break a Goose roasted*, by taking off the Legs very fair; then cut off the Belly-piece round close to the lower end of the Breast; lace her down with your knife clean through the Breast on each side, a thumbs breadth from the Breast-bone; then take off the wings on each side, with the flesh which you first laced, raising it up clear from the bone, then cut up the merry-thought, and having cut up another piece of flesh which you formerly laced, then turn your Carcase, and cut it asunder the Back-bone, above the Loyn-bones; then take the rump-end of the Back-bone, and lay it at the fore-end of the merry-thought, with the skinny side upward; then lay your Pinions on each side contrary, set your Legs on each side contrary behind them, that the bone-end of the Legs may stand up cross in the middle of the Dish, and the wing-Pinions on the outside of them; put under the wing-Pinions on each side the long slices of flesh which you did cut from the Breast-bone, and let the ends meet under the Leg-bones.

If you would cut up a *Turky* or *Bustard*, raise up the leg very fair, then open the Joint with the point of your sharp Knife, yet take not off the Leg; then lace down the Breast on both sides, and open the Breast-pinion, but take it not off; then raise up the Merry-thought betwixt the Breast-bone and the top of the Merry-thought, lace down the flesh on both sides of the Breast-bone, and raise up the flesh called the Brawn, turn it outwards on both sides, but break it not nor cut it off; then cut off the Wing-pinion at the Joint next the Body, and stick on each side the Pinion in the place where you turned out the Brawn, but cut off the sharp end of the Pinion, take the middle piece and that will just fit the place. You may cut up a *Capon* or *Pheasant* the same way; but be sure you cut not off the Pinion of your *Capon*, but in the place where you put the Pinion of the *Turky*, place there your divided Gizard on each side half.

In the *dismembring of an Hern*, you must take off both the Legs, and lace it down the Breast; then raise up the flesh, and take it clean off, with the Pinion; then stick the head in the Breast, set the Pinion on the contrary side of the Carcase, and the Leg on the other side, so that the bones ends may meet cross over the Carcase, and the other Wing cross over upon the top of the Carcase.

If you will *Unbrace a Mallard*, raise up the Pinion and the Leg, but take them not off; raise the Merry-thought from the Breast, and lace it down sloppingly, on each side the Breast with your Knife.

Turn the Back downwards, if you unlace a *Coney*, and cut the Belly-flaps clean off from the Kidneys; then put in the point of your Knife between the Kidneys, and loosen the flesh from each side the bone; then turn up the back of the Rabbat, and cut it cross between the Wings, and lace it down close by the bone on each side; then open the flesh from the bone, against the Kidney, and pull the Leg open softly with your hand, but pluck it not off; then thrust in your Knife betwixt the Ribs and the Kidney, slit it out, then lay the Legs close together.

In the *allaying of a Pheasant*, and *winging a Partridg*, you must raise their Wings and Legs as if they were Hens.

If you mince your Partridg, sauce him with Wine, powder of Ginger and Salt, and so set him on a Chafing-dish of Coals to keep Warm. Use a Quail after the same manner.

Display a Crane thus: Unfold his Legs, and cut off his Wings by the Joints; then take up his Wings and Legs, and sauce them with powder of Ginger, Mustard, Vinegar and Salt: *Dismember a Hern* in the same manner, and sauce him accordingly; so likewise unjoint a Bittern, but use no sauce but salt.

I shall now proceed to give you some Instructions in the art of *Cookery*; which I shall rank in an Alphabetical order compendiously.

Artichoaks Fried.

Boil your Artichoaks, and sever them from the bottom, then slice and quarter them; having so done, dip them in Butter, and fry them in Butter. For the sauce, take Verjuice, Butter, and Sugar, with the juice of an Orange, lay Marrow on them, and having garnisht them with Marrow, serve them up.

Artichoaks Stewed.

Artichoaks being boil'd, take out the core, and take off the leaves, cut the Bottoms into quarters, splitting them in the middle, then put them into your flat stewing-pan, with Manchet-toasts therein, laying the Artichoaks on them, with an indifferent quantity of Marrow, five or six large Maces, half a pound of preserved Plumbs with the Sirrup, Verjuice, and Sugar; let them thus stew two hours, if you stew them in a Dish, stir them not thence, but serve them up in it, laying on some Barberies preserv'd, and such-like, so sippet it and serve it up; Instead of preserved Plumbs, you may stew those which are ordinary, and will do near as well, and are much cheaper.

An Almond-Pudding.

Take a pound of Almond-paste, some grated Bisket-bread, Cream, Rosewater, yolks of Eggs, beaten Cinnamon, Ginger, Nutmeg, some boiled Currans, Pistaches and Musk, boil it in a Napkin, and serve it in a Dish, with beaten Butter and Sugar scrap'd thereon.

An Almond-Pudding in Guts.

Get a pound of Almonds blanched, beat them very small with Rose-water, and a little good new Milk, or Cream, with two or three blades of Mace, and some sliced Nutmegs; when it is boiled, take the Spice clean from it, then grate a penny-loaf, and seirce it through a Cullender, put it into the Cream, and let it stand till it be pretty cool; then put in the Almonds, five or six yolks of Eggs, Salt, Sugar, and good store of Marrow, or Beef-suet, finely minced, and so fill the Guts.

An Almond-Tart.

Strain beaten Almonds with Cream, yolks of Eggs, Sugar, Cinnamon and Ginger, boil it thick, and fill your Tart therewith.

Almond-Cream.

Take half a pound of Almond-paste, beaten with Rose-water, and strain it with a quart of Cream, put it in a Skillet with a stick of Cinnamon, and boil it, stir it continually, and when it is boiled thick, put Sugar to it, and serve it up cold.

Apple-Cream.

Take a dozen Pippins, or more, pare, slice, or quarter them, put them into a Skillet, with some Claret-wine, and a race of Ginger sliced thin, a little Lemmon-peel cut small, and some Sugar; let all these stew together till they be soft, then take them off the fire, and put them into a Dish, and when they be cold, take a quart of boil'd Cream, with a little Nutmeg, and put in of the Apple as much as will thicken it; and so serve it up.

Apricocks green Baked.

When your Apricocks are green, and so tender that you may thrust a pin through the stone, scald them, and scrape the outside, oft putting them in water as you peel them, till your Tart be ready, then dry them well, and fill your Tart with them, and lay on good store of fine Sugar, close it up and bake it, ice it, scrape on Sugar, and serve it up.

Barley-broth.

Boil the Barley first in two waters, having first pickt it well, then join it with a knuckle of Veal, and seeth them together; to the Broth add Raisins, sweet herbs, large Mace, and the quantity of a fine Manchet sliced together, then season it with salt.

B I S K.

There are divers ways to make a Bisk, but the best is this; Take a Leg of Beef, and knuckle of Veal, boil them in two Gallons of fair water, scum them clean, and put to them some Cloves and Mace, then boil them from two Gallons to three quarts of broth; being boiled, strain it thin, put it into a Pipkin; when it is cold, take off the fat and bottom, and put it into a clean Pipkin, and keep it warm till the Bisk be ready; boil the Fowl in the liquor of the Marrow-bones of half a dozen peeping Chickens, and as many peeping Pidgeons in a clean Pipkin.

Then have pallats, noses and lips, boil'd tender, blanch'd and cut into pieces as big as a six-pence; also some Sheeps-tongues boil'd, blanch'd, larded, fried, and stewed in gravy, with some Chesnuts blanched; also some Cocks-combs boiled and blanched, with some yolk of hard Eggs. Stew all the aforesaid in some roast Mutton, or Beef-gravy, with some Pistaches, large Mace, a good big Onion or two, and Salt. Then take Lamb-stones blanch'd and slic'd also sweet-breads of Veal and sweet-breads of Lamb slit, some great Oysters parboil'd, and some Cock-stones: Fry the aforesaid Materials in clarified Butter, some fried Spinnage, or Alexander-leaves, and keep them warm in an Oven, with some fried Sausages made of minced Bacon, Veal, yolks of Eggs, Nutmegs, sweet-Herbs, salt, and Pistaches; bake it in an Oven in cauls of Veal; and being baked and cold, slice it round, fry it, and keep it warm in the Oven, with the aforesaid baked things. Having prepared all these things in readiness, take a great eight pound Dish, and a six-peny *French* loaf, chip it and slice it into large slices, and cover all the bottom of the Dish, then steep it well with your strong broth, and upon that some Beef-gravy; then dish up the Fowl on the Dish, and round about it the fried Tongues, with the Lips, Pallats, Pistaches, Eggs, Noses, Chesnuts, and Cocks-combs, and run them over the Fowls with some of the gravy, and large Mace. Then again run it over with fried Sweet-breads, Sausages, Lamb-stones, Cock-stones, fried Spinnage, and the Marrow over all; next the carved Lemmons on the Meat, and run it over with the beaten Butter, yolks of Eggs and gravy beaten up till it be thick; lastly, garnish the Dish with little Pyes, Dolphins of puff-paste, Chesnuts, boil'd and fried Oisters, and yolks of hard Eggs.

Gentlewomen, I must crave your pardon, since I know I have tired your patience in the description of a Dish, which though it be frequently fed in Noblemens houses, and with all this cost and trouble put together by some rare whimsical *French* Cook, yet I cannot approve of it, but must call it a Miscellaneous hodg-podg of studied vanity; and I have here inserted it not for your imitation, but admiration.

Beef hashed.

In the making of a Hash of Beef, take some of the Buttock and mince it very small with some Beef-suet, or lard, and some sweet herbs, some beaten Cloves and Mace, Pepper, Nutmeg, and a whole Onion or two; stew altogether in a Pipkin, with some blanched Chesnuts, strong broth, and a little Claret; let it stew softly for the space of three hours, that it may be very tender, then blow off the fat, dish it, and serve it on sippets, you may garnish it with Barberries, Grapes, or Gooseberries.

Beef A-la-mode.

Cut some Buttock-beef a quarter of an inch thick, and lard it with Bacon, having hackt it before a little with the back of your Knife, then stew it in a Pipkin with some gravy, Claret-wine, and strong Broth. Cloves, Mace, Pepper, Cinnamon and Salt; being tender stewed, serve it on *French*-bread sippets.

Beef Carbonadoed.

Steep your Beef in Claret-wine, Salt, Pepper, and Nutmeg, then broil it on the Embers over a temperate and unsmoaky fire, in the mean while boil up the liquor wherein it was steeped; and serve it for sauce, with beaten Butter.

Beef baked, red-Deer-fashion, in Pies or Pasties, either Surloine, Brisket, Buttock or Fillet, larded or not.

Let your Surloine be boned, and take off the great sinew that lies on the back, lard the leanest parts of it with great lard, being season'd with Nutmeg, Pepper, four ounces of each, two ounces of Ginger, and a pound of Salt, which seasoning you must put into the Pye, but first lay a bed of good sweet Butter, and a bay-leaf or two, half an ounce of whole Cloves, lay on your Beef, then put on the rest of the seasoning, and a few more Cloves, good store of Butter, and a Bay-leaf or two, close it up and bake it, it will require eight hours soaking; if you will eat it hot, half the seasoning will serve, and then let your paste be fine, other-wise coarse.

To this quantity of flesh you must have three Gallons of fine flower heapt measure. But the best way to bake red Deer is in coarse paste, either Pye, or Pasty; if Rye-meal, it will keep long, otherwise you may make it of Meal, as it comes from the Mill, using only boiling-water, without any other stuff.

Beef Collar'd.

In the right making of a Collar of Beef you must take the flank and lay it in Pump-water two or three days; shift it twice a day, then take it out, and dry it very well with clean Clothes, cut it in three layers, and take out the bones and most of the fat; then take three handfuls of Salt, and good stoore of sweet Herbs chopped very small, mingle them, and st[r]ew them betwixt the three layers, and lay them one upon another; then take an ounce of Cloves and Mace, and another of Nutmegs, and beat them well, and strew it between the layers of Beef, rowl it up close together, then lay some splices about it, and with pack-thread tye it up very close and hard, put it in a long Earthen-pot, which are made on purpose for that use, tying up the top of the pot with cap-paper; set it into the Oven, let it stand eight hours, draw it, and taking it out of the pot, hang it up for use.

Brawn, how to make a Collar.

Take a fat Brawn of two or three years growth and bone the sides; cut off the head close to the ears, and cut five Collars of a side, bone the hinder-leg, or else five will not be deep enough; cut the Collars an inch deeper on the belly than on the back, because the belly will shrink more in the boiling; make your Collars very even before you bind them up, not big at one end, and small at the other, but fill them equally, and lay them a-soaking in fair water; be sure that they be watered two days before you bind them up, shift and scrape them twice a day in that time, then bind them up with white tape; having your Boiler ready with the water boiling put in your Collars of the biggest bulk first, a quarter of an hour before those which are less. Boil them an hour with a quick fire, keeping the Boiler continually filled up with warm clean liquor and scum the fat clean off as it riseth. After an hour, let it boil still, but more leisurely; being fine and tender boiled, so that you may thrust a straw through it, draw your fire, and let your Brawn remain till the next morning; between hot and cold, put your Brawn into moulds of deep hoops, and bind them about with pack-thread; when cold take them out and put them into souce made of boil'd Oatmeal ground or beaten, and brawn [*recte* bran] boil'd in fair water, which you must strain through a Cullender when it is cold, into that thing you intend to lay your Brawn; then put salt thereunto, and close up the mouth of the Vessel from the Air. When you use it, dish it up with a sprig of Rosemary on the top, dipt in the white of an Egg well beaten to froth, sprinkled with flower, or with a straight sprig of Ew-tree.

Brawn made of a Sucking-Pig, otherways called souced Pig.

Chuse not a spotted Pig for handsomeness-sake, but one that is white; Scald him, and cut off his head, parting him down the back, draw and bone him, the sides being throughly cleansed from the blood, and soaked in several clean waters, dry the sides thereof, season them with Nutmeg, Ginger and Salt, rowl them, and put them up in clean Clothes; then take as much water as will cover it in the boiling-pan two inches over and above, and add two quarts of White-wine thereunto. When the liquor boils, put in your Collars with Salt, Mace, sliced Ginger, Parsley-roots, and Fennel-roots scraped and picked; being half boil'd, put in a quart of White-wine more, being quite boil'd, put in slices of Lemon to it with the whole peel. Having souc'd it two or three days, dish it out on plates with Vinegar; or serve it in Collars with Mustard and Sugar.

A Calves-head roasted.

Take the Head, and cleave it, and remove from thence the Brains, purge it well from the blood, then steep the Head in fair water warm five hours, in that time shift it twice or thrice; the last time cleanse the head; then boil the Brains and with it make a Pudding with some grated Bread, Beef-suet, and some Veal minced small together with some Sage; let the pudding be seasoned with Cloves, Mace, Salt, Ginger, Sugar, five yolks of Eggs and Saffron; fill the Head with this Pudding, then close it up, and bind it fast with pack-thread, spit it and bind on the Caul with some of the Pudding round about it; as it roasts save the gravy; but when you use it for the sauce, blow off the fat, and add thereunto a little White-wine, a Nutmeg sliced, the juice of an Orange, Salt, and Sugar, and a piece of sweet Butter; before you take up the head, dredg it with grated Bread, beaten Cinnamon, minced Lemmon-peel with a little Salt.

Calves-foot Pye, or Neats-foot Pye.

Take two pair of Calves feet, boil them tender and blanch them; being cold bone them, and mince them very small, and season them with Pepper, Nutmeg, Cinnamon, a little Ginger and Salt, and a pound of Currans, a quarter of a pound of Dates sliced, a quarter of a pound of fine Sugar, with a little Rose-water, and Verjuice, stir all together in a Dish or Tray, laying a little Butter in the bottom of the Pye; then lay on half the meat in the Pye; take then the Marrow of three Marrow-bones, and lay that on the meat in the Pye, and the other half of the meat on the Marrow, and stick some Dates on the top of the meat, so close up the Pye and bake it; being half baked, liquor it with Butter, White-wine or Verjuice, and ice it with Butter, Rosewater and Sugar, then set it in the Oven again till it be iced.

Capons Souced.

Take a good young fat Capon, finely pulled, drawn, and trussed, lay it in soak two or three hours, with a Knuckle of Veal well jointed, and after set them a-boiling in a deep Brass-pan, or large Pipkin in a gallon of fair water, when it boils, scum it, and put in four or five blades of Mace, two or three races of Ginger sliced, some Fennel and parsley roots scraped and pickt, season all with Salt. The Capon being tenderly boiled take it up, and when almost cold put it to your souced broth which you must boil with a quart of White-wine to a Jelly; putting this liquor into a convenient Vessel, place your Capon therein, with two or three sliced Lemmons, cover it close and serve it at your pleasure, garnishing your Dish with slices of Lemmon, Barberries, and som of the Jelly.

Calves-Chaldron-Mince-Pyes.

Let your Chaldrons or Muggets be boiled tender, & being cold mince them small, with Beef-suet, or interlarded Bacon, some yolks of hard Eggs, Veal, Mutton, and Lamb cut small; season it with Cloves, Mace, Nutmeg, Pepper, a little Onion, and minced Lemon-peel, with salt, and Juice of an Orange; then lay on some slices of interlarded Bacon and Butter, close it up and bake it; and when you draw it, liquor it with White-wine beaten with Butter.

Capon or Chicken in white-Broth.

First boil the Capon in water and salt, then take three pints of strong Broth, and a quart of White wine, and stew it in a Pipkin, with a quarter of a pound of Dates, half a pound of fine Sugar, four or five blades of large Mace, the Marrow of three Marrow-bones, an handful of white Endive; stew them very leisurely; having so done, strain the yolks of ten Eggs with some of the Broth. Before you dish up the Capon or Chickens, put the Eggs into the Broth, and keep it stirring that it may not curdle, and let it be but a little while on the fire; the Fowls being dished up, put on the Broth, and garnish the Dish with Dates, large Mace, Endive, preserved barberries. You may make a Lere of Almond-paste, and Grape-verjuice.

Chicken-Pye.

Truss the Chickens, then season them lightly with pepper, Salt and Nutmeg, lay them in the Pye, and lay on them some sliced Dates, with the Marrow of two or three Marrow-bones, some large Mace, a quarter of a pound of Eringo-roots, some Grapes or Barberries, with Butter, close it up and put it into the Oven; being half baked, liquor it with a Cawdle made of a Pint of White-wine or Verjuice, the yolks of five or six Eggs, with Sugar and Butter; shake liquor well in it, which you may colour green with the juice of Spinage: It is proper to ice these Pyes, or scrape Sugar on them.

Clouted Cream.

Take a gallon of new Milk from the Cow, two quarts of Cream, and twelve spoonfuls of Rosewater, put these together in a large Milkpan, and set it upon a fire of Charcole well kindled, (be sure the fire be not too hot) and let it stand a day and a night; then take it off and dish it with a slice or scummer, let no Milk be in it, lay it in a Cream-dish, with Sugar scraped thereon, and so serve it up.

Cabbedg-Cream.

Set over the fire six quarts of new Milk, and when it boils, pour it out into half a score of Earthen-pans or bowls, as fast as you can without frothing, set them apart, and when they are a little cold, gather the Cream that is on the top with your hand, rumpling it together, and lay it on a flat dish; when you have laid three or four layers one on the other, wet a feather in Rosewater and Musk, and stroke over it, then searce a little grated Nutmeg, and fine Sugar, then lay three or four lays more on, as before, thus doing till you have all the Cream in the bowl, and then put all the Milk together and boil it again; and when it boils, do with it as you did before; it will yield thus four or five times seething, with which you must do as before, that it may lie round and high like a Cabbedg. You will do well to let one of the first Bowls to stand till last, that the Cream may be thick and crumpled, and that use for the uppermost lay, and so scrape Sugar in it. This must be made overnight for Dinner, and in the morning for Supper.

Carp Stewed.

Dress the Carp and take out the Milt, put it in a Dish with the Carp, take out the Gall, then save the blood, and scotch with your knife the back of the Carp. If the Carp be large, take a quart of Claret, or White-wine, four or five blades of large Mace, ten Cloves, two large races of Ginger sliced, two sliced Nutmegs, with the tops of Time, Marjoram, Savory, and Parsley chopped very small, four great Onions whole, three or four Bay-leaves, and some Salt; Stew them all together with the Wine when the liquor boils: Put in the Carp, with a quarter of a pound of sweet Butter; being stew'd enough, take a large Dish, and laying the Carp therein, pour the Sawce thereon with the Spices; lay on sliced Lemon, with some of the peel cut small, and run it over with beaten Butter; Garnish the Dish with Manchet grated and searced, and carved sippets laid round the Dish. You may for variety, the Carp being scaled, garnish the body with stewed Oisters, some fried in white Butter, some in green, made by the juice of Spinnage.

Carp Marinated.

Take a Carp, scale it, and scrape off the slime, wipe it clean with a dry Cloth, and split it down the back, flowre it, and fry it in sweet Sallet-oyl, or clarified butter; being fried crisp, lay it in a deep Dish, or Earthen-pan, then take some white Claret-wine, white-wine-Vinegar, and put it into a broad-mouth'd Pipkin, with Rosemary, Time, sweet Marjoram, Parsley, Winter-Savory, Bay-leaves, Sorrel and Sage, a like quantity of each, with some large Mace, sliced Ginger, gross Pepper, sliced Nutmeg, whole Cloves and Salt, with as much Wine and Vinegar as will cover the Fish; boil all these together a little while, and then pour it on the Fish hot, and cover it close to detain the spirits from evaporating for an hours space, and then lay on your Lemon with Orange-peel. Thus you may marinate Soles, Plaice, or any other, whether Sea or fresh-water Fish; if you barrel or pack it up close, it will be as good, and keep as long as Sturgeon.

Carp roasted.

Take a live Carp, draw and wash it, taking away the Gall, Milt or Spawn, then make a Pudding with some grated Manchet, some Almond-paste, Cream, Currans, grated Nutmeg, raw yolks of Eggs, Sugar, Carraway-seed candied, some Salt and Lemon; make a stiff-Pudding, and put it through the Gills into the belly of the Carp; then spit it, and when it is roasted, make Sauce with the Gravy that falls from it, with juice of Orange, Sugar and Cinamon; beat up the Sauce thick with the Butter, and dish it up.

Deer, Red and Fallow, roasted.

Take a side or half-Haunch, and parboil it, then farce or stuff it with all manner of sweet Herbs minced with Beef-suet; lay the Cawl over, and so roast it; when ready, dish it up with a Gallendine-sauce made with strained Bread, Vinegar, Claret-wine, Cinamon, Ginger and Sugar, boil up these with a few whole Cloves, and a sprig of Rosemary.

Deer Baked.

Take a side of Venison, bone and lard it with great lards as big as your little finger, and season it with two ounces of Pepper, two ounces of Nutmeg, and four ounces of Salt, then make your Pye, and lay some Butter in the bottom thereof, then lay in your flesh the inside downward, coat it thick with seasoning, adding a few Cloves and good store of Butter, so close it up and bake it, first basting it with Eggs.

Egg-Mince-Pye.

Boil your Eggs hard, then mince and mix them with Cinamon, Currans, Carraway-seed, Sugar and Dates, minced Lemon-peel, Verjuice, Rosewater, Butter and Salt, with these fill your Pyes; when baked, liquor them with Butter, White-wine, Sugar and ice them.

Florentines on Paste, or without Paste.

Take a Leg of Mutton or Veal, shave it into thin slices, and mingle it with some sweet Herbs, as sweet Marjoram, Time, Savory, Parsley and Rosemary; being minced very small, a Clove of Garlick, some beaten Nutmeg, Pepper, a minced Onion, some grated Manchet, and three or four yolks of raw

Eggs, mix all together with a little Salt, some thin slices of interlarded Bacon, lay the Meat round the Dish, on a sheet of Paste, or in the Dish without Paste; being baked, stick Bay-leaves round the Dish.

Flowers of all sorts Pickled.

Put them into a Gally-pot, or Glass, with as much Sugar as they weigh, fill them up with Wine-Vinegar. To a pint of Vinegar a pound of Sugar, and a pound of Flowers: so keep them for Sallets and boil'd Meats.

Grapes and Goosberries Pickled.

Pick them and put them in Verjuice, and so barrel them up.

Geese Boiled.

Take them being powder'd, and fill their bellies with Oatmeal, being first steeped in warm Milk, then mingle it with some Beef-suet, minced Onions and Apples, season'd with Cloves, Mace, some sweet Herbs minced, and Pepper, fasten the neck and vent, boil them, and serve them with Brewis, and Colliflowers or Cabbedg, running it over with beaten Butter; thus you may dress any sort of Sea-fowl.

Hashes several ways.

First, of raw Beef, mince it very small with Beef-suet or Lard, some sweet-Herbs, Pepper, Salt, some Cloves and Mace, Ches-nuts or Almonds blanch'd, put in whole, some Nutmeg, and a whole Onion or two, and stew it in a Pipkin with some strong broth two hours, put a little Claret to it, and serve it on Sippets, blowing off the fat, and garnish it with Lemon or Barberries.

Otherways.

Cut your Beef, fat and lean, into Gobbets, as big as a Pullets Egg, and put them into a pot or Pipkin with some Carrots cut into pieces as big as a Walnut, some whole Onions, some Parsnips, large Mace, a faggot of sweet herbs, Salt, Pepper, Cloves, with as much water and wine as will cover them, let them thus stew three hours.

Hashes of Neats-feet, or any feet, as Calves, Sheep, Deer, Hogs,
Pigs or Lambs.

Boil them very tender, and being cold, mince them small,
then put Currans to them, beaten Cinamon, hard Eggs minc'd,
Capers, sweet Herbs minced small, Cloves, Mace, Sugar, White-
wine, Butter, sliced Lemon or Orange, sliced Almonds, grated
Bread, Saffron, Grapes, or Barberries, to serve them on fine
carved Sippets.

Hashing of any feet.

Mince them small, and stew them with White-wine, Butter,
Currans, Raisins, Marrow, Sugar, Prunes, Dates, Cinamon,
Mace, ginger, Pepper, and serve them on toasts of fried
Manchet.

Hares roasted without and with the Skin.

Take an Hare and flay him, then lard him with small lard,
stick him with Cloves, and make a Pudding in his belly, with
grated Bread, grated Nutmeg, Cinamon beaten, Salt, Currans,
Eggs, Cream and Sugar; having made it stiff, fill the belly of the
Hare and so roast it. If you will have your Pudding green,
colour it with Spinage; if yellow, with Saffron. Let the Sauce be
made of beaten Cinamon, Nutmeg, Ginger, Pepper, Prunes,
Currans, a little grated Bread, Sugar and Cloves, all boiled up
as thick as Water gruel.

If you roast an Hare with the Skin on, draw out the Bowels,
and make a farsing, or stuffing of all manner of sweet Herbs
minced very small, then roul them in some Butter, and make a
ball thereof, put it into the belly, and prick it up close, baste it
with butter, and being almost roasted, flay off the Skin, and stick
on some Cloves on the Body, bread it with fine grated Manchet,
Flower and Cinamon, froth it up, and dish it on Sawce, made of
grated Bread, Claret-wine, Wine-vinegar, Cinamon, Ginger, and
Sugar, being boiled up to an indifferency.

Ipocras.

To make good Ipocras, you must take a gallon of Wine, three
ounces of Cinamon, two ounces of sliced Ginger, an ounce of
Nutmegs, a quarter of an ounce of Cloves, twenty corns of
Pepper, an handful of Rosemary-Flowers, three pounds of
Sugar, and two quarts of Cream.

Jellies of several colours for all sorts of Soust Meats, and to be eaten alone.

Take four pair of Calves-feet, a knuckle of Veal, a good fleshy Capon, take out the bones and fat, and cast them into fair water, shift them three or four times in a day and night, then boil them in three gallons of fair water till six quarts be wasted, then strain it into an Earthen-pan, let it cool, then take off the fat at top, and pare the bottom; then dissolve it again in broth, and divide it into four equal parts, every part in a particular Vessel; put a little Saffron into one of them, into another Cutcheneel, into a third Turnsole, let the last alone to its own natural whiteness; let each Vessel have a quart of White-wine, and the juice of two Lemons. To the white Jelly add one race of Ginger pared and sliced, and three blades of large Mace. To the red Jelly two Nutmegs, and the like quantity of Cinamon and Ginger. To the yellow or Amber-colour the same spices, and the like quantity; and to the Turnsole the same with a few Cloves. Then take eighteen whites of Eggs, and beat them with six pound of double refined Sugar, beaten small and stirred together in a Tray, or great Bason; with a rowling-pin, divide it equally into four parts, and distribute one to each Vessel, being well mixed with Wine, and a little Musk, or Ambergriece, stir it about with your Jelly. Then set on your Jelly again on a fine Charcole fire, and let it stew near an hour, then make it boil up a little, so take it off; being somewhat cold, strain it, and so let it stand for your use, casting it into what mould you please.

Land or Sea-fowl, how to boil them.

Half roast the Fowls, sticking on them some Cloves as they roast, save the Gravy, and when they are half roasted, put them into a Pipkin with the Gravy, some Claret-wine, as much strong broth as will cover them, Mace, Cloves, Pepper, Ginger, some fried Onions and Salt; stew all well together and serve them on carved sippets.

Land-Fowl, the smaller sort, how to boil, as Plovers, Quails, Blackbirds, Rails, Thrushes, Snipes, Wheat-ears, Larks and Sparrows.

Take them and truss them, or cut off the Heads and Legs, and boil them, scum your Pipkin, and put therein large Mace, White-wine, Currans well pickt and washt, Dates, Marrow, Pepper and

Salt; being well stewed, dish them on carved Sippets; thicken the broth with strained Almonds, Rosewater, and Sugar; garnish them with Lemon, Barberries and grated bread.

Marrow-Pudding in a Dish baked, garnished with Puff paste.

Take the Marrow of four Marrow-bones, two *French* breads, half a pound of Raisins of the Sun ready boiled and cold, Cinamon a quarter of an ounce beaten, two grated Nutmegs, a quarter of a pound of Sugar, the like of Date, Sack half a pint, Rosewater a quarter of a pint, ten Eggs, two grains of Amber-griece. Now take a deep large dish, and lay a lay of sliced *French*-bread therein, and strew it with Cinamon, Nutmeg, and Sugar, mingled together; also sprinkle the slices of bread with Sack and Rosewater, and then some Raisins of the Sun, sliced Dates, and good big pieces of Marrow, and thus make two or three lays of the aforesaid ingredients with most Marrow on the top; then take two quarts of Cream, and strain it with half a quarter of fine Sugar, with about a spoonful of Salt, and twelve Eggs, six of the whites taken away, then set the Dish into the Oven, temperate, and not too hot, and bake it very white, then strew some Sugar on so serve it.

Mutton hashed the French way.

Take a Shoulder of Mutton, and roast it three quarters and save the Gravy; slice the one half and mince the other, and put it into a Pipkin, with the Shoulder-blade, put to it some strong broth of Mutton or Beef-gravy, large Mace, some Pepper, Salt, a big Onion or two, a faggot of sweet Herbs, and a pint of White-wine; stew them all together close covered, then take away the fat, and put some Oyster-liquor thereunto; add also three pints of great Oysters parboiled in their own liquor; these Materials being well stewed down, dish up your meat, pouring your liquor thereon, and uppermost lay your stewed Oysters with sliced Lemon and fine carved sippets.

Marinated Mullet, Bace, Gurnet, or Rochet.

Take a gallon of White-wine-Vinegar, a quart of fair water, a good handful of Bay-leaves, as much Rosemary, and a quarter of a pound of beaten Pepper, put these together, and let them boil softly, season it with Salt, then fry your Fish in the Best Sallet-oyl; this done, put the Fish in an earthen Vessel or

Barrel, lay the Bay-leaves and Rosemary between every layer of the Fish, and pour the broth upon it; when it is cold, close up the Vessel.

Mullets Fried.

Scale, draw, and scotch them, after washing wipe them dry, and flowre them, fry them in Clarified Butter; being fried, put to them some Claret-wine, sliced Ginger, grated Nutmeg, and Anchovee, Salt, and sweet Butter beaten up thick, but first rub the dish with a Clove of Garlick: Chuse the least Mullets to fry.

Mullets or Bace baked.

Scale, garbedg, wash and dry the Bace or Mullet very well, lard it with Salt-Eel, season it and make a Pudding for it of grated Bread, sweet Herbs, and fresh Eel minced, put also the yolks of hard Eggs, Anchovee washt and minced very small, some Nutmeg and Salt, fill the belly herewith, or cut it into quarters and season them with Nutmeg, Ginger and Pepper, lay them in your Pye and make Balls, and lay them on the pieces of Mullet, then put on some Capers, Prawns, or Cockles, yolks of Eggs minced, Butter, large Mace, and Barberries, close it up; being baked, cut it up and fill it with beaten Butter, and garnish it with sliced Lemon. This is a very good way for Tench or Bream.

Mushrooms Fried.

Blanch them and wash them clean; if they be large, quarter them, and boil them with Salt, Vinegar, and water, sweet Herbs, large Mace, Cloves, Bay-leaves, and two or three Cloves of Garlick, then take them up, dry them, dip them in butter, and fry them in Clarified butter till they be brown; make your sauce for them of Claret-wine; the juice of two or three Oranges, Salt butter, the juice of Horse-radish-root beaten and strain'd, sliced Nutmeg and Pepper, put these into a Frying-pan, with the yolks of two or three Eggs, with some Mutton-gravy, beat or shake them well together in the Pan, that they curdle not, then rub a dish with Garlick, and lay the Mushrooms therein garnisht with Oranges and Lemons.

Mushrooms stewed.

Take them fresh gathered, and cut off the end of the stalk; and as you peel them, put them in a dish with White-wine; after they have layn half an hour, drain them from the Wine, and put them between two Dishes, and set them on a soft fire without any liquor, and when they have stewed a while, pour away the liquor that proceeded from them, then put to your Mushrooms a sprig of Time, a whole Onion, four or five corns of whole Pepper, two or three Cloves, a piece of an Orange, a little Salt, and some sweet butter, with some pure gravy of Mutton; cover them and set them on a gentle fire, so let them stew softly till they are enough and very tender; when you dish them, blow off the fat from them, and take out the Time, the Spice, and Orange, then wring in the juice of Lemon, and strew some Nutmeg thereon.

Neats-Tongues boiled.

Salt a Tongue twelve hours, or boil it in water and salt till it be tender, blanch it, serve it on carved Sippets and Brewis, with boiled Turnips and Onions, run it over with beaten Butter, and garnish it with Barberries or Grapes.

Neats-tongues Stewed.

Take a Tongue & put it a-stewing between two Dishes, being raw and fresh, put some strong broth and White-wine to it, with some whole Cloves, Mace, and whole Pepper, some Capers, Salt, with Roots, as Carrots or Turnips, and stew them all together leisurely the space of two hours or more; then blanch it, and put some Marrow to it, give it a walm or two, then Serve it on Sippets finely carved, and strew on some minced Lemon, Barberries or Grapes and run it over with beaten Butter: Garnish your Dish with Manchets finely searced.

Neats-tongues, an excellent way how to dry them.

Take Salt beaten very fine, and salt-Peter, of each a like quantity, rub your tongues very well with the Salts, and cover them all over with it; and as it wasts, supply them with more, then roul them in Bran, and dry them before a soft fire; before you boil them, lay them in Pump-water one night, and boil them in Pump-water.

Neats-Tongues roasted.

Take a Neats-tongue tenderly boiled, blanched, and cold, cut a hole in the butt-end, and mince the meat that you take out, then put some sweet Herbs, finely minced to it, with a minced Pippin or two, the yolks of Eggs sliced, some-minced Beef-suet, beaten Ginger and Salt, fill the Tongue and stop the end with a Caul of Veal, lard it and roast it, make your Sawce with Butter, Nutmeg, Gravy, and juice of Oranges: Garnish the Dish with sliced Lemon and Barberries.

Neats-tongue-Minc'd-Pye.

Take a fresh Neats-tongue, boil, blanch, and mince it, then mince four pound of Beef-suet by it self, mingle them together and season them with an ounce of Cloves and Mace beaten, some Salt, half an Orange preserved, and a little Lemon-peel, shred with a quarter of a pound of Sugar, four pound of Currans, a little Verjuice and Rosewater and a quarter of a pint of Sack, stir all together, and fill your Pyes.

A Norfolk-Fool.

Take a quart of thick sweet Cream, and set it a-boiling in a clear scoured Skillet, with some large Mace and whole Cinamon; having boiled a little while, take the yolks of five or six Eggs beaten well and put to it; being off the fire, take out the Cinamon and Mace; the Cream being pretty thick, slice a fine Manchet into thin slices as many as will cover the botom of the Dish, and then pour on the Cream; trim the Dish with carved Sippets; and stick it with sliced Dates and scrap Sugar all over it.

Oysters stewed.

Take a pottle of large Oysters, parboil them in their own liquor, then wash them from the dregs in warm water, and put them in a Pepkin, with a good big Onion or two, and five or six blades of large Mace, a little whole Pepper, a sliced Nutmeg, a quarter of a pint of White-wine, as much Wine-vinegar, a quarter of a pound of sweet Butter, with a little Salt, stew them together on a soft fire the space of half an hour, then dish them on Sippets of *French*-bread, sliced Lemon on that and Barberies, then run them over with beaten Butter, and garnish the dish with grated Manchet searced.

Oysters Fried.

Strain the liquor from them, and parboil them in a Kettle, then dry and roll them in Flower, or make a batter with Eggs,

Flower, a little Cream and Salt, dip them therein, and fry them in Butter. For the Sawce, boil the juice of three or four Oranges, some of their own liquor, a sliced Nutmeg and Claret; being boiled a little, put in a slice of Butter, beating it up thick; having warm'd the Dish, rub it with some Garlick, and lay therein the Oysters; garnishing the Dish with slices of Orange.

Oyster-Pyes.

Parboil your Oysters in their own liquor, then take them out and wash them in warm water, dry them, and season them with Pepper, Nutmeg, yolks of hard Eggs and Salt; the pye being made, put a few Currans in the bottom and lay on the Oysters with some sliced Dates in halfs, some large Mace, sliced Lemon, Barberries and Butter, close it up, and bake it, then liquor it with White-wine, Sugar, and Butter.

Otherways.

Take a pottle of Oysters, being parboiled in their own liquor, beard and dry them, then season them with large Mace, whole Pepper, a little beaten Ginger, Salt, Butter, and Marrow, then close and bake it, then make a Lear with White-wine, Oyster-liquor, and one Onion; boil these with a pound of Butter, minced Lemon, and a faggot of sweet herbs, and liquor the Pye therewith.

Oysters Pickled.

Take eight quarts of Oysters, and parboil them in their own liquor, then take them out and cleanse them in warm water, then wipe them dry, then take the liquor, they were parboiled in, and clear it from the grounds into a large Pipkin, or Skillet, put to it a pottle of good White-wine, a quart of Wine-Vinegar, some large Mace, whole Pepper and a good quantity of Salt, set it over the fire and boil it leisurely, scum it clean, and being well boiled, put the liquor into Barrels, that will hold a quart or more, and when it is cold, put in the Oysters, and close up the head.

Ox-cheeks baked in a Pye.

Being first cleansed from the slime, filth and blood, cut them in pieces, take out the bones, and season them with Pepper, Salt, and Nutmeg, then put them in a Pye with a few whole Cloves, a little seasoning, slices of Butter and Bacon over all; bake them very tender, and liquor them with Butter and Claret-wine.

A Calves-head Pye.

Take a Calves-head, soak it well, and take out the brains, boil the head and take out the bones; being cold, stuff it with sweet Herbs and hard Eggs chopped small, minced Bacon, and a raw Egg or two, Nutmeg, Pepper, and Salt; and lay in the bottom of the Pye minced Veal raw, and Bacon; then lay the Cheeks on it in the Pye, and sliced Bacon on that, then Spices, Butter and Grapes, or a Lemon, then close it up, bake it, and liquor it with butter only.

Puff-paste, the best way how to make it.

Take a pottle of Flower, mix it with cold water, half a pound of Butter, and the whites of five Eggs, work these together very well and stiff, then roul it out very thin, and put Flower under it and over it, then take near a pound of butter, and lay it in bits all over it, then double it in five or six doubles; this being done, roul it out the second time, and serve it as at the first, then roul it out and cut it into what form you please, and for what use, you need not fear the curle, for it will divide as often as you have doubled, ten or twelve times is enough for any use.

Panado's.

Boil fair water in a Skillet, put to it grated bread or cakes, good store of Currans, Mace, and whole Cinamon; being almost boil'd, and indifferent thick, put in some Sack or White-wine, Sugar, and some strained yolks of Eggs. Otherways, with sliced Bread, Water, Currans, and Mace; and being well boiled, put to it some Sugar, White-wine, and Butter.

Posset of Sack, Claret, or White-wine, the best manner.

Take twenty yolks of Eggs, with a little Cream, strain them, and set them by; then have a clean-scoured Skillet, and put into it a pottle of sweet Cream, and a good quantity of whole Cinamon; set it a-boiling on a soft Charcole-fire, and stir it continually; the Cream having a good taste of the Cinamon, put in the strained Eggs and Cream into your Skillet, stir them together, and give them a walm, then have in readiness some Sack or other Wine in a deep Bason, or Posset-cup, good store of fine Sugar, and some sliced Nutmeg; the Sack and Sugar, being warm, take out the Cinamon, and pour your Eggs and Cream very high into the Bason, that it may spatter in it; then strew on Loaf-sugar.

Pompion-Pye.

Take a pound of Pompion, and slice it; an handful of Time, a little Rosemary, sweet Marjoram stripped off the stalks, chop them small; then take Cinamon, Nutmeg, Pepper, and a few Cloves, all beaten; also ten Eggs, and beat them all together, with as much Sugar as you shall think sufficient; then fry them like a Froise; and being fried, let them stand till they are cold; Then fill your Pye after this manner: Take Apples sliced thin round-wise, and lay a layer of the Froise, and another of the Apples, with Currans betwixt the layers; be sure you put in good store of sweet Butter before you close it. When the Pye is baked, take six yolks of Eggs, some White-wine or Verjuice, and make a Caudle thereof, but not too thick; cut up the lid and put it in, and stir them well together whilst the Eggs and Pompions are not perceived, and so serve it up.

Pig roasted with the Hair on.

Take a Pig, and draw out his Entrails, Liver and Lights, draw him very clean at vent, and wipe him, cut off his Legs and truss him, and prick up the Belly close, Spit it, and lay it to the fire; have a care of scorching it; when it is a quarter roasted, the skin will rise up in blisters from the flesh, then with your hands or knife, pull off the skin and hair; being cleanly flay'd, cut slashes down to the bones, baste it with Butter or Cream, then bread it with grated white-bread, Currans, Sugar and Salt, all together; and thus baste it and dredg it till the Body be covered an inch thick, then the Pig being thoroughly roasted, draw it and serve it up whole, with Sauce made of Wine-Vinegar, whole Cloves, whole Cinamon, and Sugar boiled to a Syrrup.

Pidgeons boiled.

Being trussed, put them into a Pipkin or Skillet, with some strong broth, or fair water, boil and scum them, then put in some Mace, a faggot of sweet Herbs, white Endive, Marigold-flowers and Salt, and being finely boiled, serve them on sippets; and garnish the Dish with Mace and white Endive-flowers.

Pike boiled.

Take your Pike and wash it clean, then truss it whole, round, with the tail in his mouth, and his back scorched, or cut it in three pieces, and divide the middle-piece into two; then boil it in Water, Salt, and Vinegar, put it not in till the liquor boil, and then make it boil apace, and that will crisp your Pike; but afterwards softly. For the Sauce, put into a Pipkin a pint of White-wine, sliced Ginger, Mace, Dates quartered, a pint of large Oysters with their liquor, a little Vinegar and Salt; boil them a quarter of an hour, then mince a few sweet Herbs and Parsley, stew them till half the liquor be consumed; the Pike being boiled, dish it, and garnish the Dish with grated White-bread, or Ginger fine beaten, then beat up the Sauce with half a pound of Butter, minced Lemon or Orange, and pour it on the Pike with Sippets.

Pike stewed.

Take a Pike, slat it, and lay it in a Dish; when the blood is clean washed out, put to it as much White-wine as will cover it, and set it a-stewing; when it boils, put in the Fish, and scum it, and put to it some large Mace, whole Cinamon and some Salt; when thorowly stewed, dish it on Sippets finely carved.

Pike Souc'd.

Draw and wash it clean from the blood and slime, then boil it in fair Water and Salt; when the liquor boils, put it to it, and boil it leisurely and simpering, season it savourily of the Salt, boil it not too much, nor in more water than will just cover it: If you intend to keep it long, put as much White-wine as Water, of both as much as will cover the Fish, some Wine-vinegar, sliced Ginger, large Mace, Cloves, and some Salt; when it boils put in the Fish, Spices, and some Lemon-peel, boil it up quick, and not too much, then take it up in a Tray, and boil down the liquor to a Jelly; lay some sliced Lemon on it, pour on the liquor, and cover it up close; when you serve it in Jelly, melt some of the Jelly, and run it over therewith; garnish your Dish with Bar-berries and sliced Lemon.

Pike Roasted.

Take a Pike; scour off the slime, and take out the Entrails, lard the back with pickled Herring, (you must have a sharp bodkin to make the holes to lard it) then take some large Oysters and Claret-wine; season the Oysters with Pepper and Nutmeg, stuff the Belly with the Oysters, and intermix the stuffing with Rosemary, Time, Winter-savory, sweet Marjoram, a little Onion and Garlick, sow these in the belly of the Pike; then take two sticks about the breadth of a lath, and with packthread tye the Pike to the Spit, tye also along the side of the Pike which is not defended with the Spit, Rosemary and Bays; baste the Pike with Butter and Claret-wine; when it is roasted, rip up the Belly, and take out the Herbs quite away, boil up the Gravy with Butter, and dish it up.

Quaking Pudding.

Slice the Crum of a Peny-manchet, and infuse it three or four hours in a pint of scalding hot Cream, covering it close, then break the bread with a spoon very small, and put to it eight Eggs (but four whites), and beat them together very well, then season it with Sugar, Rosewater and grated Nutmeg; if you think it too stiff, qualifie that fault with cold Cream, and beat them well together, then wet the bag or napkin, and flower it, put in the Pudding, and ty it hard, boil it half an hour, then dish it and put Butter to it, Rosewater and Sugar, and so serve it to the Table.

Quince-Pyes.

Make choice of fair Quinces to make your Pye withal, pare them very thin, and core them, and lay them within your paste; add thereunto two races of Ginger sliced, as much Cinamon broken into bits, and eight or ten whole Cloves; lay these with the Quinces close packed, with as much refined Sugar as the Quinces weigh, close it up; and having soaked four or five hours in the Oven, take it out and ice it.

You may otherwise make a Quince-Pye thus: Take a gallon of Flower, a pound and half of Butter, six Eggs, thirty Quinces, three pounds of Sugar, half an ounce of Cinamon, the like quantity of Ginger and Cloves, and some Rosewater, then make it into a Pye or Tart; when it is baked, strew on some double refined Sugar.

An excellent restorative for a weak back.

Take Clary, Dates, the pith of an Ox, and chop them together, put some Cream to them, Eggs, grated Bread, and a little white

Sanders, temper them all well together, fry them, and let it be the first thing you eat in a morning. You may also take the leaves of Clary, and Nepe, and fry them for Breakfast.

A most incomparable broth or drink for a sick person.
Procure a good fleshy Capon, and take the flesh from the bones, or chop it in pieces very small, and not wash it, then put it in a Rose-Still, with slices of Lemon-peel, Wood-sorrel, with other restorative herbs, being distilled, give it the sick person to drink.

Rice-Tart.
Boil your Rice in Milk or Cream; being tender boiled pour it into a Dish, and season it with Nutmeg, Ginger, and Cinamon, Pepper, Salt, Sugar and the yolks of six Eggs; put it in the Tart when it is baked scrape Sugar thereon.

Rice-Cream.
Take a quart of Cream, two handfuls of Rice-flower, and a quarter of a pound of Sugar, mingle the Flower and Sugar very well together, and put it in the Cream, then beat the yolk of an Egg with a little Rosewater; put it to the Cream and stir them all together, set it over a quick fire, and keep it continually stirring till it be as thick as Pap.

Another excellent and rare Cream.
Take a pound of Almond-paste, fine beaten with Rosewater, mingle it with a quart of Cream, six Eggs, a little Sack, half a pound of Sugar, and some beaten Nutmeg, strain them, and put them in a clean scoured Skillet, and set it on a soft fire, stir it continually, and being well incorporated, dish it and serve it up with juice of Orange, Sugar and stick it full of candied Pistaches.

Several excellent Sauces for several Dishes, and first for green-Geese.
Take the juice of Sorrel mixed with scalded Goosberries, beaten Butter and Sugar, then serve it on Sippets. Or fill their bellies with Goosberries, and so roast them, then take them out, and mingle them with Sugar, Butter, Vinegar, Cinamon, and served on sippets.

For Land-fowl, take boiled Prunes, and strain them with the blood of the Fowl, Cinamon, Ginger, and Sugar, boil them to an indifferent thickness, and serve it in Sawcers, with the Gravy of the Fowl.

For roast Mutton divers sorts of Sawces; 1. Gravy, Capers, Samphire, and Salt, stew them well together. 2. Water, Onion, Claret-wine, sliced Nutmeg and Gravy boiled. 3. Whole Onions stewed in Gravy, White-wine, Pepper, pickled Capers, Mace, and three or four slices of Lemon. 4. Take Vinegar, Butter, and Currans, put them into a Pipkin with sweet Herbs finely minced, the yolks of two hard Eggs, some Cinamon, Ginger, Sugar, Salt, with some of the meat minced very small, and boiled up with the aforesaid ingredients. 5. Salt, Pepper, juice of Oranges, and an A[n]chovee. 6. Preserve the liquor of the Oysters you stuff your Mutton with, and add thereto Onions, Claret, Capers, or Broombuds, Gravy, Nutmeg, and Salt boiled together. These for a taste: for brevity I shall omit many more for Mutton, which might be here inserted.

For roast Veal several Sawces. 1. Gravy, Claret, Nutmeg, Vinegar, Butter, Sugar and Oranges. 2. Only Vinegar and Butter. 3. All manner of sweet Herbs chopped small, with the yolks of three or four Eggs, and boil them in Vinegar and Butter, a few bread-crumbs, Currans, beaten Cinamon, Sugar, and a whole Clove or two, put it under the Veal with slices of Orange and Lemon to garnish the Dish.

For Red-deer. 1. The Gravy and sweet Herbs chopped small and boiled together. 2. White-bread boiled in water pretty thick without spice, and put to it some Butter, Vinegar and Sugar. 3. The juice of Oranges or Lemons, with the Gravy. A Gallendine sawce I have already described in the roasting of Red-deer.

For Rabbets several sawces. 1. Beaten Butter, with the Liver, and Parsley cut very small. 2. Sage and Parsley minced, rowl it in a ball of Butter, and stuff the belly therewith.

For roast Hens divers Sawces. 1. Take the yolks of three hard Eggs minced small, salt, grated Bread, Gravy, juice of Oranges, with Lemon-peel shred small. 2. Gravy and Claret boiled with a piece of an Onion, Nutmeg and Salt. 3. Oyster-liquor, an Anchovee or two, Nutmeg and Gravy, and rub the Dish with a Clove of Garlick.

Sawces for roast Chicken. Butter and Vinegar boiled together with a little Sugar; then make thin sops of Bread, then lay the roast Chicken on them, and serve them up.

For roast Pidgeons, or Stock-doves. 1. Boil'd Parsley minced, and put amongst some Butter and Vinegar beaten up thick. 2. Vine-leaves roasted with the Pidgeons, minced and put into Claret with Salt, Butter and Gravy boiled together. 3. Minced Onions boiled in Claret-wine almost dry, then put to it Nutmeg, Sugar, Gravy of the Fowl and a little Pepper.

An excellent way to roast Salmon.

Take a Rand or Jole, cut it into four pieces, and season it with a little Nutmeg and Salt, stick a few Cloves, and put it on a small Spit, put between it some Bay-leaves, and stick it with little sprigs of Rosemary, roast it and baste it with Butter, save the Gravy, and add to it for Sawce some Vinegar, sweet Butter, and some slices of Orange.

Salmon Fried.

Take a Jole, Chine, or Rand, and fry it in clarified Butter; being stiff and crisp fried; make Sauce with a little Claret-wine, sweet Butter, grated Nutmeg, slices of Orange, and Oyster-liquor, stew them all together, and pour on the Sauce, and on that Parsley, Ellick-sander, and Sage-leaves fried in Butter.

Soust Veal, Lamb, or any joint of Mutton, Kid, Fawn or Venison.

Bone a breast of Veal, and soak it well from the blood, then wipe it dry, and season the side of the breast with beaten Nutmeg, Ginger, some sweet Herbs minced small, whole Coriander-seed, minced Lemon-peel and Salt, and lay some broad slices of sweet Lard over the seasoning, then roul it into a Collar, and bind it up in a white clean cloth, put it into boiling liquor, scum it well, and then put in sliced Ginger, sliced Nut-meg, Salt, Fennel, Parsley; being almost boiled, put in a quart of White-wine, and when it is quite boiled, take it off, and put in slices of Lemon, the peel of two Lemons whole, and a dozen Bay-leaves, boil it close covered, that the souse may look white.

Taffety-Tart.

First, wet your paste with Butter, and cold water, roul it very thin, then lay Apples in lays and between every lay of Apples strew some fine Sugar, and some Lemon-peel cut very small; you may also put some Fennel-seed to them, let them bake an hour or more, then ice them with Rosewater, Sugar, and Butter beaten together, and wash them over with the same, strew more fine Sugar over them, and put them into the Oven again; this done, you may serve them hot or cold.

Venison, how to recover when tainted.

Take a clean cloth and wrap your Venison therein, then bury it in the Earth one whole night, and it will take away the ill scent or savour.

To make Beef, Ram, or Mutton pass for Venison.

Take your Beef, &c., and dip it in Pigs-blood, or any new blood, then take Small-beer and Vinegar, and parboil it therein, let it steep all night, then put some Turnsole to it; when it is baked, a good judgment shall not discern it from Red or Fallow-deer.

Warden-Tarts.

Take twenty good Wardens, pare them and cut them into your Tart, and put to them two pound of refined Sugar, twenty whole Cloves, a quarter of an Ounce of Cinamon broke into little bits, and three races of Ginger pared and sliced thin; then close up the Tart and bake it; it will require five hours baking; then ice it with a quarter of a pound of double refined Sugar, Rosewater and Butter.

Thus Ladies and Gentlewomen I have cursorily run through the whole body of the art of Cookery; I have only toucht here and there upon some excellent Receipts, and now much in fashion, leaving it to your industry to supply my deficiency: I shall now proceed to the rest of those accomplishments which best become a Gentlewoman.

A Bill of Fare of suitable Meat for every Month in the Year.

January.
1. Brawn and Mustard.
2. Two boiled Capons in White-broth.
3. A Turky roasted.
4. A Shoulder of Mutton hasht.
5. Two Geese boiled.
6. Goose roasted.
7. Ribs or Surloyn of Beef.
8. Minced Pyes
9. A Loyn of Veal.
10. A Pasty of Venison.
11. A Marrow-pye.
12. Roasted Capons.
13. Lamb.
14. Woodcocks, Partridges, with smaller Birds.

Second Course.
1. A Soust Pig.
2. A Warden-Pye.
3. Dried Neats-tongues.
4. A Soust Capon.
5. Pickled Oysters, and Mushrooms together
6. Sturgeon
7. A Goose, or Turky-pye.

February.
1. A Chine of roast-Pork.
2. Veal or Beef roasted.
3. A Lamb-Pye, and Mince-Pyes.
4. A couple of wild Ducks.
5. A couple of Rabbits.
6. Fried Oysters.
7. A Skirrot-Pye.

Second Course.
1. A whole Lamb roasted.
2. Three Widgeons.
3. A Pippin-Pye.
4. A Jole of Sturgeon.
5. A cold Turkey-Pye.

March.
1. Neats-tongue and Udder.
2. Boil'd Chickens.
3. A Dish of stew'd Oysters.
4. A Dish of young Rabbits.
5. A grand Sallet.

Second Course.
1. A Dish of Soles, or Smelts.
2. Marinate Flounders.
3. A Lambstone-Pye.
4. An hundred of Asparagus.
5. A Warden-Pye.

April.
1. Green Greese, or Veal and Bacon.
2. Haunch of Venison roasted.
3. A Lumber-Pye.
4. Rabbits and Tarts.

Second Course.
1. Cold Lamb.
2. Cold Neats-tongue-Pye.
3. Salmon, Lobsters and Prawns.
4. Asparagus.

May.

1. Boil'd Chickens.
2. Roast Veal.
3. Roasted Capons.
4. Rabbits.

Second Course.

1. Artichoak-Pye hot.
2. Westphalia Bacon, and Tarts.
3. Sturgeon, Salmon and Lobsters.
4. A Dish of Sparagrass.
5. A Tansie.

June.

1. A Neats-tongue, or Leg of Mutton and Colliflowers.
2. A Steak-Pye.
3. A Shoulder of Mutton.
4. A fore-quarter of Lamb.
5. A Dish of Pease.

Second Course.

1. Sweet-bread-Pye.
2. A Capon.
3. A Goose-berry Tart.
4. Straw berries and Cream. Or Straw-berries, White-wine, Rosewater and Sugar.

July.

1. A Westphalia Ham and Pidgeons.
2. A Loyn of Veal.
3. A Venison-Pasty.
4. Roast Capons.

Second Course.

1. Pease or *French* beans.
2. A Codling-Tart.

3. Artechoaks, or a Pye made thereof.
4. Roast Chickens.

August.

1. Calves-head and Bacon.
2. An Olio, or grand boil'd meat.
3. A Haunch of Venison roasted.
4. A Pig roasted.

Second Course.

1. Marinate Smelts.
2. A Pidgeon-Pye.
3. Roast Chickens.
4. A Tart.
5. Some Creams and Fruit.

September.

1. Capon and White-broth.
2. Neats-tongue and Udder roasted.
3. A powder'd Goose.
4. roast Turky.

Second Course.

1. A Potato-pye.
2. Roast Partridges.
3. A Dish of Larks.
4. Creams and Fruit.

October.

1. Roast Veal.
2. Two brand-Geese roasted.
3. A grand Sallet
4. Roasted Capons.

Second Course.

1. Pheasants, Pouts and Pidgeons.

2. A Dish of Quails, or Sparrows.
3. A Warden-Pye, Tarts or Custards.

November.

1. A Shoulder of Mutton and Oysters.
2. A loyn of Veal.
3. Geese roasted.
4. A Pasty of Venison.

Second Course.

1. Two Herns, one larded.
2. A Soust Turbut.
3. Two Pheasants, one larded.
4. A Roll of Beef.
5. A Soust Mullet and Base.
6. Jellies and Tarts.

December.

1. Stew'd broth of Mutton and Marrow-bones.
2. Lambs-head and White-broth.
3. A Chine of Beef roasted.
4. Mince-Pyes.
5. A roast Turky stuck with Cloves.
6. Two Capons, one larded.

Second Course.

1. A young Lamb or Kid.
2. Two brace of Partridg.
3. Ballonia Sausages, Anchovees, Mushrooms, Caviare, and pickled Oysters, in a Dish together.
4. A Quince-Pye.
5. Half a dozen of Woodcocks.

Bills of Fare for fasting days or Lent; Out of these following Dishes, you may compose what Messes you please of several sorts and kinds.

Oysters, if in Season. Pole of Ling. Greenfish and Eggs. Prawns butter'd, or Craw-fish. Pike boil'd. Carp stew'd with Oysters. Soles fried. Spitchcock Eels roasted. Fried Smelts, Salmon, Lobsters, and Sturgeon. Butter'd Eggs. Barley-broth, or Rice-pottage. Stew'd or fried Oysters. Boil'd Gurnet. Haddocks, fresh Cod, or Whitings, Eel or Carp-Pye. Soust Turbut. Potato's baked, or Oyster-Pyes. Butter'd Crabs. Fried Flounders. Joles of fresh Salmon. Fried Turbut. Fried Skirrets. Soust Conger; with what else your own judgments shall think proper for that Season.

Thus Ladies I have given you an Essay, or small pattern of Cookery, not desiring to tye you too strictly to the observation of those rules I have here laid down for your imitation; but desire to give your fancy all convenient liberty in correcting what you may find amiss herein. There are many excellent Books in Cookery already extant, to which I shall refer you, and your own ingenious experiments in the amending what in this you find erroneous, and that you may know (though a Woman) I am not altogether ignorant of that tongue I have advised you to learn, give me leave to quot an ancient Poet very applicable to this purpose.

> ————*Si quid novisti rectius istis,*
> *Candidus imperti, si non, his utere mecum.*

If thou know'st ought than this more right or wise,
Impart it freely, or let this suffice.

Now because I have promised to give an Essay to everything which concerns the virtuous and good Education of your Ladies and Gentlewomen, I shall endeavour their instruction in the most considerable matters of Physick and Chyrurgery, Candying, Preserving and Distilling.

An Introduction to Physick and Chyrurgery.

AS it is a very commendable quality in Gentlewomen, whether young or old, to visit the sick; so it is impossible to do it with that charity some stand in need of, without some knowledg in Physick, and the several operations of Herbs and Spices: But since it will take up too much room to insert here what may make you a compleat Herbalists I shall refer you to such who have largely treated on that Subject; *viz.* Mr. *Gerhard*, and Mr. *Parkinson*, with many more expert in the knowledg of Vegetables. Wherefore, since the knowledg of sundry sort of Spices is very requisite both for persons diseased, and in health, I shall begin with them.

Pepper is a spice of the most common use, hot and dry to the fourth degree almost. The black is that which is generally coveted; but inconsiderately by the younger sorts of people, it being hurtful to them, though comfortable to old Age. When you use it, beat it not too small for fear of inflaming the blood, otherwise it cutteth gross flegm, dispelleth Crudities, and helpeth Digestion.

The next thing, which is hotter than Pepper, is Ginger; not that it is really so, but because the biting heat of Ginger is more lasting and durable. This spice is not so much used in dressing meat, as the other; however it is very good for concoction, and opens obstructions, and is very expedient for the expulsion of Wind. Green ginger in the *Indies* preserved, is excellent good for a watry and windy stomack, if taken fasting; the better sort is unsteaky, and so clear you may almost see through it; but there is little good made in *England*.

Cloves is an excellent spice for the head, heart, stomack, and the eyes, which are much benefited thereby, and Nature strengthned. In Swoonings and Fainting-fits they are very good, or against the Plague, or any other infectious disease whatsoever, or fluxes of the belly proceeding from cold humors. They are good against strengthning the retentive faculty, and sweetning the breath; but let young Sanguine and Cholerick Complexions use them and all other spices very sparingly.

Nutmeg is hot and dry in the second degree, and is accounted a spice of the like nature and property, with what are before mention'd. It is astringent, and good for Flegmatick Constitutions, cold Diseases and Fluxes. Nutmegs whilst green and covered over with an husk or shell like our Walnuts, are preserved in the *Indies* as Ginger is, and are very comfortable to the Head and Stomack.

The covering of the Nutmg is the Mace, which partakes of the same nature with it, strengthning the animal parts, and it is good against fluxes and spitting of blood.

Cinamon is the inward bark or rind of a Tree growing in the *Indies*, and is accounted to be hot and dry in the third degree. This spice by reason of its fragrancy and palatable taste, may justly challenge the precellency of most other Spices; it comforteth the Spirits, and opens obstructions both in Men and Women; it helpeth a Woman in her delivery, furthereth Urine, and is good for Concoction.

We have a spice growing here at home called Saffron, which need not give place to any of the former; it is hot in the second, and dry in the first degree: It is a great Cordial, and a help against obstructions; it is good against the Jaundies, and unstuffs the pipes of the Lungs: It is good to bring down the Menstruum, and facilitates the Birth, if taken moderately. And since I have spoken of a thing of our own growth, let me add another, which is Honey, hot and dry in the second degree, and is better boiled than raw; it is very restorative, and therefore good against Consumptions, and Phlegmatick Constitutions, but dangerous to be used much by hot Complexions, for thereby it is soon converted into Choler. The best is very sweet, pleasant of smell, of a cleer and yellowish colour, pretty stiff and firm, and yieldeth but little scum on the top when boiled. Garden-honey is the best and is clarified by adding a little water to it, about the fourth part, and so scum it whilst any froth ariseth, or till the water be evaporated, which is known by the bubbles rising from the bottom; if you will have it more pure, put into every pound of Honey the white of an Egg, and afterwards scum it again in the boiling; then use it against all pectoral infirmities, as the Cough, shortness of breath, the Pleurisie &c.

Sugar is the next thing we treat of which is generally esteemed and used, and more now than ever; since the Ancients knew not the right way of preparing it as it is done now-a-days.

Sugar is neither so hot and dry as Honey; the brownest or coarsest is most cleansing, and is good for abstersions in diseases of the Breast or Lungs; but as it is opening and cleansing, so the immoderate use thereof is dangerous; for it will rot the Teeth, and taint the Breath, ingender Jaundies and Consumptions; and Physicians verily believe, that the major part of those who die of the Consumption in the City (the constantly great numbers whereof may be seen in the Weekly Bills of Mortality) are such who eat Confections, and such-like sweet things immoderately.

And since I have spoken of Sugar, pray take special notice of this remark, That the most part of our finest Sugar, and which is most coveted, is refined and whitened by the means of the Lee of Lime; how prejudicial that may be to the body, I will leave it to the Rational to consider.

Thus I have given you a small touch of the nature of spices; I think I need not acquaint you, that we have here at home in our own Gardens many excellent Aromatical Plants, such as Rosemary, Lavender, Time, Savory, Sage, Mint, Penny-royal, Basil, sweet Cerfuel, Avens, Angelica, with many more which you may find in *Culpepers* English Physician, with their nature, use, and disposition.

The great plenty we have of these excellent Plants hath made many judicious persons admire, that being supplied at home with such admirable Simples, we should hunt so eagerly after Outlandish Spices, which by difficulty of transportation, length of way, and carelesness of the Merchant, are frequently imported rotten, or worm-eaten; or so long before they come to our hands, that they have lost half their virtue.

What is to be observed by a Gentlewoman before she undertakes the administration of Physick.

The first inconvenience you must shun (which I have observed in most Physical Practitioners) is the vulgar error of not suffering the diseased or sick person to change his linnen often; and I know not by what unreasonable prescription they will not suffer a diseased female to change her head-clothes, till it too sensibly offend the noses of the Visitants. Their common objection is, That the sick by that means may catch cold; and next, That their shifting much weakneth them.

To this I answer, That it is only the foolish conjecture and groundless fear of some old Dotard of our sex; for a good fire will easily prevent catching of cold; and in the next place, their often shifting hath apparently proved the means of their strengthning; besides it much discourageth and dejecteth the sick person to lie in foul linnen, making them even loath themselves in that stinking condition. To make this the more easily understood, take notice, that in humane bodies there is a threefold Concoction the first in the stomack, which is commonly called the Chyle, and hath for its excrement that which is convey'd to Colon or the great Gut; the second concoction is in the Liver, and hath for its excrement the Urine; the last is called Nutrition, and hath for its excrement certain fuliginous vapours, which by insensible transpiration do breath out themselves through the pores of the body, and by the sweat, which is apparent to the eye. Now in times of Sickness, especially in all sorts of Fevers (which are the usual diseases which invade *English* bodies) this last excrement doth very much abound, and doth extreamly and speedily foul the Linnen of the sick person; for which cause reason tells us, that the Linnen should be often shifted, especially if they sweat much, lest the sweat continuing about the body, it should be drawn in by the same way it had its passage out. For know the Arteries of the body have a double motion, one whereby they expel the Excrements, already mention'd; and the other whereby they attract into the body the ambient Air to refresh the blood: Now observe, whatsoever Air is next unto them, whether good or bad they draw it in; and therefore if this foul sweaty Linnen do lie about, or upon them, undoubtedly the noisome airs will be drawn in by the Arteries, and so prolong the distemper. To make further proof hereof, I have heard it reported by an eminent Physician, that let any person newly come out of the Bath, go into a place where a quantity of dust is rais'd, and he shall instantly feel an universal pricking over his whole body which is nothing else but the Atoms of dust drawn in by the Arteries. By this then you may understand, that the skin ought to be cleansed from all corruption, and the pores and passages to be kept open and clean; for which cause it was that the *Romans* of old had their bodies frequently rubbed with a coarse cloth. Thus much I have added likewise, to let Gentlewomen see how much they are abused by their credulous and ignorant Nurses.

Should I add other observables, with the Symptoms of Diseases, I should swell this small Treatise into a greater volume than is requisite. I shall therefore desist and give you my collection (with my own observation) of the choicest receipts in Physick and Chirugery I could meet with in my strictest indigation.

Choice and Experimental Observations in Physick and Chyrurgery, such which rarely fail'd any who made trial thereof.

A most approved Receipt for a Quartane Ague.

PRocure a white flint-stone (for that will best endure the fire without breaking) and let it lye in a quick fire till it be red-hot, then take some small beer and quench it therein; when the fit is coming, let the diseased drink a good draught thereof, and another in the midst thereof; let this be done four several days both in the fit, and when the fit is coming. This I have been credibly inform'd was a receipt a woman had her livelihood from, in curing several when all other means proved ineffectual.

For a sudden and violent bleeding at the nose.

Take an Egg-shell and burn it to a coal, then pulverize or beat it to a fine powder, and let the person snuff it up his Nostrils or take your two thumbs and press them hard against the Temples of the Bleeder, and you would admire how speedily it will divert the course of the blood. For those that are accustomed thus to bleed, let them make an ordinary Posset taking off the curd, let the juice of Liverwort beaten be added thereunto, and so drink morning and evening.

To stop the Bleeding of a Wound.

Take Vervine dried, and reduce it to powder; or take the sole of an old stocking and burn it, put the ashes of the one, or powder of the other, to the wound, and it will leave bleeding.

An approved Medicine of London-Midwives to break and heal Womens sore breasts.

Take red Sage and Oatmeal the finest you can get, and boil them together in Spring-water, till you have boil'd them to a consistency, that is as thick as to make a Plaister; then add thereunto a fit proportion of Honey; having boil'd a little while together, take it off the fire, and whilst it is boiling-hot, make it indifferent thick with the best *Venice*-Turpentine, then spread it on fine leather, or linnen-cloth, and laying it on the sore breast it will first break it, and afterwards perfectly heal it.

An excellent way to dry up a Womans breast.

Of Linseed-Oyl and *English* Honey, take of each a peny-worth, of white-wax half a peny-worth, and half a quarter of a pound of sweet butter, boil all these together, spread a Plaister thereof, and lay it on the breast. *Probatum est.*

An infallible receipt to increase milk in Womens breasts.

Take Chickens and make broth of them, then add thereunto Fennel and Parsnip-roots, then take the newest-made Butter you can procure, and butter the roots therewith; having so done let her eat heartily, and her expectations therein will be speedily satisfied,

Against a Stinking-breath.

To prevent a Stinking-breath, you ought to keep your teeth very clean by rubbing them every morning with water and salt, which will also cure the Scurvy; you may if you please try Mr. *Turners* Dentifrices, which are every-where much cryed up. But if your breath be tainted, proceeding from some other cause, take Rosemary-leaves with the blossoms, if to be had, and seeth them in White-wine, with a little Myrrh and Cinamon, and you will find the effect to answer your desires if you use it often.

For a Cancer in a Womans Breast.

Take Goose-dung and Celidony, stamp them well together, and lay them Plaisterwise on the sore; this shall cleanse the Cancer, kill the Worm, and heal the Sore. For a Cancer in the Mouth take the juice of Plantane-Vinegar, and Rosewater, mingle together of each a like quantity, and wash the mouth often with them.

For young Children who by reason of the weakness of their Limbs can neither stand nor go.

Take Marjoram and Sage, of each a like quantity, beat them very well together, then strain out the juice, and put it into a double Glass-Vial, filling the Glass as full as it will hold; stop it then with paste very close all over, set it into an Oven, and there let it stand the time of an Houshold-loafs baking; taking it out, let it stand till it be cold; then breaking the paste round about it, see if the juice be grown thick; if so, break the Glass, and put what was therein contain'd, into a Gally-pot, and keep it. When you use it, take the quantity of two spoonfuls at a time and as much Marrow of an Oxleg, melt them together, and mingle them well, and both morning and evening anoint therewith (as warm as can be endur'd) the tender parts of the Childs legs, knees and thighs, chafing them well with your hands; and in a short time (*Deo volente*) the child will be able to go and stand; this receipt hath been ever found successful.

An approved China-broth for a Consumption.

Take two ounces of China-root sliced thin, and let it be steept twenty-four hours in fair water, let it stand warm all the time close covered in an Earthen Pipkin; add thereunto a couple of Chickens or a Cockerel, cleanly dressed, to these put half an handful of Maiden-hair, the like quantity of five-leav'd grass and Harts-tongue; twenty sliced Dates, three or four blades of Mace, and the bottom of a Manchet; let all these stew together till there be but a quart of liquor left, then strain it and take all the flesh and bones, and beat them in a Stone-Morter, then strain out the juice into the aforesaid broth, then sweeten it with two ounces of powder'd Sugar-Candy. Take hereof half a pint in the morning warm, and sleep after it if you can; you will not do amiss to add two drams of white and red Sanders to steep with your China-root.

A most excellent Jelly for the Consumption.

Take a new-kill'd Cock, scald him, and wash him clean, then take a Leg of Veal, and take away all the fat from it, and let them lie in water five or six hours, then seeth them together in a gallon of Spring-water, scum clean the fat off; thus let it seeth over a soft fire till the liquor be half consumed; then put in a pottle of White-wine, let it boil to a quart; add hereunto the whites of new-laid Eggs, clarifie it and let it run through a Jellybag; then set it on the fire again, and put into it an ounce of gross Cinamon, and a pound of fine Sugar, and let it run twice or thrice through a Jelly-bag again; having made a Jelly hereof, eat thereof cold.

An excellent Comforter of the Stomach, and helper of Digestion.

Take two ounces of good old Conserve of Red-roses, of chosen Mithridate two drams, mingle them together, and when you are going to bed eat thereof the quantity of an Haselnut. This will expel all flatulency or windiness off the Stomach, drives away raw humours, and venemous vapours, helpeth Digestion, drieth the Rheum, and strengthneth the Sight and Memory.

A well-tried Medicine for the Corns on the Feet or Toes.

Pare your Corns well, then take a black snail and bruise it, and put a drop or two thereof on the place grieved; adding thereto a little powder of Samphire; this I can assure with constant use in a little time will take away the Corn.

An excellent Diet-drink for the Spring to purge the Blood, and cleanse it.

Of Scurvy-grass take half a peck, Broodlime [*recte* Brooklime], Water-cresses, Agrimony, Maiden-hair, Liverwort, Borrage, Bugloss, Betony, Sage, sweet Marjoram, Sea-wormwood, Tops of green-hops, Fumitory, of each a good handful; of Ivory, Harts-horn, and yellow Sanders, of each one unce; Red dock-roots two ounces. Parsley, Fennel, Asparagus-roots of each an ounce, Raisins half a pound; boil these very well in a gallon of Beer, then stamp and strain them, and put it into three gallons of new Beer to work together.

A Remedy for the Dropsie, whether hot or cold.

Take of the tops of red Mint, of Archangel, or blind nettles, and red Sage, of either a small quantity, stamp them together, and strain the juice of them into some stale Ale, so much as will serve to drink morning and evening; do this for ten days together, and (God willing) it will effect the Cure.

Another for the Dropsie, which hath cured many a Person when they were left and forsaken by Physicians.

Take green Broom and burn it in some clean place, that you may save the Ashes of it; take ten or twelve spoonful of the same Ashes, and boil them in a pint of White-wine till the virtue thereof be in the Wine, then cool it, and drain the Wine from the dregs, and make three draughts of the Wine, one fasting in the Morning, the other at three in the Afternoon, and the other when you go to Bed, this seldom fails in his desired effect.

For the Web or Pin in the Eye.
Take the Gall of a Hare and clarified Honey, of each a like quantity, mingle them well together, and anoint the Web with a feather dipped in the same, and in three or four days it will be gone.

To cleanse the skin of the face, and make it look beautiful and fair.
Take Rosemary and boil it in White-wine, with the juice of Erigan put thereunto, and wash your face therewith Mornings and Evenings. If your Face be troubled with heat, take Elder-flowers, Plantane, white Daisie-roots, and Herb-Robert and put these into running-water, and wash your Face therewith at night, and in the Morning.

How to ripen and heal a Felon or Whitelof.
Take some white flower and boil it in Claret-wine to a Poultess, then spread it very thick, and apply it as hot as you can endure it; this will asswage the throbbing pain of the Whitelof, break and heal it.

How to cure the bloody Flux.
There are two sorts of Fluxes, the one proceedeth from the evil quality or temperament of the Liver, and is called in Latin, *Fluxus Hepaticus*; the other cometh from the great heat and distemperament of Nature, and is called *Dysenteria*; that is, the distemper of the Guts; some cure this distemper with repression and restrictives, but many more hundreds are cured by *Aromaticum Leonardi*, with three or four doses of his *Syrupus solutivus*. You may try this way, which I shall assure you is both safe and good: Take Frogs and distil them as you do Herbs and Flowers, or any thing else, but put nothing to them but a little water; take two or three spoonfuls of this distillation in any thing you drink, and it will give you present ease.

A Cure for every sort of Gout.
The Gout whether hot or cold, or of whatever temperature, ariseth from one and the same cause, though the effects seem

different. As for example, Fat-men have it with much inflammation, redness and great pain, in leaner Persons it is discovered
with less inflammation, though not with lesser pain; it afflicteth
Cholerick and Melancholick men with nodes and tumors. The
cause of this distemper cometh from an evil quality engendred
in the Stomack, Blood and Liver, the cure thereof must be then
the removal of this ill quality from the Stomack, and the purga-
tion of Blood and Liver. Wherefore when you perceive the pain
approaching, take two Doses of *Pillule Magistrales Leonardi* in the
morning fasting, one day after another; or if you will intermit
a day, then take drams of *Quinta essentia solutiva Leonardi*, in half
a Porringer of Veal-broth sweetned with Sugar; take this five
hours before you eat any thing; then every night after Supper
take a little of the *Unguentum Leonardi*, and anoint your grief,
and you will find your speedy recovery.

How to cure the Green-Sickness.

Laziness and love are the usual causes of these obstructions in
young women; and that which increaseth and continueth this
distemper, is their eating Oat-meal, chalk, nay some have not
forbore Cinders, Lime, and I know not what trash. If you
would prevent this slothful disease, be sure you let not those
under your command to want imployment, that will hinder the
growth of this distemper, and cure a worser Malady of a love-
sick breast, for business will not give them time to think of such
idle matters. But if this Green-sickness hath already got footing
in the body, use this means to drive it away: Take a Quart of
Claret-wine, one pound of Currans, and a handful of your
Rosemary-tops, with half an ounce of Mace, seeth these to a
pint, and let the Patient drink thereof three spoonfuls at a time,
Morning and Evening, and eat some of the Currans after.

An Universal Medicine of wonderful use both for Man and Woman.

Take ten ounces of the seeds of Quinces, six ounces of the pills
of Citrons; Balm and Nettles, of each four ounces; beat all
these grosly, and infuse them in six quarts of good White-wine,
thus let it remain six days, then distil it with six ounces of
Honey, and fifteen ounces of Sugar, until you have received a
quart of water; then put it in a place to cool, then add thereunto eight grains of Musk dissolved, with about two ounces of

Rose-water; put thereunto two scruples of oyl of Vitriol, and incorporate them well together; then keep this water in a Glass well-closed to keep out the air; and of this take one ounce in the Morning, and fast thereon two hours. This Experiment is a wonderful preserver of health, and continuer of life to long age, if constantly used, which may appear by the excellency of the Ingredients, for the Quince-seeds are admirable for the removing of ill humours which clog the Stomach, and are very cordial; the Pomo-citron-pills preserve and help digestion; the Balm purifieth the Blood, healeth the Liver, incourageth Concoction, and comforteth the heart; the Nettles provoke Urine, mundifie the Reins, and correct the malignity of the sinews; as for the Wine, you cannot be ignorant of its Virtues; Musk purgeth the Blood of Windiness; the oyl of Vitriol healeth all the excoriations of the Mouth, Breast, and Stomach, and is excellent against malign humours that oppress it.

An admirable Remedy against the yellow Jaundies.
Take an handful of Red-nettle-tops, Plantane, and Saffron, and boil them well in a pint of Ale, then strain it, and drink five or six days thereof, and you will find it a present remedy; let not the cheapness of its ingredients occasion this composition to be slighted.

Against the Itch.
Take sweet Butter, unwrought Wax, Vinegar, Brimstone, a little Rose-water & red Cloves whole, boil them together till they be like Salve, then anoint the flesh three sundry nights by the fire therewith, and no more, and you need not question a cure.

Against Kibed Heels a certain Remedy.
Make a hole in the top of a Turnip, take out some of the pith, & pour into the hole oyl of Roses, then stop the hole close, and roast it under hot Embers; when it is soft, apply it Plaisterwise to the Kibe as hot as can be endured.

What is best to be administred to one sick of the Measels.

In this distemper, as in the small Pox, it is only necessary to defend the Heart, and preserve the Stomach, from putrefaction, and corruption; if young, to hinder the hands from murdering a good face; and then give the diseased a Julip, made of two ounces of Violets, four ounces of Rose-water, and four grains of Oyl of Vitriol, mix them and let them be drunk cold: It is as good a receipt as any for this distemper.

To cure the Fits of the Mother.

Some, nay most use burnt Feathers, or *Assafœtida*, applyed to the Nose of the Distempered person, not without success; but your better way is to take six or seven drops of the spirit of Castoreum, in the beginning of the fit, in two or three spoonfuls of Ale-posset, and apply a Plaister of Gavanum to the Navel.

To take away the Heat of a Burn or Scald.

Roast Eggs as hard as a Stone, then take out the yolks of them, then fry the yolks of these Eggs in a Frying-pan till they turn to an Oyl; then strain it, and anoint the Burn or Scald therewith, then lay on a Bladder anointed with Sallet-oyl, and this will speedily asswage the pain, and heal the Scald or Burn.

For a Scald head.

Take a Candle, and let it drop upon it as Hot as you can, in so doing it will scale off; then take the Stale of a Cow, and the furring of Chamber-pots, boil these together and wash the place, and it will speedily cure it.

A very good receipt for one hurt with Gun-powder.

Take twelve heads of Housleek, one handful of Groundsel, one pint of Goose-dung, as much Chicken-dung of the newest that can be gotten; stamp the Herbs very small, then put the dung into a Mortar, temper them together with a pottle of Bores-grease, stir them together half an hour, then strain it through a Canvas-bag and so preserve it for your use; it will keep two years, and be not the worse.

A very safe Clister to be used by either Man or Woman who is much bound or costiv.

Take Mallows and Mercury unwasht, of each two handfuls, half an handful of Barley; clean rubbed and washed, and boil them in Spring-water, from a pottle to a quart, then strain out the Water, and put it in a Skillet, and put to it three spoonfuls of Sallet-oyl, two spoonfuls of Honey and a little Salt, then make it luke-warm, and with your Pipe administer it.

How to cure old Sores on the Legs, which have been of so long standing that the Bones have appeared.

Take a quantity of sweet Cream, and as much Brimstone beaten into fine powder as will make it thick like Paste; then take so much sweet Butter as will work it into the form of an Oynment, and here-with anoint the place grieved twice a day, and in a short time the cure will be effected. *Probatum est.*

An excellent way to dissolve the Stone.

Take a peck of Green-bean-cods without dew or rain, and two good handfuls of Saxifrage, lay the same into a Still, one row of Saxifrage, and another of the Green-bean-cods; and so distil in this manner a quart of Water; and then distil another quantity of Water from the Bean-cods alone, and use to drink of these two Waters. If the Patient be most troubled with the heat of the Reins, then let him most frequently drink of the distilled Bean-water, and upon coming down of the sharp gravel of stone, let him drink the other.

A way not only to prevent but to cure the Toothach, or to make an aking-Tooth fall out of it self.

Every Month, twice or theice [*recte* thrice] therein, wash your Mouth with White-wine, in which Spurge hath been boil'd, and you shall never be troubled with the Tooth-ach. If your Tooth be hollow, & paineth you much, take this Herb called Spurge and squeeze it, and mingle Wheat-flower with the Milk which issueth thence; with this make a Paste and fill the cavity of your Tooth therewith, leaving it there a while, changing it every two hours, and the Tooth will drop out.

How to order a Woman with Child, before, in, and after her Delivery.

To preserve the Infant, and prevent Abortion, take Coriander-seed prepared two drams, of the roots of Bistort, the shaving of Ivory, & red Coral, of each a dram, of white Amber and Crystal, of each a Scruple; Alkermes half a Scruple, Sugar dissolv'd in four Ounces of Rose-water; make tables each of them weighing a dram. Let the Woman with Child take one of them every other day morning and evening; between whiles let her sup a new-laid-Egg, thickened a little with Magisterium of Pearl, or red Coral. But if her Breasts after their filling should begin to lessen or fall, it is a sign of future Abortion; to prevent which let her take root of Bistort and Corianders, of each two drams; of unripened Galls, and red Sander, and Hippocestidos, of each one dram; Gum-Laudanum and Mastick of each half an ounce; choice Frankincense and Bdelium of each two drams; of Coral, Amber, one dram of each powder those which are to be powdered, and with Oyl of Turpentine and Wax, make two or three Cere-cloths, apply them sometimes to her Loines and Sides, and sometimes under the Navel. She must avoid all violent and sudden motions, both of the Mind and Body, as Coughs, Sneezing, Frights, also Spices and Wine. Thus much before Delivery.

In Labour, if you will facilitate the Birth, and give speedy ease, take three or four drops of the distilled Oyl of Nutmegs in a spoonful of White-wine or take white Dictamn-root, stones of Dates, and Borax, of each two Scruples; Cinamon, Cassia-Lignea, Amber, fine Pearl, of each one Scruple, Saffron half a Scruple, make a small powder of these, and divide them into two equal parts, and let her take the one part in a draught of Lilly-water, or Ale-posset made with Rhenish-wine and the other part let her take in like manner six hours after if need require. If she be subject to swooning or fainting before or after Labour, give her a spoonful of this excellent Cordial following.

An excellent Cordial for Women troubled with Swooning-fits in Travel.

Take Borage-water, Rose-water, Strawberry-water, and Rhenish wine, of each two Ounces; Species of Diamargaricum frigidum, one Scruple; make a warm infusion for the space of an hour, then strain it, and add thereunto *Manus Christi*, made with Pearl, four Ounces; Oriental Bezoar Unicorns-horn, and Ambergreece, of each six Grains; of these make a Cordial-Julip.

Great pains frequently follow Women newly brought to Bed; for which, there is nothing better than this plain receipt; *viz.*, Drink a good draught of Beer boil'd with a spoonful of Camomile-flowers; and in greater pains let her drink six Ounces of the Oyl of sweet Almonds fresh drawn.

If the Woman delivered have no mind to give suck, and that she will have her Milk speedily dried up, a quick and safe remedy is, new Spunges wet in Vinegar, where a handful of Cummin-seed boiled is bruised, tyed close to the Breasts, anointing them with Unguentum Populeum.

To procure store of Milk, use Posset-drink boiled with Fennel, with the seeds thereof, and Anniseeds. These remedies are known to be safe and effectual.

Thus much for Physick and Chyrurgery; having given you only some of the choicest Receipts I could procure; if you desire a larger knowledg herein, you would do well to acquaint your self with the Composition of Mans Body, and the Diseases incident to every part; which you may gather from several Books of Anatomy, either that of Dr. *Read*, or Dr. *Riolanus*, I think as good as any extant.

If you would know the nature of Plants, *Gerhard* and *Parkinson* write incomparably on that Subject; but if they are too bulky, and so may seem tedious you may make choice of lesser Herbals, as *Adam in Eden*; or a small Manual, written by Mr. *Lovel*. If you would have a Salve for every sore, as the Proverb expresseth, and a receipt for every Distemper, consult the general practice of Physick, *Riverius* his practice of Physick translated by Mr. *Culpepper*; with many more of the like Subject.

The next Qualifications which accomplish a Gentlewoman, are, Candying, Conserving, Preserving, and Distilling.

And first of Candying, Conserving and Preserving.

THese are Curiosities which are not only laudable, but requisite and necessary in young Ladies and Gentlewomen: To represent them at large, would require more art and time than I have either the ability or leisure to perform; however I shall give you a *Specimen* hereof or an Essay of my own Experiments; and first,

How to preserve Barberries.

Select the largest and fairest bunches, picking off the withered or shrunk Barberries, and wash them clean, drying them in a clean Cloth. After this, take a quantity of Barberries, and boil them in Claret-wine till they be soft; then strain them well through a Strainer, wringing the juice hard through it; boil this strained liquor with Sugar, till it be thick, and very sweet; let it then stand till it be cold, then put your branches of Barberries into Gally-pots, and fill them up with this liquor; by this means you will have both the Syrrup of Barberries, and their Preserves.

Pears Preserved.

Take Pears that are found, and newly gathered from the Tree, indifferent ripe, then lay in the bottom of an Earthen-pot some dried Vine-leaves, and so make a lay of Pears and leaves till you have filled the pot, laying between each lay some sliced Ginger, then pour in as much old Wine as the pot will hold, laying some heavy thing on the Pears that they may not swim.

Green Pippins Preserved.

Take half a score of Green Pippens, (from the Tree if you can) pare them, and boil them in a pottle of water, till they are like a Pulpe; strain them from the Cores, then take two pound of Sugar, and mingle it with the liquor or pulp so strained, then set it on the fire, and as soon as it boileth, put in your Pippins you intend to preserve, so let them boil leisurely; till they be enough; when they are preserved, they will be green; in like sort you may preserve Quinces, Plumbs, Peaches and Apricocks, if you take them green.

Black-Cherries Preserved.

Take them fresh, or as they come from the Tree, and cut off the stalk; take one pound of Sugar for double the weight of Cherries, seeth and clarifie them, and when they are half boil'd put in your other Cherries, and let them seeth softly together, until the Sugar may be drawn between the fingers like small threads; when the broth is almost cold, put the Cherries in the pots with the stalks upward.

Mulberries Preserved.

Take Mulberries, and add to them their weight of Sugar; having wet your Sugar with some juice of Mulberries, then stir your Sugar together, and put in your Mulberries and boil them till they are enough, then take them off and boil the Syrrup a while, then put in the Mulberries, and let them stand till they be cold.

Oranges and Lemons Preserved.

Take the fairest you can get, lay them in water three days and three nights, to take away their bitterness; then boil them in fair water till they be tender; make as much Syrrup as will make them swim about the pan; let them not boil long, for then the skins will be tough; then let them lye all night in the Syrrup, that they may soak themselves therein; in the morning boil the Syrrup to a convenient thickness, then with it and the Oranges and Lemons, fill your Gally-pots, and keep them all the year; in this manner you may preserve Citrons.

Goosberries Preserved.

Let your Goosberries be gather'd with their stalks on, cut off their heads and stone them, then put them in Scalding-water, and let them stand therein covered a little while; then take their weight of Sugar finely beaten, and lay first a layer of Sugar, then one of Goosberries in your Preserving pan or Skillet till all be in, putting in for every pound of Goosberries a spoonful of fair water, set them on the Embers till the Sugar be melted, then boil them up as fast as you can, till the Syrrup be thick enough; when cold, put them up. In this manner you may preserve Raspices and Mulberries.

Preserved Roses, or any other Flowers.

Take one pound of Roses, three pound of Sugar, one pint and a little more of Rose-water; make your Syrrup first, and let it stand till it be cold; then take your Rose-leaves, having first clipt off all the white, put them in the cold Syrrup and cover them; let your fire be very soft that they may only simper two or three hours; then whilst they are hot, put them out into pots or glasses for your use.

Cherries Preserved.

Take Cherries fully ripe, and newly gather'd, put them to the bottom of your Preserving-pan, let the Cherries and Sugar be of equal weight, then throw some Sugar on the Cherries, and set them over a quick fire; and as they boil, throw on the rest of the Sugar till the Syrrup be thick enough; then take them out and put them into a Gally-pot whilst they are warm; it will not be amiss to add two or three spoonfuls of Rose-water to them.

Apricocks Preserved.

Let the weight of your Sugar equal the weight of your Apricocks, what quantity soever you mind to use; pare and stone your Apricocks, and lay them in the Sugar in your Preserving-pan all night, and in the morning set them on the Embers till the Sugar be all melted, and then let them stand and scald an hour; then take them off the fire and let them stand in that Syrrup two days, and then boil them softly till they be tender and well colour'd; and after that, when they are cold, put them up in glasses or pots, which you please.

Green Walnuts Preserv'd.

Take Walnuts and boil them till the water taste bitter, then take them off and put them in cold water, and peel off the rind, and put to them as much Sugar as they weigh, and a little more water than will wet the Sugar, set them on a fire and when they boil up, take them off, and let them stand two days, then boil them again once more.

Eringo-roots Preserv'd.

Take Eringo-roots fair, and not knotty, one pound, and wash them clean, then set them on the fire, and boil them very tender, peel off their outer-most skin, but break them not as you pare them; then let them lye a while in cold water; after this you must take to every pound of roots three quarters of a pound of clarified Sugar and boil it almost to the height of a Syrrup, and, then put in your roots, but look that they boil but gently together, and stir them as little as may be, for fear of breaking; when they are cold, put them up and keep them.

Ennula-Campana-roots Preserved.

Wash them, and scrape them very clean, and cut them thin to the pith, the length of your little finger; and as you cut them, put them in water, and let them lye there thirty days, shifting them twice every day, to take away the bitterness; then weigh them, and to every pound of Roots add twelve Ounces of Sugar, clarified first, boiling the Roots very tender, then put them into this Sugar, and let them boil upon a gentle fire until they be enough; having stood a good while off the fire, put them up between hot and cold.

Conserve of Roses.

Take red-Rose-buds, clip all the white, either bruised or withered from them; then add to every pound of Roses, three pound of Sugar, stamp the Roses very small, putting to them a little juice of Lemons or Rose-water as they become dry; when you think your Roses small enough, then put your Sugar to them, so beat them together till they be well mingled, then put it up in Gally-pots or Glasses. In this manner is made the Conserve of Flowers of Violets, which doth cool and open in a burning Fever or Ague, being dissolved in Almond-milk, and so taken; and excellent good for any inflammation in Children.

Thus you may also make the Conserve of Cowslips, which strengthens the brain, and is a Preservative against Madness; it helps the Memory, asswageth the pain of the head, and helpeth most infirmities thereof. In like manner you may also make Conserve of Marigolds, which taken fasting in the morning is very good against Melancholy; cureth the trembling of the heart, and very good against any Pestilential distemper.

Thus make Conserve of Sage and Scabious, the one is good against Melancholy, drieth and comforteth the Stomack, cureth an old Cough, and openeth the stopping of the Liver: the other, that is Scabious, cleanseth the Breast and Lungs, takes away old Coughs, and imposthumes of the Breast and inward parts.

How to Candy all sorts of Flowers as they grow with their stalks on.

Take the Flowers, and cut the stalks somewhat short; then take one pound of the whitest and hardest Sugar you can get, put to it eight spoonfuls of Rose-water, and boil it till it will rowl between your finger and your thumb; then take it from the fire, and cool it with a stick, and as it waxeth cold, dip in all your Flowers, and taking them out again suddenly, lay them one by one on the bottom of a Sieve, then turn a joined Stool with the feet upward; set the sieve on the feet thereof, then cover it with a fair linnen-cloth, and set a Chafing-dish of coals in the midst of the stool underneath the sieve, and the heat thereof will ['will' repeated] dry your Candy speedily, which will look very pleasantly, and keep the whole year.

Candyed Eringo-roots.

Take of your Eringo-roots ready to be preserved, and weigh them, and to every pound of Roots you must take of the purest Sugar you can get two pound, and clarifie it with the whites of Eggs exceeding well, that it may be as clear as Crystal; it being clarified, you must boil it to the height of *Manus Christi*, and then dip in your Roots two or three at once till they are all Candyed; put them in a Stove, and so keep them all the year.

The best and most approved way to dry Plumbs.

Take Plumbs when they are fully grown, with the stalks on them; however let them be green, split them on the one side and put them in hot water (but not too hot,) and so let them stand three or four hours; then to a pound of them take three quarters of a pound of Sugar beaten very fine, and eight spoonfuls of water to every pound; set them on hot embers till the Sugar be melted; and after that, boil them till they be very tender, letting them stand in that Syrrup three days to plump them; then take them out, and wash the Syrrup from them in warm water, and wipe them dry in a fine Linnen-cloth, then set them on plates, and let them dry in a Stove; dry them not in an Oven, for then they will be tough.

Proper colours for fruitage.

Saffron is the best Yellow, Sap-green the best Green, Indian-lake the best Red; all your Colours must be temper'd with Gum-water made of Rose-water.

Quince Marmelade.

Take of the fairest Quinces, wash them very clean, grate them very small, and wring out as much juice as you can; then take other Quinces and cut them into six pieces, put them into a pot, let them be evapoured with hot water, until they be throughly mellow; then take half a pot-full of the former juice, and pour it upon the former, stew'd and cut to pieces; break it well together, and put the rest of the juice amongst it, then wring it through a clean thin cloth; seeth no more of this juice at once than will fill a box therewith, and put white Sugar to it, as much as you please.

How to make Syrrup of Violets.

Boil fair water, and scum it, and to every ounce so scum'd and boil'd, take six ounces of the blew of Violets, only shift them as before nine times, and the last time take nine ounces of Violets; let them stand between times of shifting twelve hours, keeping the liquor still on hot embers, that it may be but milk-warm; after the first shifting, you must stamp and strain your last nine ounces of Violets, and put in only the juice of them, then take to every pint of this liquor thus prepared, one pound of Sugar finely beaten, boil it, and keep it stirring till all the Sugar be melted, which you must do, if you can, before it boil, afterwards boil it up with a quick fire.

Syrrup of Roses.

Take Damask Roses, and clip of the white of them, for every pint of water take six ounces of them, boil your water first, and scum it, then let them stand twelve hours, wringing out the Roses, and putting in new eight times, then wringing out the last, put in the juice of four ounces of Roses only, and so make it up as before.

Syrrup of Coltsfoot.

Take the leaves of Coltsfoot, and wash them very clean, then wipe them with a clean cloth leaf by leaf, then dry them well with a cloth, then beat them in a Mortar, and put them in a Strainer and wring all the juice you can out of them, and put it into Glasses, and let it stand in them to settle all night, the next day pour out the clearest of the Juice from the Grounds into a clean Bason, and take for every pint thereof a pound of Sugar finely beaten; boil the Juice of Coltsfoot softly on a Charcoal fire, and when you have well scum'd it put in the Sugar according to its proportion, and so let them boil together, keeping it with due scumming, until it will stand on a stiff purl, dropping it on a plate; then take it from the fire, and pour it through a Jelly-bag into a fair Bason, putting first a branch or two of Rosemary into the Bag's bottom, then keep it stirring with a spoon till it be luke-warm; otherwise it will have a Cream upon it; so letting it stand all night, put it in what Vessels you think fit to keep it in, for your future use and service.

Let these forms suffice to furnish you with the knowledg of making any other Syrrups; you need no better a pattern than this, for the making of a many others, as is the Syrrup of Wormwood, take the like quantity of Sugar, with the Juice of the said Wormwood, the Sugar being first clarified, and so make it up according to art; in the like manner you may make Syrrup of Betony, Borage, Bugloss, Cardis, Cammomel, Succory, Endive, Strawberries, Fumitory, Groundear, Purslain, Sage, Scabious, Scordium, Housleek, with many more. But enough of this; and therefore I shall next treat of Distillation.

Of DISTILLATION.

Ladies, before you come to the knowledg of distilling Waters, you ought in the first place to be furnished with good Stills, which Stills must either be of Tyne, or sweet Earth, wherein you may distil all manner of Waters, either for the health of your own Family or others.

Now by the way observe, you may easily make your waters look of what colour you please, if you will first distil your Water in a Stillatory, and then put it in a great Glass of strength, and fill it as full of those Flowers whose Colours you desire, then stop it and set it in the Stillatory, and let it distil, and you shall have their perfect colour.

Of precious and excellent Waters there are thousands, wherefore I shall only set down here some of the choicest and most valuable.

Dr. Stevens *his famous Water.*

Take a gallon of Gascoin-wine, of Ginger, Gallingal, Cinamon-Grains, Cloves, Mace, Nutmegs, Anniseeds, Carraway-seed, Coriander-seed, Fennel-seed, and Sugar, of every one a dram; then take of Sack and Ale a quart of each, of Camomile, Sage, Mint, Red-roses, Time, Pellitory of the Wall, wild-Marjoram, wild-Time, Lavender, Penneroyal, Fennel-roots, Parsley-roots, and Set-wall-roots, of each half a handful; then beat the Spice small, and bruise the Herbs, and put them all together into the Wine, and so let it stand sixteen hours, stirring it now and then, then distil it in a Limbeck with a soft fire, the first pint of the Water by it self, for it is the best.

The principal use of this water is against all cold Diseases, it preserveth Youth, comforteth the Stomack, cureth the Stone of what nature soever using but two spoonfuls in seven days: It preserved Dr. *Stevens* ten years Bed-rid, that he lived to ninety eight years.

Aqua Mirabilis.

Take three pints of White-wine, of Aquavitæ, and Juice of Saladine, of each a pint; one dram of Cardamer, and one dram of Mellilot-flowers, Cubebs a dram, of Gallingale, Nutmegs, Cloves, Mace and Ginger, of each a dram; mingle all these together over night, the next morning set them a Stilling in a Glass-Limbeck. This admirable Water dissolveth the swelling of the Lungs, and restoreth them when perished; it suffereth not the Blood to putrifie; neither need he or she to breach a Vein, that useth this Water often; it cureth the Heart-burn, and purgeth Melancholy and Flegm it expelleth Urine; it preserveth a Colour in the Face; and is an utter enemy to the Palsey; take three spoonfuls of it at a time, morning and evening twice a week.

A most approved Water for the Eyes.

Take a new-laid Egg and roast it hard, then cut the shell in the midst, and take out the yolk and put some white Copporice where the yolk was, then bind the Egg together again, and let it lye till it begin to be a Water, then take the white forth from both sides of the Egg, and put the same into a Glass of fair running-water, and so let it stand a while; then strain it through a fair Linnen-cloth, and keep it close stopped in a Glass, and therewith wash your Eyes morning and evening.

An admirable Water against the Stone in the Kidneys.

Take of the middle rind of the Root of Ash bruised two pound; Juniper-berries bruised, three pound; Venice-Turpentine of the best, two pound and an half; put these into twelve pints of Spring-water in a Glass-vessel well closed, and there let them purifie in Hors-dung three Months then distil them in Ashes, and there will come forth an Oyl, and a Water; seperate the one from the other; ten or twelve drops being taken of this Oyl every morning in four or six spoonfuls of the said Water, dissolves the Stone and Gravel in the Kidneys most wonderfully.

An excellent Water for the Worms.

Take of Worm-seeds bruised, eight ounces; the shaving of Harts-horn, two ounces; of Peach-flowers dri'd, an ounce; of

Aloes bruised, half an ounce; pour on these the Waters of Tansie, Rue, Peach-flowers, and of Worm-wood of each a pint and half; let them be digested in a Glass-Vessel three days, then distil them; cohobate this Water three times. This Water may be given from half an ounce to three ounces, according to the age and strength of the person. A small quantity for young Children will work the desired effect; it infallibly kills Stomack-worms, May-worms, or any other inwardly infesting the Body.

An excellent artificial Wine like Claret, but much better, and by many degrees brisker.

Take two gallons of your best Sider, (some esteem *Worcestershire* Red-streak the best) and mingle it with six gallons of Water, put thereunto eight pound of the best *Malaga* Raisins bruised in a Morter; let them stand close covered in a warm place, for the space of a fortnight, stirring them every two days well together; then press out the Raisins, and put the liquor into the same Vessel again; to which add a quart of the juice of Raspberries, and a pint of the juice of black Cherries; cover this liquor with bread, spread thick with Mustard, the Mustard-side being downward, and so let it work by the fire-side three or four days; then turn it up, and let it stand a week, and then bottle it up, and it will taste as quick as the briskest liquor whatever, and is a very pleasant drink, and much wholsomer than *French*-Wine.

An Ointment for any Wound or Sore.

Take two pound of Sheeps-suet, or rather Deers suet, a pint of Candy-Oyl, a quarter of a pound of the newest and best Bees-wax, melting them all together, and stirring them well; and put to them one ounce of the Oyl of Spike, and half an ounce of the Goldsmiths Boras; then heat them again, and stir them all together; put it up in a Gally-pot, and keep it close stopped, till you have cause to use it. This is an approved Ointment for any Wound or Sore, new or old.

A Searcloth for all Aches.

Take Rosin one pound, Perrosin a quarter of a pound, as much Mastick, Deers Suit the like, Turpintine two ounces, Cloves bruised one ounce, Mace bruised two ounces, Saffron two drachms, boil all these together in oyl of Camomile, and preserve it for your use. This hath done many good when nothing else would.

Now, that I may not seem wholly to apply my discourse and study for the benefit of young Court Ladies and City Madams, I shall descend into the Country, and find out something worthy the observation of a Rural Gentlewoman.

What things belong to a Country Gentlewoman: Of Daries, and making Butter and Cheese.

GEntlewomen, that you may be delighted with your own experience, as well as satisfied in the labours of your servants, I shall give you an account of what must be pre-observed in the keeping of a Dayry.

Let your Kine be of the best choice and breed that possibly can be procured; and the larger the Cow is the better she is, whereof *Lincolnshire* and *Cheshire* afford great plenty. The reason why I advise you to chuse large Cattel, is, that when they grow old, and will yeild but little milk, you may then feed and fatten them for the Shambles. The common and most known signs of a Cow that gives good store of Milk, are, a wreathed, Horn, a thin neck, and a large hairy Dewlap, a full Udder, and the Teats long and thick.

The best Black Kine are said to come from *Cheshire, Lanca-shire, Derbyshire, Yorkshire*; the best red Cows (whose Milk is so much esteemed above all other of that kind for its extraordinary nourishing quality), come from *Gloucester-shire, Somerset-shire*; the Pied-kine come commonly from *Lincoln-shire*, and are little inferior to the rest.

Thus you see *England* affords variety enough of extraordinary good Cows for the good Housewife to make choice of as she pleaseth; but withal let her be careful that the Bull be of as good a breed as the Kine themselves, otherwise the encrease will degenerate, and your Dairy in time run to ruin.

If at any time you buy any Kine to encrease your dairy, you must be careful they come not from a Soil that is more fruitful than your own; but rather not so fertile, or being not so good pasture, for then they will the better prosper and thrive, with you; otherwise it is ten to one they will pine away, and fall into many Distempers: Cows are said to give most Milk when they have newly Calved. If a Cow gives a gallon at a time constantly, she may pass for a very good Milch-Cow; there are some Cows which give a gallon and half, but very few who give two at a time.

You cannot design a better time for your Cow to calve in than at the latter end of *February*, or in the Months of *March* or *April*, for then the Grass is coming on, or springing up in its perfect goodness.

The hours or times most approved and commonly used for Milking, are in the Spring and Summer between five or six in the morning, and six in the evening. Some very unprofitably with the pretence of reason, milk their Cows in the Summer-season, betwixt the hours of twelve and one; but I would not have it to be a president for any to follow. There is an old Proverb very pertinent to what is here related; *That two good meals are better than three bad ones*: It is the worst point of Hus-wifry that can be to leave the Cow half milked; for besides the loss of Milk, it is the ready way to make the Cow dry and so become unprofitable to the Dairy.

Now the profits arising from Milk are chiefly three; *viz.* Cream, Butter, and Cheese; the Cream is the very heart and strength of the Milk, which must be skimmed very cleanly: Cleanly, I say, for Cleanliness is such an ornament to a good Huswife, that if she want any part thereof, she loseth both that and all other good names whatsoever. Cream is not to be kept above two days in Summer, and not above four in the Winter, if you wil be always provided with the best and sweetest Butter: But before we speak of that, I shall here insert some excellent Receipts for made-Cream, & Milk made better by art.

How to make your ordinary clouted-Cream.
Take a quantity of Milk from the Cow, and put it into a broad Earthen-pan, and set it over a slow fire, letting it stand there from morning to night, suffering it not to boil by any means; then take it off the fire, and set it in some place all night to cool, in the morning dish off your Cream, for it will be very thick.

To make fresh Cheese in Cream.
Take a pottle of new Milk as it cometh from the Cow, and half a pound of blanched Almonds beaten very small, and make a thick Almond-milk, with a pint of Cream strained; and a little before you go to Dinner make it blood-warm, season it with a little Sugar, Rose-water, and searsed Ginger, and put to it a little Runnet, and when it is scummed, bread [*recte* break] it up, and

whey it, and put it into a Mould, and press it with your hand and when it is well wheyed put it into a Dish with Cream.

Cream of Codlins.

After you have scalded your Codlins and peel'd off the skins, and scraped the pulps from the cores, with a little Sugar and Rose-water, strain them, and lay the pulp of your Codlins in a Dish, with as much raw Cream as you please about them; there are several other ways propounded, but this is most satisfactory to the Palat.

To make a Junket.

Take Ews or Goats-milk; if you have neither of these, then take Cows-milk, and put it over the fire to warm, then put in a little Runnet to it; then pour it out into a Dish, and let it cool, then strew on Cinamon and Sugar, then take some Cream and lay upon it scraping Sugar thereon, serve it up.

Here note by the way, that you cannot keep Cream above three days in Summer, and six days in Winter without prejudice.

I need not tell you how to make Butter, since there are very few in the Country that can be ignorant thereof; wherefore I shall only say, that the best time to pot your Butter is in the Month of *May*, for then the air is most temperate, and the Butter will take Salt best; however, it may be done at any time betwixt *May* and *September*. In preserving thus your Butter, you may not only supply your House therewith, but to your profit furnish others.

There is another profit which ariseth from the Dairy, and that is Cheese; of which there are three kinds, Morning-Milk-Cheese, Nettle-Cheese and floaten-Milk-Cheese: The first is the fattest and best that is made in this Kingdom; the Nettle Cheese is so called, because when the Cheese is new-made, Nettles are put upon it; which Nettles are to be renewed ounce [*recte* once] in two days: The floaten-Milk-Cheese is the worst of all Cheeses, & indeed so coarse, that as I like not to feed thereof so I love not to write of it. What is further to be spoken of a Dairy, I shall refer it to my advice to that Maid who desires to be a Dairy-Maid in a great House.

I have hitherto, Ladies, endeavoured the accomplishment of Gentlewomen well extracted; but as you cannot do all things your selves, so you must have Attendants & Servants about you, such whose good Qualifications may not only render them fit for your employments, but in the performance thereof they may credit the House wherein they live, and profit their own selves, to such therefore I direct my following advice.

And first to all Gentlewomen, who though well born are notwithstanding by indigency necessitated to serve some person of Quality.

In the first place, I would not have you look upon your condition as to what it hath been but what it is; learn what ever you can, and slight no opportunity which may advance your knowledg to the height of your birth, for want of which some by reason of their Parents negligence, think they have enough to maintain their Children in a good equipage, & therefore slight those arts which may not only be ornamental, but beneficial to their Children hereafter, vainly imagining that poverty will never approach their Gates; by which cross mistake their Daughters are often exposed to great hardships, many times contenting themselves to serve as Chamber-maids because they have not the Accomplishments of a Waiting-woman, or an House-keeper; and so whereas their own natural and acquired parts might raise in every ones opinion a great esteem of their worth and merit, and incline Ladies to covet their company, sit at Table, and have a command in the House, respect from the rest of the Servants; wear good Clothes and have a considerable sallary; instead thereof, the meanness of their qualifications render them only fit companions for Grooms and Footboys.

Wherefore in the first place I shall advise all Parents (be their Estates never so good, and their Revenues large) to endeavour the gentile education of their Daughters, encouraging them to learn whatever opportunity offers, worthy a good estimation. *For riches hath wings, and will quickly fly away*; or Death comes and removes the Parents, leaving the Children to the tuition of merciless and unconscionable Executors or others in trusted, who only study how to rob the Orphants of their due, and afterwards thrust them into the world, giving them neither their own money, not [i.e. nor] half the education they deserved; now if there be a treasury laid up within by education, by which they may live (without an Estate their Parents shall leave them) in some honest and creditable imployment, their condition will be so establisht, that nothing almost but death or sickness can make an alteration therein, and may boldly defie and scorn the various vicissitudes of common misfortunes. For this reason I would have you to lose no time, but improve all you may in learning whatever may befit a Woman.

If your Father hath had large Revenues, and could talk loudly of his Birth, and so may think this servile life beneath you, yet thank God you can do something for an honest livelihood, and be never the less submissive; for if you are a Servant, you must do what becomes a Servant; if your extraction be mean, and have attained to serviceable preferment, give God the glory, and be more careful to please.

If you desire to be a Waiting-Gentlewoman, it will be expected that you can Dress well; Preserve well; and Write well a legible hand, good language, and good *English*; have some skill in Arithmetick; Carve well, and let your behaviour be modest & courteous to all persons accord[ing] to their degree; humble and submissive to your Lord and Lady, or Master and Mistriss; neat in your Habit; loving to Servants; sober in your Countenance and Discourse; not using any wanton gesture, which may give Gentlemen occasion to suspect your levity, and so court you to Debauchery, and lose a reputation irrecoverable.

If you would be an House-keeper, it will be required that your behaviour be grave and solid, which will inculcate in their beliefs that you are able to govern a Family. And as I told you before, you must Preserve well; so you must have a competent knowledg in Distilling, making Cates, all manner of spoon-meats, and the like. Be careful in looking after the Servants, that every one perform their duty in their several places, that they keep good hours in up-rising and lying down; and that no Goods be either spoil'd, or imbezel'd.

That all Strangers be nobly and civilly used in their Chambers; and that your Master or Lady be not dishonoured through neglect or miscarriage of Servants.

To be first up, and last in bed, to prevent junketing.

To make Salves and Ointments, to dress the wounds of the poor about you, with other things of your own composition, with which you may compassionate the sick and indigent: for commonly all good and charitable Ladies do make this part of their House-keepers business.

To all Maidens, who desire to be Chamber-Maids to persons of Quality.

IT will be required of you, that you Dress well that you may be able to supply the place of the Waiting-woman, should she chance to fall sick, or be absent from your Lady; you must wash fine Linnen well and starch Tiffanies, Lawns Points, and Laces, mend them neatly; and wash white Sarcenets, with such like things.

You must make your Ladies bed; lay up, and lay out her Night-clothes; see that her Chamber be kept clean, and nothing wanting which she desires or requires to be done. Be modest in your deportment, ready at her call, always diligent, answering not again when reprov'd, but with pacifying words; loving & courteous to your fellow-servants not gigling or idling out your time, nor wantoning in the society of men; you will find the benefit thereof; for an honest and sober man will sooner make that woman his Wife whom he seeth continually imployed about her business, than one who makes it her business to trifle away her own and others time; neither will a virtuous and under-standing Mistress long entertain such a servant whom she finds of such a temper.

Be not subject to change, *For a rouling stone gathers no moss*; and as you will gain but little money, so if you ramble up and down you will lose your credit.

It may be a fellow-servant may court you; but before you entertain the motion, consider how you must live; by incon-siderately marrying you may have one joyful meeting, and ever after a sorrowful living, and have time to repent of your rash matching,

Instructions for all Nursery-Maids in Noble Families.

YOU ought to be naturally inclined to love young Children or else you will soon discover your unfitness to manage that charge; you must be neat and cleanly about them, and careful to keep good hours for them: Get their Break-fasts and Suppers in good and convenient time; let them not sit too long, but walk them often up and down especially those who cannot go well of themselves; take heed they get no falls by your carelessness for such means many (the cause first being unperceivable) have afterwards grown irrecoverably lame or crooked; wherefore if any such thing should happen, conceal it not, though you may justly incur a great deal of blame therefore.

I knew a Gentlewoman absolutely spoil'd by such a concealment; her Nurse by negligence let her fall (being very young) from a Table, and by the fall her thigh-bone was dislocated, the Nurse fearing the indignation and displeasure of the Childs Parents, who where rich and potent, concealed it a long time, under the pretence of some other indisposition; endeavouring in the mean time the reducing of the bone to its proper place; but by reason of an interposition of a Jelly between the dislocations, it could not be done, and then when it was too late, the Parents were acquainted with the said condition of their beloved Child; and hereupon all means imaginable used for its recovery, but all in vain, although they had been at some hundreds of pounds charge for the cure.

She is now as lovely a young Gentlewoman as a ravisht eye can feast upon; but it would break the heart of that body the eye belongs unto to see her go; her back-side-walking would force a man from her to the *Indies*, and yet her face would attract him to her twice as far.

But to my purpose; be not churlish or dogged to them, but merry and pleasant, and contrive and invent pretty pastimes, agreeable to their age; keep their linnen and other things always mended, and suffer them not to run too fast to decay. Do not shew a partiality in your love to any of them, for that dejects the rest: Be careful to hear them read if it be imposed upon you, and be not too hasty with them; have a special care how you behave your self before them, neither speaking nor acting misbecomingly, lest your bad example prove the subject of their imitation.

Instructions for all Chamber-maids to Gentle-women in City and Country.

FRom you it will be required that you wash and starch very well both Tiffanies, Lawns, Points and Laces, and that you can mend what is amiss in them.

That you work Needle-work well, and all sorts of Plain-work, or any other work with the Needle which is used in such Houses.

That you wash black and white Sarsnets; that you dress well, and diligently perform what you are commanded by your Mistress; be neat in your Habit, modest in your Carriage, silent when she is angry, willing to please, quick and neat-handed about what you have to do.

You must know how to make all manner of Spoon-meats, to raise Paste, to dress Meat well, (though not often required thereunto) both of Fish and Flesh; to make Sauces, garnish Dishes, make all sorts of Pickles, to see that every thing be served in well and handsomely to the Table, in due time, and to wait with a graceful *decorum* at the Table if need should require.

Keep your Mistresses Chamber clean, and lay up every thing in its due place; you ought to be skillful in buying any thing in the Market, if you be intrusted therewith; these things will be expected from you in those Houses where there is no Head-cook. If there be no Butler, you must see all things decent and fitting in the Parlour and Dining-room.

In a word, you must divest your Mistress from all the care you can, giving to her a just and true account of what moneys you lay out, shewing your self thrifty in all your disbursements; be careful in overlooking inferiour servants, that they waste nothing which belongs to your Master and Mistress.

If you are thus qualified, and be of an humble and good disposition, your merit will deserve a good Salary, and a great deal of love and respect. If you have not these accomplishments, endeavour their procuration by sparing some money from superfluous expence, and over-gaudy clothes; for to see a Maid finely trickt up, having a fine show without, and not one good qualification within, is like a jointed *Bartholomew*-Baby bought for no other use than to be look'd upon.

Instructions for Nursery-Maids to Gentlewomen, both in London, *or elsewhere.*

Let me advise you, first to consider the charge you take in hand, and not to desire it as too many do, because it is an easie kind of life, void of labour and pains-taking, Children are easily pleas'd with any thing: I can assure you the contrary;

for it is a troublesome employment, and the charge is of greater weight than such vainly imagine.

You ought in the first place to be of a gentle and good disposition, sober in your Carriage, neat in your Apparel; not sluggish nor heavy-headed, but watchful and careful in the night-season, for fear any of the Children should be ill; and keep due hours for their up-rising and going to bed.

Take special care that they eat nothing which may over-charge their Stomacks. If you observe their Faces at any time paler than ordinary, or complain of pain in their Stomach, conclude it is the Worms that troubles them, and therefore give them remedies suitable to the distemper, do this often whether you see those Symtoms or no, the neglect of which hath been the destruction of many hopeful Children.

Keep them (whatever you do) sweet and clean, and moderately warm; teach them some good forms of prayer, and to read as they are capable; refrain them from drinking too much Wine, strong Liquors, and eating over-much Fruit.

Be loving and chearful with them, not thumping or beating them as many do, contrary to the knowledg and pleasure of their Parents: That Mother is very unwise that will give liberty to Servants to strike her Children; and that Servant is over-sawcy and ill natur'd who dares do it without her Mistresses privity and consent.

This is your duty; and unless you can and will do this, never undertake this charge.

Instructions for such who desire to be absolute Cook-maids in good and great houses.

IT is a common thing now-adays for Cook-maids to ask great Wages, although they are conscious to themselves of their inability of performing almost any thing; which as it is unconscionable so to do, so in the end it will prove disgraceful to them: I shall therefore tell you what in reason may be required from you, and what justly you ought to perform.

Your skill will chiefly consist in dressing all sorts of Meat, both Fish, Flesh and Fowl, all manner of Baked-meats, all kind of Sawces, and which are most proper for every sort of Dish, and be curious in garnishing your Dishes, and making all manner of Pickles, of all which I have treated of before, as you will find it in the Chapter of my Instructions for young Ladies and Gentlewomen in the Art of Cookery, wherein you may be supplyed with the Customary and *a-la-mode* ways of dressing all sorts of Meat.

And as you must know how to dress Meat well, so you must know how to save what is left of that you have dressed, of which you may make both handsome and toothsome Dishes again, to the saving of your Masters purse, and the credit of his Table.

Be as saving as you can, and cleanly about every thing; see also that your Kitchen be kept clean, and all things scoured in due time; your Larders also and Cupboards, that there be no bits or meat or bread lye about them to spoil and stink.

That your Meat taint not for want of good Salting.

That you keep good hours for your Meals, else you put an house quite out of order; do not covet to have the Kitchin-stuff for your vails, but rather ask the more wages, for that may make you an ill Huswife of your Masters goods, and teach you to be a thief, for you will be apt to put that which goes into the tried suet into your pot.

Lay not all your Wages on your back, but lay up something against sickness, and an hundred other Casualties; assure your self, it is more commendable for one of your profession to go decent and clean, than gaudily fine.

Take this in part of that good counsel I could give you, had I time; which if you follow, the greatest benefit will be your own at last.

Instructions for under-Cook-Maids.

IT behoves you to be very diligent and willing to do what you are bid to do; and though your employment be greasie and smutty, yet if you please you may keep your self from being nasty, therefore let it be your care to keep your self clean. Observe every thing in Cookery that is done by your Superiour, treasure it up in your memory; and when you meet with a convenient opportunity, put that in practice which you have observed; this course will advance you from a drudg to be a Cook another day.

Every one must have a beginning; and if you will be ingenious and willing to learn, there is none will be so churlish or unkind as to be unwilling to teach you; but if you are stubborn and careless, who do you think will trouble themselves with you? Beware of Gossips, for they will misadvise you; beware of the sollicitations of the flesh, for they will undo you; and though you may have mean thoughts of your self, and think none will meddle with such as you; it is a mistake, *Hungry Dogs will eat dirty Puddings*; and I my self have known a brave Gallant to fall foul with the Wench of the Skullery, when some others would have hazarded their life for one sole enjoyment of that incomparable Lady his Wife, he so ingratefully slighted.

Instructions for Dairy-Maids in great Houses.

Have a care that all your Vessels be scalded well, and kept very clean; that you milk your Cattel in due time; for your Kine by custom will expect it, though you neglect it, which will tend much to their detriment.

Waste not your Cream by giving it away to liquorish persons; keep certain days for your Churning, and be sure to make up your Butter neatly and cleanly, washing it well from the Buttermilk, and then salt it well.

Be careful to make your Cheeses good and tender, by well ordering them; and see that your Hogs have the whey, and that it be not given away to idle or gossiping people, who live meerly upon what they can get from Servants: That you provide your Winter-Butter and Cheese in the Summer, as in *May*; and when your Rowens come in, be sparing of your Fire; and do not lavish away your Milk-butter or Cheese.

If you have any Fowls to fat, or Pigs, look to them that it may be your credit, and not your shame, when they come to the Table.

When you milk your Cattel, stroke them well, and in the Summer-time save those strokings by themselves, to put into your morning-Milk-cheese.

Instructions for Laundry-Maids in great Houses.

Your duty will be to take care of all the Linnen in the house, excepting Points and Laces; whatever you wash, do it up quickly, that it may not stink and grow yellow, and be forced to the washing again before it be used.

Let all the bracks in the Linnen, or rents, be duly mended; and keep your certain days of washing, and other days for the making clean of such Rooms as are appointed you.

Be sparing of your Soap, Fire and Candle.

Entertain no Chare-woman unknown to your Lady or Mistress.

Be careful that your Tubs and Copper, or whatever else you make use of, be kept clean, and in good repair.

That you rise early every morning, but more especially on Washing-days.

Instructions for House-Maids in great Houses.

YOur principal Office is to make clean the greatest part of the house; and so that you suffer no room to lie foul; that you look well to all the stuff, and see that they be often brushed, and the Beds frequently turned.

That you do not misplace any thing by carrying it out of one room into another, for that is the way to have them lost, or you soundly chid for their being not in their proper places.

That you be careful for, and diligent to all Strangers, and see that they lack nothing in their Chambers, which your Mistress or Lady will allow; and that your Close-stools and Chamber-pots be duly emptied and kept clean.

That you help the Laundry-maid in a morning on a Washing-day.

That in the Afternoon you be ready to help the House-keeper or the Waiting-woman in their Preserving and Distilling.

To Scullery-Maids in great Houses.

THere are several Rooms that you must keep sweet and clean, as the Kitchen, Pantry, Wash-house, &c.

That you wash and scowre all the Plates and Dishes which are used in the Kitchen, also Kettles, Pots, Pans, Chamber-pots, with all other Iron, Brass, and Pewter materials that belong to the Chambers or Kitchen; and lastly, you must wash your own Linnen.

Thus Ladies; I have endeavoured to shew your Servant their duties in their respective places and what qualifications they ought to have, which may enable and fit them for your service. I shall now return to the Compleatment of those Accomplishments which best become your noble and gentile extraction.

I have already declared how you ought to be educated from your Minority to better Maturity of years, and from thence what your deportment ought to be to all persons in all places; there remaineth only some instructions how you may talk and that elegantly, to the same persons at a distance whether relations, friends or acquaintance, and that is by Letter; having given you some general instructions how to pen them, I shall lay you down some choice patterns of Letter upon several occasions for your imitation. I shall conclude at present this Treatise with some witty Dialogues, or interchangeable Discourses between several of your Sex emi-nent for birth, worth, and ingenuity.

Some general and choice Rules for writting of Letters.

First, what a Letter is? It is or ought to be the express image of the Mind, represented in writing to a friend at a distance; wherein is declared what He or She would do or have done. This excellent use we have of Letters, that when distance of place, will not admit of Union of persons, or converse *Viva voce*; that deplorable defect is supplied by a Letter or Missive; and indeed the necessity of conversing one with another as long as we live, layeth an unavoidable cogency of communicating our affairs each to other, without which friends at a distance could have no correspondence one with the other.

Though it lieth not in the power of every one to make use of these excellent means for reciprocal Communication; yet we see daily the illiterate and ignorant will make hard shifts rather than go without the benefit thereof, applying themselves to friends that can write; or if they have none, to Scriveners or other strangers, venturing their secrets with them, rather than their friend shall go without the knowledg of them.

But as for you, Ladies, for whose use this Book was framed, I question not your writing well; but without inditing well it will signifie but little; to the intent therefore you may polish your Epistolical compositions, observe these two things therein, that is, the Matter and Form.

The Matter of Letters is any thing that may be discoursed of without any exception; or that which you would freely discover to your Relations, or discourse to your friend when present the same you would do by Letter when he is absent, if it stands with conveniency. For sometime it is not convenient to trust that in a sheet of paper which is lost or miscarried may be the great detriment, if not the utter ruin of the person. This matter you must know varieth much according to the subject you write upon. I shall endeavour to treat a little of all the common subjects which are the usual occasions of Letter-writing.

Of Intelligence or Advice.

THese Letters are the informers of our friends, of our own, or others concerns. There is no great matter of invention required in them, for the very subject will afford you matter enough; all that is required of you in this, are these two things; the first, that you word your Matter well, and that you write not any thing unadvisedly, which you cannot justifie; but above all, have a care of News-writing if it nearly concern the State, or any great person thereunto belonging.

Of Friend chastisement.

IF you have a dear female-friend whom you suspect of any youthful excursions, especially levity, and would reduce her to a better understanding, mildly lay open her errors; and therein discover what an enemy she hath been to God and to her own reputation; that there is no way to reconcile her self to God and the World, but by her future exemplary modest carriage. And that she may not think, your reproofs have their original from malice or hatred to her person, declare what a great esteem you ever had for her excellent parts, and rare endowments of mind; and what a pity it is, such excellencies should be eclipsed by such foul miscarriages; that is not your sorrow alone, but the grief of several of her friends; and then subtilly insinuate this, That had it not been a friend you so dearly loved, you could have been well content to have been silent; but contrary, the love you bear her, obliged you to reveal the evil reports you have heard of her, and how troubled you are to see her commendations so limited with exceptions. Were it not that she is ——— she is absolutely one of the finest Gentlewomen in *Europe*. Then conclude, that you hope she will take all in good part; and that she will highly oblige you, to use the same freedom as you have done with her, if she hears ought amiss.

Of giving good Counsel.

YOu may in the first place excuse your rash intrusion, in giving counsel before it be required, but the bonds of freindship were so strong that you could not forbear, and therefore hoped she would take all in good part; and then inculcate this, that you did not doubt the sufficiency of her judgment, but being tender of her welfare and knowing of what weighty concern the business in hand imported, that it was not for a year or a day, but for life, you could do no less, being full fraught with a most entire affection, but tell her, she must consider ——— then tell her what your advice is, and be sure you back it with the best reasons and arguments you can summon together; making it appear, that your counsel is both honest and profitable, and not self-interested; and it only tends to her lasting good here, and eternal hereafter; husbanding your reasons according to the person you deal with. Conclude with an hearty ejaculation to God, that he may direct her for the best, following the good advice you have given, &c.

If you are a Mother of Children, and would write to them, or to your Servant, you need not have rules in so doing, the plainer you write, the better it is and they will more readily understand you; you need no more than signifie to them what you would have done, and what undone; as for reasons, you need not alledg any to encourage them in their duty, your power is sufficient, and your command is the only reason why they should do so, or so; however, if you see any refractoriness in your Children, it will not be amiss, to urge how just your commands are, and how easily performed, adding the promise of a reward, if they fulfil your desire; but threats and menaces of punishment, if they disobey; but concluding, you hope to find them so towardly, that they will not need correction.

Of requesting a kindness.

LEtters of this nature, are of two kinds; the first is, when one Gentlewoman of quality sends to another, her very good friend, either for some courtesie to her self; or for another; and then she must begin with an acknowledgment of her love and how confident she still remains in the assurance thereof; then make known your request, and how easily it may be done, and end with a promise of being sensible of the courtesie, and retaliation.

If the person requesting be somewhat a stranger, but much inferior to the person of whom she entreats the kindness, then she must begin with an insinuation, excusing her boldness in daring to request a favour of a person whom she never obliged by any former service; yet adding withal, that knowing her goodness, and the delight her Ladiship takes in bestowing courtesies on the undeserver, she fears not a denial. If it be upon an urgent occasion, let her endeavour to move her, to compassionate her misery, exaggerating the greatness thereof; insisting, that she hath no other way to retrive her misfortune; that if she cannot hereafter find any way a requital, yet she shall notwithstanding retain the remembrance of her love or charity fixed in her heart. Conclude with a Prayer to God, so to increase her felicity here, that she may never stand in need of a kindness from any till the Almighty hath fixed on her head a Crown of Glory.

Of Recommendation.

IN the recommending of a person, you must shew your motives for so doing, as first, either as she is a Kinswoman, or Friend, and a person so worthy as deserving all favour, that were it not for her goodness and virtue, you would not utter a word in her behalf; and conclude, that what kindness is done her, is shewn to your self.

How elegantly to complain of injuries done.

THis may be done several ways, if you would mildly complain of a friend and yet not break with him or her; let your complaint be mixt with praises, saying, that you are sorry the persons deportment hath not been such as your friendship required; however, you are so charitable as to believe the offence was commited willingly, but rather through misprision or ill-perswasion. But let the offence be ever so great, do not rail in opprobrious terms, though in smart and significant expressions; saying, that you have connived too long patiently at the injuries done you, but finding, instead of amendment, the person growing worse, you would be more sensless than stones if you should not speak; referring your self to his own judgment, if passion hath not quite extinguisht the eye of reason, whether you are not very much wrong'd; however, upon a just acknowledgment, you are willing to forget all, and retain him or her still in the estimation of a friend.

Forms of Address or Visit.

IN the first place, insinuate your contentment in discoursing with your friend face to face, but since you are deprived thereof, you are happy still in having the opportunity and conveniency of writing: That you desire to hear of her welfare, both as to health and other concerns; that your desire is earnest to see her, and that those dayes wherein you see her not, are years; and those years seem ages, especially when you receive no Letters from her; that if she will continue that correspondence, she shall find occasion of finding fault on your side more of importunity than carelessness or neglect; and so conclude with a protestation of the continuance of an inviolable friendship.

Forms of Congratulation.

THis is done when we desire to rejoice with our friend for some great good that hath befaln him or her, either by escaping from some eminent danger, or sickness. There are several other subjects of this nature which you may treat on as they happen, and therefore I cannot prescribe you exact rules; only you must testifie the great satisfaction you receive in your friends welfare, and that your joy is not particular, but all in general have it when good and virtuous persons are advanced, and do prosper.

Of Consolation.

LEtters of Consolation seem to mitigate any evil or adversity that hath befaln a friend, which being various cannot well have one remedy applied to them. If the evil be but small, alledg they have no such great cause for their sorrowing, the subject not deserving it; that they ought to have courage; for pusillanimity wrongs the reputation; or if it be great, insist that it will not last long: But if the disaster be very great indeed, you must then aknowledg how much you are concerned in his or her sufferings, and that having so great a share in her misfortune, you are fitter to condole than comfort her therein, yet however the interest of alliance or friendship obliges you to apply some lenitive: That you cannot perswade her from grieving, for that would argue inhumanity; having sustain'd so great a loss of a Husband, a Wife, Father, Mother, &c. but hope she or he will not be so heartless as to be carried away in the torrent of a fruitless grief; that Reason must be used: for Nature is not obliged to alter its course to please him or her particularly, and exempt it self for the sake of one from those Laws to which the whole world is subject. In short, when a misfortune cannot be withstood, immoderate grief doth but exasperate it; and that being a Christian, there ought to be a submission to Gods Will, and subscribe with a prayer to the Almighty, to give him or her patience to overcome this great affliction.

Form of thanks for Courtesies received.

THanks we must apply as well to the nature of the Courtesie, as to the quality of him that hath done it. You must begin with a commemoration of the Courtesie received, acknowledging the receiver not worthy thereof, having never done any obliging service; or if you have, yet this hath made double satisfaction; then promise that the remembrance of her love shall be deeply engraven in your heart; and that you will always retain a resentment of her kindness: This you may write, if the kindness be so highly qualified that the person looks for no other satisfaction than acknowledgment only.

I have given you several forms of Letters, let me now shew you the parts of a Letter; the common ones are Superscription and Subscription.

The Superscription of Leters is twofold; the one external, the other internal; the outward Superscription is that when the Letter is folded up, and containeth the name, title, and abode of the person we write unto; but above all you must have a care that you give proper titles, such as befit the quality of the person.

The Title of a King is, *To His most Excellent Majesty.* To the Queen the same, altering the article. To all Sons or Brethren of the King of *England*, *To His Royal Highness*. To a Duke, *To His Grace*. To a Dutchess the same. To all Earls, Marquesses, Viscounts and Barons, *To the right Honourable*. To Marchionesses and Countesses by Patent, *To the right Honourable*. To all Lords, *To the right honourable*. To Knights, *To the right Worshipful*. To all Justices of Peace, High-Sheriffs, Counsellors at Law, Esquires, either by birth or place, &c. *To the Worshipful*.

The Subscription is placed at the lower end of the Letter; and in writing to great Persons you must Subscribe thus,

My Lord, or Madam,
   Your most humble, and most obedient Servant.
or *Your most faithful, and most obliged Servant.*
                  S. G.

To persons of meaner degree, subscribe your self thus,

               Your Servant.
      or   *Your Friend and Servant.*

If kindred write one to another, the greater may express the relation in the beginning of the Letter; but she that is of the meaner quality must be content to specifie it in the Subscription.

Besides Superscription and Subscription, you must set down what year and day you writ this Letter in, and the place from whence it came; yet it is not always convenient to mention the place, nor the relation the person hath to you to whom you write.

The beginning of all your Letters ought to contain some small Complements by way of insinuation, with a short proposal of what you intend to say; this is only observed in long Letters, otherwise you may fall upon the Matter immediately.

As for the Matter that is according to your Concern, and I need not use much order in the discoursing it, but write what falls under your pen, not standing much upon connexion, unless it be in Letters of Answer, and then you must follow the order of those letters, using some small transition. In the Conclusion it is requisite that you testifie your affection with hearty wishes and prayers for the person you write unto.

For the stile of your Letters, let is not be affected but careless, not much differing from our usual way of speaking. In Letters of Complement supply the barrenness of your matter with the smoothness of your rhetorical exornations; but have a care that in striving to avoid affectation you do not run into improprieties of speech, or barbarisms.

Consider seriously what best befits the things you are to write of, regarding person, time and place. It would be absurd for any one to write to a superiour as to a familiar, and that which would suit very well with an ancient man, or a person in Authority, would be ridiculous for to use to a man of mean degree, or of the younger sort; surely we are not to use the like expressions to a Soldier, as we do to a Scholar or Lady.

Be not too prolix in your writing, nor too short; but observe a mediocrity or mean betwixt them: In the avoiding of tautologies, do not omit any thing that may conduce to the illustration of your matter.

Do not study for hard words, but such as are either plain, or very significant; this perspicuity of writing is to be measur'd according to the capacity of the person to whom the Letter is directed; for some will easily conceive what is difficult and hard for others to comprehend.

Have especial care of blotting your paper, giving it a large Margent; and be curious in the cutting your Letters, that they may delight the sight, and not tire the Reader.

Lastly, be curious in the neat folding up your Letter, pressing it so that it may take up but little room, and let your Seal and Superscription be very fair.

Having given you general instructions how to compose and indite Letters, it follows that I here insert some of the best patterns for your imitation.

Letters upon all Occasions.

Of Complement.

Madam,

I Am by so many Obligations yours, that the only want of occasion to give you testimony thereof alone breeds in me all my discontent; esteeming my self unfortunate in nothing so much; and that the passion which carrieth me to your service, proves as unprofitable as extream; which forceth me to have recourse to intreaties, beseeching you to honour me with your commands, that (other means failing) my obedience may oblige you to believe that I am,

Madam,
Your most humble and
affectionate Servant.

Another of the like nature.

Madam,

T Hough I have told you a thousand times by word of mouth how much I am your Servant; yet my Pen shall once more assure you of the same; I only wait for some eminent proofs to demonstrate the truth of my profession; I do heartily wish that you would not longer make me expect an opportunity, but lay your command, which may satisfie my impatience, to make you know and confess at the same time, that you may have more powerful and more considerable Servants, but never,

Madam,
One more obedient and faithful.

Their Answers.

Madam,

I Will be so presumptuous (since you desire it) as to believe you love me, but on condition that you will acknowledg the passion I have to serve you. For as it only makes me merit the honour of your friendship, so I should be very glad that you would everlastingly conserve the memory thereof. Continue then in loving me as much as you plese, and likewise esteem infallibly that I am more than all the world besides,

Madam,
Your very Servant.

Another Answer.

Madam,

I Am not so unfortunate as I thought I was, since I see I hold some place still in your memory; yet the grief which I entertain for not deserving the honour, hath reduced my thoughts to such a moderation, that I am in doubt whether I should complain or rejoyce. It remains in you only, to allay the discontent of my mind, by giving me some employment in your service, which may witness the passion I have to maintain the quality of,

Madam,
Your faithful Servant.

A Letter from a Gentlewoman at a Boarding-School in Hackney, *to her* quondam *School-fellow in* London.

Indeared Friend,

I Have laid aside the exercise of my Needle, that I may employ my hand some little time in the management of my Pen, that herein I may assure you, that the strong inclinations I have to manifest my self your friend upon all accounts, will not permit me to let slip any opportunity wherein I may evidence this truth. I am troubled that you are not always as ready to honour me with your commands, as I am zealous and forward to obey them. That cordial respect I bear you, hath so strongly link'd me to you, that into whatsoever condition fortune shall throw me, I shall still retain the memory of your affection, and must not live when I cease to love you, whom above mine own welfare I esteem, and therefore must subscribe my self, dearest friend,

Your most affectionate, &c,
M. G.

The Answer to it.

Most Obliging Friend,

I Am ravisht with content, to see how your curious art, and delicateness thereof, can so happily translate your hand and fancy from on[e] flower to another, the one as the draught of your Needle, the other of your Pen; were I to be judg, I knew not which to give the greatest praise or encomium, the Flourishes of the Pen, or the Flowers of the Needle; the one might make *Arachny*'s Maids of Honour (I mean those delicate fingered Nuns) to blush, to be out-done; and from the other, a Secretary to a Queen may gather eloquence and fancy. You need not make the least question of my love, or the integrity thereof, for although I want the art of Rhetorick to represent it, yet my deeds and services shall be the elaborate Elocutors which shall express my self to be,

Your most cordially affectionate Servant,
S. L.

From the above-nam'd M. G. *to the said* S. L. *acknowledging her and her School-fellows sorrow for her absence, giving an account of the accustomed care of her Governess.*

Dear Friend,

WE remain in the state and condition you left us, there being no access as yet, of any more numbers, but only of your [*recte* our] griefs for your absence, which increase, as our desires do increase, or our daily discourses of you. We understood not our happiness till your departure from us, being now made sensible of the good we enjoyed, by being deprived thereof. Our Governess is as active and watchful as ever, down with the Sun and up with the Lark, and then doth her messenger summon us to desert our beds; if she perceives any unwilling, she subtilly tempers the unpleasantness of her early importunity; she perswades them thereunto, by alledging, what benefit thereby will accrew to their healths; nor is her accustomed care to be discommended, since therein she aims not only at the benefit of our Bodies, but the eternal welfare of our Souls in the performance of our duties to God and our Parents. She continues her former jealousie, not suffering a Letter to come into the house without her knowledg thereof; and herein her prudence is highly to be commended, for by her strict examination of these Paper-messengers, she shuts the doors against a great many which might be the Bawds which might betray the Obedience of some, and the Chastity of others. Neither are there any Answers returned to any Letters but what she is privy to; by which means, there is nothing we write we need be ashamed of, were it legibly written on our Foreheads as well as Papers. I question not but you have heard your old Bed-fellow Mrs. F. G. hath lately entertained a new one, being married to a Gentleman, as deserving in excellency of parts as nobility of birth; I long to hear of the like in you whose good fortunes shall always be attended with the greatest acclamations of joy which can proceed from

Your most affectionate Friend,
M. G.

The Answer.

Indearedly Beloved,

YOU honour me much with the testimony of your affection; and do glad my heart by giving me to understand, that your Governess continueth her vigilancy and accustomed care; if she reap the praise thereof, the profit will be yours and yet she will be a gainer too, for this will be the means to increase the number of her Scholars. Mrs. F. G's. marriage is no news to me, wishing her all happiness in her choice, and that her fortune may be answerable to her incomparable virtues; but for your good wishes to me in the like nature, (though I am thankful to you or for them, yet) I should not be displeased, if you did forbear to utter them, for if good Husbands are Miracles, why should I afflict my self with the vain expectation of them, since Miracles are ceased? I can best content my self with my present condition, having thereby a greater liberty to express my self to be,

> *Your passionate and most obliged*
> *Friend and Servant,*
> S. L.

To a Kinswoman discoursing about Fashions.

Beloved Cousin,

I Thank you for your Papers, and the trouble of that spruce inventory you sent me, which I desired more out of curiosity than any intention of conformity thereunto; for indeed the vanity was sufficient to satiate an ordinary appetite; and besides, mine is no way greedy of such idle kickshaws. I find fault with most of these Modes, not for their levity only but brevity also, especially such as are far-fetcht for a fortnights wearings, and leaves not a good Huswife a relique worth the keeping. I have learned in a great manner, *That the fashion of the world passeth away*, and therefore I cannot think it but a piece of great imprudence, to spend so much industry upon a frail and perishing object; yet I am not against such natural or native decencies, which may difference persons, and bring not an unprofitable expence upon their finery; no more than I discommend a sumptuous Feast, when I censure one that is ridiculous; for I know not what secret power of blandishment there is in an handsome ornament, even to court beauty it self; and therefore it must be more advantagious to those, whose small imperfections it conceals. But of all incongruities, deformity and the fashion, I take to be the uggliest: you know how indifferently I am concern'd in these cases, and therefore will easily pardon this humour of

> *Your most humble Servant.*

A Letter from one Lady to another, condemning Artificial-beauty.

Madam,

YOU are so absolute in the endowments of your mind and perfections of body, that I cannot but honour you; having formerly experienced your love to me particularly, and the greatness of your Wit to all; I hope you will excuse this rudeness if I desire your opinion concerning borrowed beauty from art; and whether it may be lawfully used by such as profess Religion and a good Conscience? I must confess my own judgment is much unsetled; nevertheless, I have been informed by many learned and godly men, that it is a great sin, and undoubtedly inconsistent with a Christian, and a good Conscience. I do find that washing and painting is condemned in holy Writ, as the practise of loose licentious and lascivious Women; who with the deforming of their Souls, and polluting their Consciences, do use the Art for embellishing their Countenances. The new Testament affirms we cannot make one hair of our head white or black; and if we have neither the liberty, nor are to assume the power to alter the complexion of our hairs, then much less the complexion of our Cheeks and Faces. It argueth, besides, ingratitude to the Almighty, when we are not content with what He hath made; and the highest presumption in thinking or daring to mend it. St. *Paul*, and St. *Peter* prescribed how Women should be clad, that is, with modesty, shamefastness and sobriety, and not with gorgeous apparel, or with braided Hair, Gold or Pearls; and if these things were forbidden, how much more is washing or painting the Face, which is suitable (some think) to none but light spirits, such as who are not yet redeemed from the vanity of their conversation. So that this Artificial beauty may appear to be divinely forbidden as an enemy to Truth, which needeth none but its own native complexion; and is so far from being beholding to Art for any addition to enliven her colour, or to put a blush upon it, that she converteth even Deformities and Decays into Advantages and Perfections. Besides, that this adding of colour and complexion proceeds from Pride, is without controversie; and should it not reflect on wantonness, yet it doth on arrogance to borrow, and then challenge that beauty to be ours, which is not but by an adventitious wealth. Moreover, this self-conceit is an enemy to humility and grace, and would degrees over-top all virtue. And now grant it were neither scandalously sinful, nor absolutely unlawful, yet the offence it giveth to the true and strict Professors of Piety is a sufficient argument, that it ought not to be practised. Although many things may be permitted in themselves, yet they become evil and are to be forborn, when others are offended at them. Neither is this all; for the very name of a painted face is enough to destroy the reputation of her that useth it, and exposeth her to all manner of reproaches. We are taught to follow things of a good report, that we may not only be good but that in all things we may preserve the reputation of a good name. If the light of Scriptures were not so clear & full against all artificial beauty, yet the light of Nature doth seem to discover an uncomeliness therein. There is none but may conclude, if God threatens to punish strange apparel, he will not spare to punish strange faces.

Madam, pardon the tediousness of my Letter, which I have extended almost to the length of a Treatise; I was the more large, because I would be the more fully satisfied in your answer, which in a labouring-expectation I attend; if your Ladiship will deign me this favour, you will infinitely oblige her, who is

Madam,
Your most humble and
affectionate Servant.

The Answer of an ingenious Lady.

Madam,

YOU have been pleas'd to impose a great task upon me, which I am resolved to discharge, not so much to shew any wit or knowledg in my self, as your power over me, by my obedience to your commands; what I shall say on this subject in the defence thereof, I shall be obliged thereunto by the rules of Reason, and not the liberty of practice. I cannot deny but that several reverend and learned persons are of a judgment opposite to mine which have prevailed on the credulity of many young Ladies, and did at first upon my own, until I began to examine the grounds of their opinions, and to value more the weight of their reasons than the gravity and number of their persons. I do not find that these persons can produce out of Scripture any reasons of force which expresly forbid the using any Art in the imbellishing the Countenance: The opinions of men are not of any power to charge the Soul with sin in things of outward use and custom, neither in this particular are the Divines themselves all of one mind; for I know many excellent persons, who wisely forbear to condemn the use of these things as sin, that are innocently helpful to the beauties of modest women; for indeed they are as far from sin or not from sin, as the minds of those that use them are disposed either to a modest decency, or to pride and vanity. Now where it is objected, that *Jezabel* was devoured by Dogs, because she painted her eyes; if your Ladiship be pleased to look again on the History, you shall find that the painting of her face or eyes was thirteen or fourteen years before the Prophet *Elisha* presaged her ruin; and it was no more a cause of her dreadful death than the dressing her head, or her looking out at the Window, which was at one and the same time, and one of them as innocent as the other. If all that *Jezabel* did is to be avoided as a sin, we may not call a solemn assembly, or keep a Fast, because she did so, as appeareth by the same History: We may not embrace or kiss a friend, because *Joab* did so when he killed *Abner*; and *Judas*, when he betray'd his Master. And as for *Herodias* dancing, which was the cause of *John Baptists* death, you shall find in the Gospel that she danced alone, which is allowed by our austerest Divines, and by the precise Matrons in the education of their Children. She danced not with *Herod*, but before him; and it was not the decent motion of her feet, but the disorderly motions of her heart, and the perversness of her spirit to the Doctrine of St. *John*, that was the cause of his murther. And as for those places in the Prophets, from whence scrupulous and censorious persons do infer that the painting of the face is a sin; we may truly answer, it is not therefore unlawful because we find it there sometimes condemned as unreasonable; or because vain and loose Women do practise it, therefore the modest must altogether disclaim it. Believe me, Madam, in the whole Scripture there is not any Moral command to be found that doth expresly forbid this artificial adorning the face. We may read that Queen *Esther* made use of sweet perfumes, of gorgeous habiliments, and beautiful colours; nay, whatsoever was then in fashion, the more to attract the eyes and affections of the King unto her; and this was in her so far from a sin, that it had been almost a sin in her not to have done it. We find that *Rebeccah* almost in the infancy of the world, received ornaments for her hands, her neck and ears, and certainly she thought it no disparagement to her modesty or her piety to wear them. Neither is it any new invention for Ladies to use Artificial helps for the advancement of their beauties; it is as general as ancient, and there is no Nation but doth practise it without any reproach of vanity or pride. And although in this Nation a commendable discretion is used in powdering, curling, and gumming the hair, and quickning the complexion; yet in forreign parts it is every-where frequently done, and as freely owned. It is strange methinks that supplies should be allowed of for bodily defects and deformities; the Shoo-maker is imployed and commended for making the body higher; and the Taylor for making it straighter; and must we account it a sin or scandal to advance the beauty of the face? Much more might be alledged to prove the truth hereof, but I have been already too tedious, and have punished your expectation with the length of my Letter, which not withstanding the innocence of the subject, is a sin or fault in her, who i, [*recte* is]

Madam,
Your most devoted Servant, &c.

A Lady to her Daughter, perswading her from wearing Spots and Black-patches in her face.

Daughter,

THE indulgent care of a loving Mother makes me keep my eye continually on you; it hath been my great comfort hitherto in that you have seem'd a profest enemy against the vices of this present age; but now it is no small grief to me that I hear you are too much addicted to its fashions; and that lately you have been seen with those deformities which are commonly called Black-patches. A fashion till of late never practiced by any, nor your half-Moons used in the *Turkish* Seraglio; no nor ever read of in all the Histories of the vanities of Women. It appeareth strange to me, that your Gentlewomen should lose their reason with their modesty, and think that they add to their beauty by substracting from it. I must deal plainly with you, I am afraid that the black Oath of God-damn-me in the mouth of a Ranter, and the Black-patch in the face of a Gentlewoman, are near of kin one to another. I shall therefore assume the freedom of power which is due unto me, and command you to wear them no more till I am better satisfied in their decency or lawfulness; thus not doubting of your obedience, I commit you with my blessing to the blessed Protection of the God of all blessings, and rest

Your tenderly loving and
careful Mother,
M. N.

The Answer of a dutiful Daughter.

Madam,

IT is as well Religion as Duty in me, To render you all observances, which I shall make my delight as well as employment. My greatest blessing is the continuance of your love, which obligeth me to encrease my thankfulness as well as my obedience. I perceive some censorious tongue hath been too busie with my face, and hath endeavoured to throw dirt on it, because it hath been lately spotted in the fashion; a fashion that hath as much innocence to plead for its excuse, as custom for its authority. *Venus* the Goddess of beauty was born with a *Motticella*, or natural beauty-spot, as if Nature had set forth a pattern for Art to imitate. You may see every day some little clouds over the face of the Sun, yet he is not ashamed of his attraction; nay, some of late with an Optick-glass have discovered some *maculæ* or spots in the very face of the Sun, yet they are not attributed as his deformities. The Moon when she is at Full and shining in her greatest lustre, hath in her face some remarkable spots, and herein is placed her chiefest glory; as being in every thing inconstant but in this. When I put on my Mask, which is no more nor better than one great patch, you do commend me for it; and will you be displeased with me for wearing a few black patches? which if they are cut into Stars, do represent unto me whither I would go; or if into little worms, whither I must go; the one of them testifying in me the sense of my unworthiness to increase my humility, and the other the height of my meditations to advance my affections. It is the unhappiness of the most harmless things, to be subject to the greatest misconstruction; and on the same subject from whence others draw their suspitions of curiosity to accuse our pride, we derive the greatest arguments of discipline and instruction to defend our innocence; neither is the ignorance of antiquity in relation to them, any argument of weight to condemn their novelty; for the Black-bags on the head are not much older than the Black-spots on the face, and much less may be said for them, only they have had the good luck in the City not to meet with contradiction, although in the Country they are much cavil'd at, unless worn by Gentlewomen of eminent note and quality. Nevertheless, according to the obligation of my duty, to give you in all things satisfaction, I am determined to wear them no more; not that I find any such vanity in them, but that by the fruits of my obedience, you may perceive what an absolute power your commands have over her, who is

Madam,
Your most humble and most
obedient Daughter,
S. N.

Love protested, with its Repulse.

Madam,

IT hath pleased Heaven you should have the sole command of my affections, with which I am joyfully content, and stand disposed to obey you in every thing, when you shall be pleased to count me worthy of your service. Enjoying you I must account my self the happiest man in the world; but being deprived of you I shall not only live, but die miserably; either then reward him who adores you, or chastise him who idolizeth you. Yet must I confess all my good to proceed from you, and that all the evil I can endure must come from your disdain; however hoping that you will commiserate my languishing condition, I shall greedily subscribe my self,

Intirely Yours, &c.

The Answer.

SIR,

IF it hath pleas'd Heaven you should love me, you cannot blame me though you suffer by it; should I accept the tenders of affection from all such amorous pretenders, I might be married to a whole Troop, and make my self a legal Prostitute. My inclinations lean not your way; wherefore give me leave to tell you, That you would do better to bestow your affections on some Lady who hath more need of a Servant than I have. And if you think your affection ought not to go unrewarded, receive the perswasions which I give you, never to trouble me more, lest you run a worse hazard by persevering in your intentions. Be advised by her who is.

Your faithful Monitor and
humble Servant, &c.

I shall swell this Volume into too great a bulk, should I give you patterns of Letters for all occasions; let what I have here set down suffice, referring you for your better information and instruction to the incomparable Letters of Monsieur *Voiture*, translated into *English*, Mr. *Howel*, and Mr. *Lovedays* ingenious Letters, with many more; every Booksellers-shop affording great plenty. And now to conclude, pray accept of these ingenious Dialogues, which will tend as well to your further instruction, as recreation.

Pleasant Discourses and witty Dialogues between Males and Females, as well gentiliz'd by Birth as accomplisht by generous Education.

The Resolute Lover: A Pastoral Dialogue.

Amyntas.

S tay, dearest, stay.
Amarillis, Shepherd, why do you thus follow me?

Amyns. I needs must follow, Sweetest, for you have my heart.

Amar. Who, I! prithee tell me where it is, and how I shall restore it?

Amynt. It hangs upon your eyes; but being there scorched with disdain, and dazled with their luster, it flies for ease unto your rosie lips; but being repulsed thence with harsh denials, it hovers still about you, hoping to rest it self within your breast; but all its endeavours have been fruitless, for your hard heart would not give it entertainment.

Amar. Well, if my heart be so hard as you would make it, I rejoice in my safety, it being then strong enough to be a fence to my honour.

Amynt. You make a fence in vain to guard the Sheep where no Wolf ever came.

Amar. O but my fears, *Amyntas*! How shall I cherish the man that would undo my Chastity?

Amynt. Then cherish me, who never attempted any thing to cast a spot on that white innocence to which I am a most religious Votary.

Amar. And canst thou love, and yet be chaste in thy desires?

Amynt. Yes, fairest, I could be content to love and have our souls united, though we are not conjoined in our persons.

Amar. Let me contain thee then within mine arms; the force of greatest winds that shake, nay root up the aged Oak, shall not divide us.

Amynt. My joys do overflow! My happpiness [sic], is too great to survive the enjoyment: O let me vent my grateful heart, or else it bursts! Here, here's a spreading *Poplar*, under whose cooler shade thou shalt seal thy promise *Amaryllis*.

Amar. 'Tis done, not to be repented of; and now methinks I here could stay, my dear *Amyntas*, till death moved his cold dart, and beckned us to follow him to the lower shades; and by his angry power, make these my warm embraces cold.

Amynt. May we never, never part,
That thy delight I may prolong,
Dear *Amarillis* hear this Song.

> 1. *Come my sweet, whilst every strain*
> *Calls our Souls into the ear,*
> *Where thy greedy listnings fain*
> *Would run into the sound they hear.*
> *Lest in desire.*
> *To fill the Quire,*
> *Themselves they tye*
> *To harmony.*
> *Let's kiss and call them back again.*
> 2. *Now let us orderly convey*
> *Our Souls into each others Breast,*
> *Where interchanged let them stay,*
> *Slumbering in a melting rest.*
> *Then with new fire*
> *Let them retire*
> *And still present*
> *Sweet fresh content;*
> *Youthful as the early day.*
> 3. *Then let us a tumult make*
> *Shuffling so our Souls, that we,*
> *Careless who did give or take,*
> *May not know in whom they be.*
> *Then let each smother*
> *And stifle the other,*
> *Till we expire*
> *In gentle fire;*
> *Scorning the forgetful Lake.*

Addresses of Love and Service, from Erotus *to* Aurelia.

Erot.

Madam, invited, or rather forced, by the just commendations which *Englands* Metropolis and other famed places attribute to your merits, I here prostrate my respects and service, which I shall desire you to esteem obedient to your will, until the time of my perserverance manifest them to be constant and faithful.

Aurel. Sir, report is commonly a Lyar, and now proves more favourable to me than truth; you know I am flatter'd, and you add thereunto by presenting feigned love and service to the honour of this imaginary merit.

Erot. Madam, you seem ingrateful to overkind and indulgent Nature, in wronging that incomparable beauty she hath prodigally bestow'd upon you, which is so Paramount, it can produce no other effects but fervent desires, and passionate endeavours to serve you.

Aurel. Sir, your Rhetorick may work Miracles, but it can never alter my belief.

Erot. Then, Madam, I see there nothing remains but my future obedience and affection, which must condemn your misbelief, and authorize this truth.

Aurel. Such expressions float commonly on the streams of this Ages affection, which usually produce nothing but Artifice, although they pretend to the greatest service.

Erot. I know it is ordinary for some to confirm Promises with Oaths, when at that instant they ne're intended to perform them; but that which will infuse a belief that I follow not the common custom of the times, is and will be the sincerity of my love, and constancy of my service.

Aurel. Sir, your enterprise will not be worth your pains; and should you obtain your desire, I know not how you will bear with the loss of being cheated in your hopes.

Erot. However, Madam, my resolution is fixt; and although you should make the end of it unfortunate or successless, yet it shall be the glory of my courage that I fell from high attempts.

Aurel. Seeing you thus ground your hope on misfortune, hope can no way harm you; for if it deceive you, it makes you notwithstanding happy.

Erot. May I be so happy!

Aurel. I shall never advise a soul of your generosity to rest upon such a design, the resolution being so mean that it must needs be followed with sorrow and repentance.

Erot. My encouragement will be the gaining of as much honour in the enterprize as difficulty in the worthy achieving.

Aurel. If you made but half the proofs of these many proffers of service, you would be famous throughout the whole Empire of Love.

Erot. Madam, have patience to see the guidance of my love by the light of that fire your fair self hath kindled, which when your Luminaries are by death extinct, shall never be extinguished.

A merry Dialogue between an ingenious Gentlewoman and a Poetaster or Rimer.

Poet.

M Adam, I'm come to tell you I have writ;
Your praise & glory wrapt up in my wit.
Then pray accept and grace it with a smile
Your humble servant I my self shall stile.

Gent. After she had read his Verses, thus she speaks; Now prithee tell me, are these lines of your own composition?

Poet. They are indeed, Madam.

Gent. Now beshrew me if I did not think so; the conceits are as poor as thy habit, and the whole matter like thy self, hunger-starved; prithee leave off riming, and beg some other way, in the ancient manner of such who haunt *Morefields* on Sundays; if thou hadst but a fore leg or arm, with a Partner, the structure of whose body is built on timber, (in plain *English*) a wooden-leg; thou ['thou' repeated] wouldst thrive on't.

Poet. Accept pray Madam, what I here have writ:
Pay first your Poet, and then shew your wit.

Gent. Then I see you are a Mercenary Scribler: Come tell me truly, how many have you presented with this *Encomium* with no other alteration than the name; I dare lay my life an hundred; your Verses are great Travellers; and yet I dare engage my life they have never been as far as *Parnassus*; but there is not a Gentlemans house in the whole Kingdom in which they have not been conversant, and yet I wonder how they came to have such universal entertainment: as for my own part, I must confess plainly they are too lousie and beggarly to lodg underneath my roof; they will infect my Foot-men.

Poet. If these do not like you, Lady, fair and bright,
Here's more I do present unto your sight.

Gent. Did you make them your self?

Poet. Did I not? What a question is that? How do you think I should come by them, unless I bought them? Some I know can buy Verses cheaper than they can make them; but I am no Sales-man in one respect though in another I may be said to be so; Sales-men use to have Clothes in their shop which Taylors make, and yet they own the work.

Gent. I marry, Sir, these savour of raptures and Poetical fancies!

Poet. Do you smell them, Madam? I hope they do not offend your Ladiships nose.

Gent. But hold Sir, how comes this about? Here is one Verse is running a race with another, and hath the start of him, three feet at least?

Poet. I did it on purpose to see which would run fastest, or in imitation of a Hare, who is swifter of foot than a Dog, and therefore is commonly before-hand with him.

Gent. I, but Sir, here his another hath ran too much, hath prickt his foot, and halts down tight.

Poet. Why, look you, there lyes the conceit, my invention is rare by way of imitation; lame halting Verses are commendable, or *Magnum Jovis incrementum* had never been writ; here lyeth the greatest art, and herein I express no small courage, making my enemies come home short by a leg; and to tell you truly, I am a sow'r Satyrist (*alias*) an *Jambographer*.

Gent. In the name of goodness, what was that you mumbled! I hope you are no Conjurer; there's a word with all my heart!

Poet. Why, this it is to be ignorant; or as we *Latins* say, *Ars nullum habet inimicum nisi ignorantem*; it is my pride and glory that I speak beyond the reach of Phlegmatick feminine capacity; but I will condescend so low as to explain this significant word of my own composition, *Jambographer*; in the first place, know it is partly *Greek*, and partly I know not what, but the signification in short, is a keen and sharp Versifier, whose lines prick worse than *Spanish* Needles or in short, you may hang your self in a pair of them.

Gent. I thank you, Sir, for your good advice; but if you and your lines are such dangerous company, pray let me have no more of their society; and so farewell.

Poet. Nay, one word more; I cannot only hang with *Jambicks*, but I can fetch blood with *Asclepiads*; cudgel and bastinado with

Sapphicks, and whip to death with *Phaleuciums*.

Gent. Pray practice, Sir, first on your self, 'tis no matter which of them you take to free the world of such an insufferable burthen. Adieu.

A form of Discourse at a casual meeting between Silvester *and* Sylvia.

Silvest.

Madam I see your inclinations to virtue so powerful, that you are ever restless but when you are in the society of such who make the greatest proof thereof.

Sylvia. Sir, your judgment concerning the company is most true; for there cannot be more accomplished persons, nor any honester content found in any society whatever: but your courtesie exceeds in attributing praises to her who least deserves them, and comparatively to the rest, hath no considerable perfection.

Silvest. Your modesty and humility (which is the crown of your excellencies) makes you speak disadvantagiously of your self, which I must not connive at, lest I run into an unpardonable errour; and I should look upon my self as most unworthy to look upon so fair an object, and not to admire its perfections, the lustre whereof can never be eclipsed by your undervaluings.

Sylvia. Sir, the higher you strain your eloquence, the more reason I have to shun those Elogies whereof you are as liberal towards me, as Heaven is sparing to me of those gifts you so much commend; wherefore pray desist, and in this company select some better subject to exercise your wit and language on.

A method of Courtship on fair and honourable terms.

Inamorato. Lusippe.

Inam.

I Shall ever account this, Madam, the happiest day I ever had in all the course of my life, which hath given me the honour and satisfaction of your acquaintance.

Lusip. Sir, if I knew ought in me worthy your merit, I should readily imploy it in your service; but being fully sensible of my imperfections and weakness, I believe the knowledg of me will yield you less happiness than you imagine.

Inam. Madam, I wonder you should wrong so much per-fection.

Lusip. I wrong not any thing in my possession, but it is your courtesie and rhetorick that would willingly excuse my defects, to make your own sufficiency to appear so much the more.

Inam. Pardon me, Madam, it is the charming power of your virtues and merits, which oblige me not only to honour and serve you, but also to desire some part and interest in your affections.

Lusip. Sir, whatsoever a Maid with honour may do, you may request of me; I should be as void of judgment as defective in beauty, did I not respect your quality, admire your virtues, and wish you a happiness equal to your demerit.

Inam. Madam, I assure you, my affections are real, and I hope sincerity doth wait on your good wishes; but if you will extend your favour, I cannot but be the happiest of all men.

Lusip. Sir, as I cannot perswade my self you will fix your affection on a person so little deserving; so I wish with all my heart your happy Stars may guide you to a Match that may become your worth.

Inam. Do not entertain so palpable a mistake: I have pro-posed to my self an unfeigned resolution to honour and serve you to my uttermost endeavour; and your refusal cannot lessen my affection; suffer me then to bear the honourable title of your servant.

Lusip. Sir, I have absolutely render'd my self up to the disposal of my dear Parents, consult them; if you prevail on their consent, you shall not doubt the conquest of my affection.

Inam. You oblige me infinitely, and I must thank you as heartily; I will not rest a minute till I know my sentence of life or death, which consists in the refusal of my love, or its accept-ance.

An impertinent and lying Travellers Discourse with his witty and Jocose Mistress.

Erraticus. Constantia.

Errat.

Madam, your Seat is so incomparable, that I have not seen a better in all my Travels.

Constant. It seems then you are a Traveller.

Errat. I am no less: Did you never travel, Lady?

Constant. I hope, Sir, you do not take me for a Lady-errant; however, Sir, I shall acknowledg I have travel'd through the Universe, and yet was never out of my own Country.

Errat. Hey day! How can that be?

Constant. I pity your want of apprehension; why, Sir, this is no such notorious contradiction, if you consider that the Cosmographers of these latter times have taught us in their Books to surround the world, and yet never stir a foot; I have read of some Countries.

Errat. And you may hear talk of many wonderful passages; but pish, talk is but talk; give me the man hath measur'd those Countries you have heard talk of; and can readily recount you the names of all the petty Towns as well as Cities in a whole Kingdom.

Constant. You have seen many Cities abroad, I pray what think you of *London?*

Errat. *London!* ha, ha, ha, like a Cock-boat to the *Royal-Soveraign*, comparatively to Cities I have seen.

Constant. I pray name one, Sir.

Errat. Why, Madam, I took shipping in the *Downs*, and had no sooner arrived to the height of the *Cape of Good-hope*, but passing by the *Grinonians, Hungarians* and *Sclavonians*, I came to *Vienna*, a pretty village, and for scituation much like *Hamsted*, its distance is about seven leagues from *Civil*, from whence we are stor'd with Oranges.

Constant. Sir, I have read that *Vienna* is in *Germany*, and *Civil* in *Spain*.

Errat. Pish, what care I for reading; however as you say, I cannot but acknowledg the people in *Spain* are as much or more Civil than any other; but if *Civil* be not in *Germany*, then I was neither in *Civil* nor *Vienna* in my life; I have been in *Paris* too, and do know the founder thereof.

Constant. Pray, Sir, inform my curiousity with the name of the Founder.

Errat. His name was *Parismus* the son of *Palmerin* of *England*, and hence the City was called *Paris*; some would have it called *Lutetia*, because the women are so well skill'd in an instrument called a Lute.

Constant. Good Sir, proceed; what observations did you make whilst you were in that famous City?

Errat. In the first place there is a famous University called *Pontneufe*, whose Students ply their business very notably; studying most part of the night, and are such notable disputants, they confute all that come that way after nine at night.

Here are excellent Comedians, the Women are the best, who act their parts notably, and take great pains to do things to the life. In the Summer-time Foot-boys and Lacquys do here swarm as flyes in *August*; and the season is so sultry-hot, that the fiery heat continues with the people all the Winter following.

Riding one day in the street, a dust arose so thick and great that I lost my way; that way I rid, the wind drove the dust, and did not leave me till I was within a league of *Naples*, and then I found where I was.

Constant. What a loss had *England* sustain'd had you never been found!

Errat. Entring this City I found the people all clad in silk, too soft and effeminate for me to converse withal. From hence I went to *Florence*, from whence we borrow the art of making Custards, which are therefore called *Florentines*. From hence I went to *Milan*, famous for Haberdashers, from thence called in *London* Millaners. Thence to *Padua*, hence come our Padding or Stroling Doctors, vulgarly called Mountebanks.

Constant. You report wonders! Go on, Sir.

Errat. Of all the Champane Countries in the world, *Venice* for my money. What lofty Mountains and pleasant Valleys! what spacious Downs for the merry hunt! Oh how I have made the Woods ring there with the Dukes dogs! And now I talk of him, I had never left the place had it not been for the excessive love of his chief Concubine towards me; who being discovered stealing the *Piezzi* to carry with her in her journey with me for *England*, was secur'd, and I forc'd to fly for't.

Constant. Is't possible?

Errat. I took poste from thence to *Genoa*, from thence to *Madrid*, and so to *Leyden*.

Constant. Excellent; and how were you entertain'd by the *Dutch?*

Errat. We were drunk together every day; but I'le say this for them, the Devil's but a Dunce to them, when they are in their drink. The last thing I heard there, was a design to charm the *Indies*, and bring it to *Amsterdam* in Butter-Firkins. Had I staid longer in *Holland* I should have dyed on a surfeit of Bore; but I washt it down with a Fox at *Flushing*; here I met with a bucksome Froe, with whom I went to *Middleburgh*, and left her as drunk as a Bitch at *Rotterdam*, and so taking shipping, from thence I landed at *Trig*-stairs.

Constant. Well, Sir, I see the difference between you and truth is so great, that there cannot be expected a reconcilement; wherefore I shall leave you.

A Gentleman accidentally hapning into a room where a Company of Ladies were well known to him.

Gent.

Your pardon, Ladies; let not my coming interrupt your Discourse, but rather give me the freedom that I may participate in the satisfaction.

Ladies. Our discourse is of no great concernment; we can take some other time to continue it, that we may now give way to yours, which we doubt not will prove every whit, if not more agreeable.

Gent. My invention, Ladies, cannot want a subject for Discourse; where the company so overflows with wit and ingenuity; but my tongue will want expressions to answer your Critical expectations.

Ladies. Sir, we acknowledg no such thing in our selves and therefore let not that we pray be the subject of your eloquence, lest we suspect you intend to laugh at us.

Gent. Ladies, you must suffer me not withstanding at this, that though modesty interdicts you the acknowledging a truth, yet the respect I bear to Ladies, commands me not only to acknowledg it, but also to divulge and maintain it.

Ladies. We confess, Sir, the frailty and weakness of our Sex requires some support; and for my own part, I cannot look upon any person so worthy as your self to be our Champion.

Gent. What power I have to vindicate your person, is derivative from your virtues; and were I so feeble, that the supporters of my body were no longer able to support that burthen; yet one propitious glance of any of your eyes would dart heat and vigor through my whole body and so my feet would be enabled to run in your service.

Ladies. Have a care, Sir, you do not strain your invention above the reach of any Hyperbole; but lore [lower] your fancy to the meanness of our capacity; if you cannot perform it at present, we will give you time.

Gent. Ladies, I am fearful my company may be troublesome, or interrupt you from more agreeable conversation, wherefore *your Servant*, Ladies.

FINIS.

An Advertisement

COncerning Doctor *Sermon*'s most Famous, Safe, *Cathartique* and *Diuretique Pills*; Proved for many years to be the only and most incomparable Medicine in all *Chronical Diseases*; wherewith was Cured his Grace the late Lord General *Monck* of the *Dropsie* in *June* and *July* 1669. Many hundreds before and since having received absolute Cure thereby.

They are also the most certain *Purgative Pills* in the World against that common and pernicious Distemper the *Scurvy*, with all other *sharp, salt* and *watry Humours*. They help the *Kings Evil*, and cause all manner of filthy *Ulcers, Cancers,* and *spreading Sores* (from what Cause soever) the sooner to become whole.

They *purifie* and *sweeten* the *Blood* to admiration; and are never failing to prevent and perfectly Cure the aforesaid Distempers, if made use of in time. Which is well known to many Noble and Honourable Persons throughout the whole Kingdom, and to those of the same *Faculty* too, though they maliciously (for interest sake) rail against them, to the great prejudice of many that cannot be cured without them.

Which *Pills* are to be had at the *Authors* House in *Eastharding-street*, between *Fetter-lane* and *Shoo-lane*, and at *Edward Thomas* his Shop at the *Adam* and *Eve* in *Little-Brittain*, a Bookseller; and at all other places mentioned in the Book delivered with each Box; the Numbers and Prices being as followeth:

The least Box containing 20 Pills, sold for 4 *s*.
The middle Box containing 40 Pills, sold for 8 *s*.
The large Box containing 60 Pills, sold for 12 *s*.

Glossary

This glossary is founded on those of earlier Prospect Books publications, for example Robert May, *The Accomplisht Cook* (1661); Sir Kenelm Digby, *The Closet of the Eminently Learned Sir Kenelme Digbie, Kt., Opened* (1669); John Evelyn, *John Evelyn, Cook*; Richard Bradley, *The Country Housewife and Lady's Director* (1736); Hannah Glasse, *The Art of Cookery Made Plain and Easy* (1747) ; and William Ellis, *The Country Housewife's Family Companion* (1750). These glossaries are available on the Prospect Books website (www.prospectbooks.co.uk). I have also found much information in volume X, the Companion, of *The Diary of Samuel Pepys*, edited by R.C. Latham and W. Matthews (1983) and in Peter Thornton, *Seventeenth-Century Interior Decoration in England, France & Holland* (1978). For medical matters, I have relied on John Quincy, *The English Dispensatory* (1749 edition). Otherwise, the usual reference books have been consulted.

This glossary includes archaic or obsolete words used by the author and identifies individuals, places and authors to whom she refers. Entries are listed as they are spelled in the text.

Tom Jaine

ABSTERSION.   The act of cleansing or purging.

ADAM IN EDEN.   This book was written by William Coles (1626–1662) and published in 1657.

AGATHOCLES.   Tyrant of Syracuse, Sicily, died in BC 289.

AGRIMONY.   *Agrimonia eupatoria*, astringent, with medical uses, also called Aaron's rod and liverwort.

A-LA-MODE.   The French phrase *à la mode*, meaning fashionable, was often applied in an anglicized form to dishes.

ALKERMES.   A sweet cordial coloured with cochineal.

AMBERGRIECE.   Ambergris, a substance produced in the sperm whale and harvested from the sea or beach in pieces that can weigh up to 200 lb. 'Griece' is a natural description of its texture, which is waxy, though the term refers to its greyish colour (*gris*, grey in French). Evidently it imparted a scent rather than a flavour to the food it was prepared with. It was much used in cookery, but is now restricted to perfumery. The perfume of ambergris has been described as 'the blending of new-mown hay with the scent of violets'.

ANGELICA. Angelica was the daughter of Galafron, king of Cathay and heroine of *Orlando Innamorato* (1487) and *Orlando Furioso* (1532), poems by Boiardo and Ariosto respectively. Orlando falls in love with her in the first, but fails to get his girl in the second.

ANNA COMNENA. She was the daughter of the Byzantine emperor Alexius Comnenus and was born in 1083. Come the end of her father's life, she was worsted in a tussle for the succession, seeking to depose her brother in favour of her husband. She retired to a monastery and there composed a history of her father's reign, *The Alexiad*.

ANNA. The mother of the Blessed Virgin Mary.

ANNA MARIA VON SCHURMAN. Anna Maria van Schurman (1607–1678) was a Dutch theologian and writer of great influence, particularly in the field of education. Her book *The Learned Maid* was translated into English in 1659. See also the introduction, above.

AQUA MIRABILIS. This distilled, medicinal water was a traditional compound found by this name in many *pharmaco-poeias*.

ARACHNY. Arachne, in Greek myth, was a woman of Lydia who challenged Athena to a contest of weaving. The victorious goddess turned her into a spider.

ARCADIA. *The Arcadia*, a romance by Sir Philip Sidney, was published after his death in 1590. It was dramatized by James Shirley in 1640.

ARCHANGEL. This usually describes either dead-nettle or black stinking horehound.

ASCLEPIADS. An ancient Greek poetic metre, named after Asclepiades.

AVENS. Herb bennet, wood avens, *Geum urbanum*. Grown as a pot herb.

BACE. This means bass, a fish of the perch family. It was sometimes spelled base.

BALLONIA SAUSAGES. This is Bologna sausage, from the city of that name in Italy. Already, by the seventeenth century, the word polony is another, more extreme, derivation.

BANQUETS. In the seventeenth century, a banquet was not the

generic term for a large meal that it is today, but described a specific type of repast consisting of sweetmeats and sweet confections, fruit, preserves and conserves. It was often laid out in a separate room, or even building (the banqueting houses of Hampton Court and Whitehall are two royal examples). It was usually a postscript to the main meal. When Woolley talks of foods fit for banquets, she is thus referring to sweet things and confectionery.

BARTHOLOMEW-BABY. This is a reference to St Bartholomew's Fair, held in West Smithfield, London every August. Dolls bought at the fair were so called.

BDELIUM. More usually bdellium. A gum or resin from the tree *Commiphora*, harvested in the Middle East. Good for digestion and a host of other problems.

BERAYING. When Woolley speaks of her fear that a greedy gentlewoman might eat her spoon-meat too hot and so beray the room with her splutterings, the word means to defile, besmirch. A bird does not beray its own nest, the naturalist John Ray observed.

BETONY. *Stachys officinalis*. Believed to be diuretic and cleansing.

BEUGLE-WORK. A bugle was a long, black bead sown on to clothing as ornament, or strung on wires pendant from candlesticks.

BEZOAR. See Oriental Bezoar.

BILLETS. A log, used for firewood. It is derived from the diminutive of the French *bille*, tree-trunk.

BISTORT. *Polygonum bistorta*. It has medicinal uses.

BORAS. Borax. There are two sorts: common or jewellers' (Woolley calls it goldsmiths'). The first occurs naturally. The second was manufactured, largely from deposits of boric acid in Tuscany, by means of crystallization. Borax is used by jewellers in soldering.

BORES-GREASE. Fat from a boar. Only the spelling makes it appear outlandish.

BRAND-GEESE. Brent goose or barnacle goose, the two being often confused (*OED*).

BRAVERY. Woolley uses this word not to signify valour or daring, as we usually do today, but to mean display in ornament or dress.

BRAWN. The term originally meant the flesh of a wild boar and by extension the preserved meat made therefrom, the fatty foreparts being usually chosen for the purpose. But even before the seventeenth century the 'boar pig' used for making brawn was a tame, not a wild, animal. The term later came to have the more general meaning of the fleshy part of a hind leg of an animal, not necessarily a pig. Nowadays, brawn just means a kind of potted meat, deriving from the way in which much brawn was prepared, i.e. boned, rolled, stuffed with herbs and flavourings and soused or pickled.

BREWIS. Brewis is a pottage, based on the juices of cooked meat, thickened with bread. By association, the word also meant the bread slices upon which joints of meat were served up. Brewis is still a culinary term in Nova Scotia and Newfoundland.

BRIMSTONE. Brimstone is sulphur.

BROOMBUDS. Buds of the broom, *Sarothamnus scoparius*, usually pickled, were used in place of capers. It was a diuretic plant.

BROOKLIME. Speedwell (*Veronica beccabunga*), growing near water, eaten as a salad plant, hot in taste.

BUGLOSS. Vipers's bugloss, *Echium vulgare*; or common bugloss, *Anchusa azurea*, thought to be antidepressant.

CABINET-WORK. This description of one of the necessary skills of a young gentlewoman refers to the art of cutting up prints and pictures and ornamenting cabinets and small rooms with them.

CAP-PAPER. Paper was an essential of the seventeenth- and eighteenth-century kitchen. Many different grades are called for, much as we use brown paper for lining cake tins, greaseproof for lining pastry cases, and so on. The cap-paper specified by Woolley was probably dense, approaching a parchment, so that it would perform the same function as the greaseproof we use to top jars of jam today.

CARDAMER. A variant spelling of cardamom.

CARDIS. The holy thistle, *Silybum marianum*, Our Lady's milky or dappled thistle, whose white striped and speckled leaves were used medicinally to increase the flow of milk, and also as vegetable and salad.

CARVING. The repertory of cant terms for carving that Woolley recites is customary in English cookery books until well into the eighteenth century. See her model, Robert May's *Accomplisht Cook*, for an instance. The historian Ivan Day has recently drawn attention to the fact that these carving instructions represent an English tradition and methods reproduced almost unthinkingly from literature dating from the fifteenth century. There was a counter tradition, more spectacular and full of showmanship, developed in Renaissance Italy which was not properly explained to the English reading public until the publication of *A Perfect School of Instructions for the Officers of the Mouth* by Giles Rose in 1682, itself a translation of a French book of that name published in 1662.

CASSANDRA, CLELIA, GRAND CYRUS, CLEOPATRA, PARTHENISSA. These are all subjects of romances, for the most part written by the French authors Mlle de Scudéry (1607–1701) and Gauthier de la Calprenède (*c.* 1610–1663). The works of each were translated into English and highly popular. *Parthenissa* was a romance in similar style, written by Roger Boyle, Earl of Orrery (1621–1679).

CASTOREUM. If musk comes from a deer, castoreum, or castor, comes from the bottom of a beaver. It is very pungent, extracted from a pair of sacs near the rectum.

CATES. Delicacies or dainties. The word is a shortening of acates, purchases (cf. the French *achats*).

CAUL. The fatty membrane surrounding the intestines, used to wrap meat, either to make a sort of sausage or pudding, or to better contain it for roasting.

CAWDLE. Also spelled caudle. It is a general term for a drink, generally made from ale, sweetened and spiced, and thickened with egg yolk and often breadcrumbs or oatmeal or something similar. A caudle could also be made with water, milk, or wine. It was used as a hot drink for invalids and was drunk out of a squat, round vessel which usually had two handles and a lid, called a caudle-cup. A hot caudle could be added to a pie, e.g. a wine caudle to a sweet meat pie.

CECILIA. One Cecilia of antiquity to whom our author may be referring was the wife of the Roman dictator Sulla, daughter of Metellus. Another, mentioned by Plutarch, was the mother of Sulla's ally Lucullus, victor over Mithridates.

CELIDONY. The celandine, *Chelidonium majus*. Good for eye problems.

CERE-CLOTH. This was a cloth impregnated with wax or sticky salve. It might be used as a winding sheet, or as a medicinal plaster.

CERFUEL. Chervil, this version of the word resembling quite closely its French original.

CHAFING-DISH. A portable brazier to hold burning coals or charcoal and designed to be set on a metal stand. Dishes of food could be finished or reheated over this, away from the fierce heat of the hearth.

CHALDRON. The spelling is more usually chawdron, although both forms are often met at this date. The word also has two meanings. In this instance it is that of entrails. Otherwise it might be referring to a cooking vessel. There are two common uses when describing guts. On the one hand there are calf's chaldrons, often cooked in puddings; on the other there are sauces of guts and spices, made particularly for swans but also for all other fowl.

CHARE-WOMEN. The earliest spelling of the word charwoman. Char or chare was a medieval word meaning job of work or task.

CHINA-ROOT. The root of *Smilax china,* an Asian plant which is closely related to plants of North and Central America which are the source of sarsaparilla.

CHINE. 'The whole or part of the backbone of an animal, with the adjoining flesh' (*SOED*).

CHIP. To chip a loaf means to chip off the crust. Often the smaller loaves, for instance the French loaves as cooked in Britain, had very hard, thick crusts. Doubtless this was something to do with the fierceness of heat in the oven, as well as the recipe. It was best to get rid of the crust before using the bread in cookery. Crusts of normal household loaves would also be tough and thick. They were cooked for long times in the bread oven, the temperature starting quite high but soon dropping. As the loaves were often large, they needed hours, not minutes, to complete their cooking. The crusts, therefore, got thicker and thicker. The chipping knife was a common implement in the contemporary kitchen.

CITRON. *Citrus medica*, it was usually employed for its peel. It is sometimes distinguished as 'green citron'.

CIVIL. A variant spelling of Seville.

CLARY. Clary, *Salvia sclarea,* was used as a remedy for eye complaints, but also had culinary uses. It is slightly bitter and was used to add flavour to wine. Clary fritters were featured regularly in seventeenth-century cookery books.

CLELIA, see CASSANDRA.

CLEOPATRA, see CASSANDRA.

CLISTER. Enema; more usually spelled clyster.

COCK-BOAT. A small boat or tender.

COCK OF THE WOOD. This is the capercaillie, the wood grouse.

CODLINS. Apples.

CODS. These are pods, the usage that survives is in the word peasecod.

COHOBATE. This means to subject to repeated distillation.

COLTSFOOT. *Tussilago farfara*, useful against coughs.

COLLAR. A collar is meat or fish boned, rolled and tied with string. Randle Holme says: 'Collar of Beef, is Beef half boiled and rowled up with Spices and sweet Herbs chopped small in it, and then baked in a Pot: Eels or Congers are so collared and souced.' Collaring was a universal method of controlling floppy joints, as well as allowing them to be stuffed, spiced, then boiled without dissolution.

CONCOCTION. Concoction is the generic word for digestion. It also described the three stages that all food went through in the body: firstly digestion, then conversion into blood, then a final excretion.

COPPERICE. This is copperas. The term embraced blue, green and white copperas, the salts of copper, iron and zinc respectively.

CORNELIA. She was the daughter of Scipio Africanus in the second century BC; she was the mother of the famous tribunes Tiberius and Gaius Gracchus and a stern upholder of republican virtues, devoted to the education of her children.

CORNELIUS AGRIPPA. Henry Cornelius Agrippa von Nettesheim (1486–1535) was a German soldier, teacher, philosopher and magician whose most famous work was *De occulta philosophia*. He also wrote *De matrimonio sacramento* and a work praising womanhood *De Nobilitate et Praecellentia Feminei Sexus* which he dedicated to his employer Margaret of Burgundy in 1529.

CORVINA. This is probably a misprint for Corinna, a female Greek lyric poet possibly a contemporary of Pindar.

CREWEL. Crewel was a worsted, two-stranded thread. Crewel-work was often used to ornament bed-hangings with 'large-leafed patterns executed usually in dark green and blue'. Beds also had finials over their four posts and these often took the form of feathers (perhaps ostrich plumes) sitting in vases or holders which were themselves pasted up or surfaced with the material of the bed-hanging.

CUBEB. The fragrant berry of the Middle Eastern plant *Piper cubeba*.

CULPEPER. Nicholas Culpeper (1616–1654) wrote *The English Physician Enlarged* (1653) as well as translating the *Pharmacopoeia*.

CUTCHENEEL. Cochineal, a brilliant red dye obtained from the dried and pulverized bodies of the insect *Coccus cacti,* a parasite of cacti in Central America. After the European colonization of America this product was adopted as a better source of red colouring than the 'sanders' (sandalwood) used in medieval cookery.

DEARN. This is an obsolete form of darn.

DEERS SUET. The suet of a deer was used like that of ox or sheep as a base for ointments and salves. Quincy (1749) did not think that one was better than the other: there was no mystic advantage in taking it from the wild beast.

DEMONAX. 'A cynic philosopher from Cyprus, second century AD, known only by the biography of him ascribed to Lucian.'

DIAMARGARICUM FRIGIDUM. This is probably a misspelling of the word diamargaritum. The prefix *dia-* means something made from; the word *margaritum* means pearl (from the Greek).

DICTAMN-ROOT. Woolley specifies the white, which means that it is the white or bastard dittany or *Fraxinella*. It was thought good for expelling weapons and (presumably) other intrusions.

DINNER. An entry is only merited by the desire to note that the main meal of the day in gentle households was dinner and that at this time it was generally eaten at approximately midday. The time of supper varied, but it was the principal evening meal. Pepys noted that late suppers disagreed with him and he gave up the meal altogether for a number of years. Lunch was not a common meal until the nineteenth century. At the time of Woolley's writing, breakfast was not an invariable beginning to the day. Attentive readers of Pepys's diary will note that he had a mid-morning drink as well as snack even if he did not have much of a breakfast.

DORCAS. Dorcas was actually called Tabitha: she was a lady of Jaffa in Palestine who did many works of charity and was raised from the dead by St Peter (*Acts*, chapter 9).

DOTTREL. Dotterel is a species of plover, so guileless that it could be taken easily.

ELLICK-SANDER. A variant spelling of Alexanders.

ENDIVE, WHITE. *Cichorium intybus,* known as endive in Britain and as endive, escarole or chicory in North America. The leaves can be blanched by keeping out the light. The reference to white endive must be to this practice, which had earlier been developed in France.

ENNULA-CAMPANA-ROOTS. Elicampane (*Inula helenium*) is an important medicinal root. Recommended against the itch or scabies, coughs and snake venom, convulsions, contusions and bad sight. It was also deemed effective against elves.

ERIGAN. The meaning is this word is uncertain. Is it a misprint for erigeron or groundsel, which was used as an emetic?

ERINGO-ROOTS. The root of the sea holly, *Eryngium maritimum*, which was widely eaten, pickled or candied, in the seventeenth and eighteenth centuries. The candied root was a celebrated sweet and aphrodisiac.

ESTHER. The Book of Esther in the bible recounts how this Jewish maiden was taken as his queen by the Persian king Xerxes.

EXCHANGES. Woolley mentions 'three great Arsenals of choice Vanities' and is presumably referring to the New Exchange in the Strand, built in 1608–1609 opposite Bedford Street, the Royal Exchange in the City which had been destroyed in the Great Fire but was reopened in 1671, and the Exchange in Gresham College which was the site to which the traders in the Royal Exchange removed during the time of reconstruction. Exchanges were retail shopping precincts as well as centres for mercantile information and encounter.

FARTHINGALS. Farthingales were hooped and bolstered skirts fashionable at the turn of the sixteenth and seventeenth centuries. The hips were broadened by means of an upholstered ring worn close to the body and the skirt hung from this extension to the girth. Farthingale chairs were armless, with the backs raised somewhat above the seat, making them more comfortable for ladies so attired.

FELON. A whitlow or abscess on the finger.

FINIFIED. To finify is to make fine, adorn.

FIRMIN, MR. Giles Firmin (1614–1697) was a presbyterian divine ejected from his living at the Restoration. His book *The Real Christian* was sold by Dorman Newman, the publisher of *The Gentlewomans Companion*.

FISH STREET, OLD and NEW. The Pepys Companion volume records the first (to the west) being absorbed into the present Knightrider Street below St Paul's, the second being the main thoroughfare from the City to London Bridge and the site of Fishmongers' Hall. They were the chief fish markets before Billingsgate. Pepys bought and ate fish in each location, although whether 'sparing no cost' is more questionable.

FORD, MR. Thomas Forde (fl. 1660) was author of *Virtus Rediviva* and *Lusus Fortunae*, both of which had much currency in the Restoration period.

FRENCH LOAF. 'French' bread in England was yeasted bread made with a dough enriched with milk and eggs. In John Evelyn's contemporary manuscript recipe book is a reference to both white and brown French bread. He also states that if no French bread is available, a smaller quantity of good white bread should be substituted.

FROE. A variant of frow, a Dutchwoman (i.e. *frau*).

FROISE. Fraise became the more usual spelling of this term. It meant a kind of pancake or omelette, often with slices of bacon.

FROTH. Woolley suggests, when roasting hare, that while it is on the spit, the cook should stick it with cloves, sprinkle it with fine breadcrumbs, flour and cinnamon then 'froth it up' before dishing it with a sauce. What she is advising that it should be basted with butter or fat which then boils and forms a nice frothy crust on the surface of the meat.

FUMITORY. The plant *Fumaria officinalis*.

GALL. 'The excrementitious tubercles' that grow upon the gall-oak were the source of gallic acid, good for stemming bleeding. It was also an important ingredient of black ink, which led to a rather dramatic treatment of people having nosebleeds involving stuffing the nostrils, presumably with a rag soaked in ink.

GALLENDINE SAUCE. Gallendine is the same word as galantine, but with a meaning different from the modern usage. Seventeenth-century galantine, in England, was a dark-coloured sauce made with vinegar, breadcrumbs, cinnamon and sometimes other spices. Earlier, in medieval times, a galantine had been a jellied dish of fish or fowl or meat; and it was this version, which lingered longer in France and eventually crossed in a somewhat new form to England at the beginning of the eighteenth century, which evolved into our present galantine.

GALLY-POT. This is a small pot of glazed earthenware mainly used by apothecaries, but also serving in the kitchen.

GAVANUM. Otherwise known as Galbanum; a yellowish gum extracted from a tree of the *Ferula* family. It was imported from the Middle East and deemed helpful against hysterical afflictions.

GERHARD, MR. John Gerard (1545–1612) herbalist and author.

GRAND CYRUS, see CASSANDRA.

GREENFISH. This is a general term for fresh fish, though it

usually refers to codling. Thomas Mouffet (Dr Muffet of tuffet fame) thought that salted codling was ling and fresh codling was greenfish.

GROUNDEAR. It is not clear which plant is meant by this name.

GUM-LAUDANUM. There were various methods of extracting and presenting opium or laudanum: pills, drops, essences and so forth. Presumably, this one was a gum.

HARTS-TONGUE. A fern, *Phylitis scolopendrium*, with prettily curled fronds, which had medicinal uses.

HERN. This is an old spelling for heron.

HEYLIN, DR. Peter Heylyn (1600–1662) was an English theological and political controversialist in the Royalist cause. His career was full of ups and downs owing to the Civil War, when he composed the virulent news-sheet *Mercurius Aulicus*. His works were 'marred by ... rancour', said one authority, but his travel account, *A Survey of France* (1625) was often reprinted and appreciated, even two centuries later, as 'one of the liveliest books of travel'.

HIPPOCESTIDOS. More properly hypocistidis. It is the juice of *Cytinis hypocistis* which is a parasitic plant of various types of Cistus. It contains gallic acid and was used as an astringent.

HOUSLEEK. Stonecrop.

HOWEL, MR. James Howell (1594?–1666) was an author and diplomatist. He was appointed historiographer royal in 1661. His most popular work was a volume of letters to imaginary correspondents, *Epistolae Ho-elianae: Familiar Letters*, 1655.

ICED. An entry would not usually need to be made for this word, for Woolley means icing of pastry or cakes much as we use the word today, though we would often call it glazing (when it is a sugar mixture finished off in the oven). However, it should be noted that she ices savoury dishes as well as sweet.

IMPOSTHUME. Or impostume; a nasty swelling, cyst or abscess.

INTERLARDED BACON. Interlarding was indeed putting lards of fat into lean meat. The use of the word here and in other seventeenth-century authors such as Digby and May is as description of streaky bacon rather than bacon that has itself been larded by a cook. The phrase 'streaky bacon' is not recorded by the *OED* before its use by Dickens and Thackeray.

JACK-PUDDING. A buffoon or clown.

JAMBICKS. That is, iambics, a classical Greek poetic metre.

JANEWAY, MR. JAMES. James Janeway (1636?–1674) was a

nonconformist divine whose *A Token for Children* was published in 1671 by Dorman Newman, the publisher and compiler of *The Gentlewomans Companion*.

JEROME. St. Jerome (d. AD 420) was the translator of the Vulgate. He was involved with a group of devout women headed by St Paula during his stay in Rome in 382–385. It was doubtless at this point that he produced the advice referred to.

JOLE. The head and shoulders of a fish.

JUDITH. The Book of Judith is in the Apocrypha. She was the heroine who seduced and slaughtered Holofernes, general of the Medes, thus delivering the Israelites from certain servitude.

KIBED HEELS. Kibes are chilblains, especially on the heels – a constant problem if early medical receipts are believed.

LACE. To slice, particularly the breast. The usage is deemed restricted by the *OED*. There is a certain parallel to the meaning which had longer currency: to lash, beat or thrash (even Charlotte Brontë uses it thus).

LACEDEMONIANS. The Spartans, renowned for their stoic reaction to discomfort and a certain puritanism of manners.

LADIES COMPANION, THE. A small collection of recipes published in 1654. The book is not long and contains receipts for pies, tarts, candying and preserving. Each receipt is from a named source.

LENTULUS. The family of Cornelius Lentulus was a powerful one at the end of the Republic in Rome although most members of it seem to have got on the wrong side of whatever struggle for power might have been going on at any one time.

LERE. In the *OED* this word is recorded as lear. It shares the same derivation as the French *lier*, to bind, and refers to a thickened sauce or to a thickening for a sauce. Its use is more common in medieval cookery texts.

LEUCTRA. This is a small village on the mainland of Greece, in Boeotia north of the Gulf of Corinth, approximately midway between Athens and Delphi.

LILLY-WATER. This is a distillation of the flowers of lily-of-the-valley. It was considered good for diseases of the head, headaches.

LIMBECK. Vessel for distillation, most usually spelled alembick: the head or cap of a still. Its beak conveyed the vaporous products to a receiver where they condensed.

LIVERWORT. The word can refer to several plants, all thought beneficial to the liver. Agrimony is one, stone liverwort

(*Marchantia polymorpha*) is another, *Anemone triloba* is a third, dog lichen (*Peltigera canina*) a fourth.

LOVEDAY, MR.   Robert Loveday (fl. 1655) was translator of the first three parts of La Calprenède's *Cleopatra*.

LOVEL, MR.   Robert Lovel (1630?–1690) was a naturalist and botanist who wrote *Enchiridion Botanicum* (1659) and *A Compleat History of Animals and Minerals* (1661).

LUMBER PYE.   The name may be a corruption of Lombard. It was a savoury pie made of meat (or fish) and eggs. Robert May's two versions called for a filling consisting of separate little puddings or forcemeat balls, but the longer recipe given by Rabisha (1682) for 'Lumbard pie' did not have this requirement; the pie filling was put altogether into the 'coffin'.

MAGISTERIUM.   The term was originally alchemical but in early modern science meant a precipitate of something, i.e. after a substance (in this instance pearl) had been dissolved in acid.

MAIDEN-HAIR.   There are several maiden-hairs but the fern *Adiantum capillus-veneris* is the one that was used most in medicine.

MANCHET.   Yeasted bread made from the whitest flour. Baked in a slightly cooler oven than household bread.

MANUS CHRISTI.   On the one hand an indication of temperature when boiling sugar: 'to manus Christi height'; on the other, it was a syrup of rose-water and sugar dispensed to invalids.

MARGENT.   An early spelling of the word margin.

MARROW.   Invariably, Woolley is speaking of bone-marrow when she uses this word.

MASTICK.   A gum extracted from trees grown on Chios. Apothecaries thought it good for many ailments, including those to do with the kidneys.

MAY'S COOKERY.   *The Accomplisht Cook*, by Robert May, was first published in 1660, with several editions over the next fifteen years. It was the most compendious and exact of Restoration cookery manuals.

MELLILOT.   This is a plant of the clover family (*Melilotus altissima*). In some places (cit. *OED*) it grew in cornfields to such an extent as to impart a rank flavour to the bread of the district.

MERCURY.   In this instance the plant *Chenopodium bonus-henricus*, otherwise known as Good King Henry; not the metal.

MERRY-THOUGHT.   This is the wishbone.

MILESIAN VIRGINS.   Miletus was a Greek city in Ionia, Asia Minor, near the mouth of the river Meander. Not only was it famous for its virgins, but the *Milesian Tales* were erotic, titillating stories akin to the Decameron and similar collections.

MITHRIDATE.   An expensive medicine in the form of an electuary, made up of many ingredients and considered to be a universal antidote against poisons and infections. It took its name from King Mithridates, see below, who was reputed to have made himself immune to poisons by constantly taking very small doses of them as antidotes. He was so successful in this that when the moment came to do the gentlemanly thing and commit suicide, he was unable to find a draught sufficiently lethal. Instead he ordered a slave to run him through with a sword.

MITHRIDATES.   There were six monarchs of Pontus (the south side of the Black Sea) by that name, steadfast enemies of Rome, locked in a struggle for the hegemony of Asia Minor. The last was the greatest, he died in 63 BC. An Oriental though Hellenized despot – the dynasty was of Persian origin – he suffered many threats from his close family (his son was his nemesis). As prophylactic, he killed his mother and his younger brother and married his sister.

MOREFIELDS.   Moorfields was an area north of the City walls, roughly where Finsbury is today. It was laid out with promenades and was a great place of resort in the seventeenth century.

MOSS-WORK.   Moss was a decorative substance in rustic arbours and similar situations, its texture and appearance was also reproduced in sugar for the adornment of banquets.

MUGGETS.   The intestines of a cow or sheep.

MUNDIFIE.   To mundify means to cleanse.

MUSK.   The perfume extracted from a gland (the size of an orange) in the male musk-deer, filled with a dark brown or chocolate-coloured secretion which is the consistence of 'moist gingerbread' when fresh, but dries to a granular texture after keeping. Much used in cookery as well as by apothecaries.

MUSTE.   To grow mouldy. The dictionary suggests it might be 'a back-formation from the adjective musty'. It is not usually spelled with the final 'e'.

NAZIANZEN.   St Gregory of Nazianzus (AD 329–289) was a father of the early church and hammer of the Arians.

NEPE.   Probably the same as nep, meaning catmint.

NIOSTRATA.   Also called Nicostrata. She was an erudite Greek woman who, according to early-modern scholarship, helped determine the form of numbers in the Greek alphabet.

OCTAVIA.   The sister of the first Roman emperor, Augustus. She was married, *inter alia*, to Mark Anthony and her conduct towards her family and friends was held up as a model.

OLIO.   The Latin word *olla*, meaning cooking pot, passed into Spanish unchanged (and into Portuguese as *olha*), and gave rise to the Spanish term 'olla podrida', meaning a spiced stew of various meats and vegetables. In England, changed to olio, this became an accepted culinary term during the seventeenth century. An olio always had a large range of ingredients, and sometimes a very large range indeed.

ORIENTAL BEZOAR.   There was also Occidental Bezoar. They both came from ruminants (goats or antelopes) either from India or from Spain and the Mediterranean. Bezoars were stones found in the stomachs or intestines of these animals and were long thought an effective antidote against poison. Quincy's *Dispensatory* (1749) thought them worthless.

ORLANDO.   The hero of *Orlando Innamorato* (1487) and *Orlando Furioso* (1532), poems by Boiardo and Ariosto respectively. Orlando's great love is Angelica.

PALLATS, NOSES AND LIPS.   The palate, not to be confused with the tongue, is the roof of the mouth. The softer parts, to the rear, were those used in cookery. Robert May brackets palates with lips and noses for recipe purposes. In the main, it was the palates, noses and lips of cattle that were used.

PARISMUS.   The character adduced by the mendacious traveller to be the origin of the name of the city of Paris was in fact a fictitious prince of Bohemia who was the hero of a romance by Emanuel Ford published in 1598 and which had great popularity through the seventeenth century.

PARKINSON, MR.   John Parkinson (1567–1650) herbalist and author of *Theatrum botanicum* (1640).

PARTHENISSA, see CASSANDRA.

PEEPING CHICKENS, PEEPING PIDGEONS.   Peepers are very young birds. The word refers not to the act of peeping from underneath the mother's wing, but rather to that of cheeping or puling. Johnson, in his dictionary, wished to make the word mean chicken just out of the egg, but it would be kindlier to think that Woolley was talking rather of chicken that had not yet broken their voices from cheep to cluck.

PELLITORY OF THE WALL.   *Parietaria diffusa*, good for the stone and urinary problems.

PENELOPE.   She was the wife of Ulysses who waited long years for his return from Troy, fending off the while a succession of suitors. Her stratagem was to protest that she must finish a shroud for her father-in-law Laertes. By unravelling her daily task each night, the task was never-ending, Sisyphean.

PERROSIN.   An old name for resin: the exudation of pine trees that was the raw material for turpentine.

PESTLE.   The word can mean leg, as in 'pestle of a lark'.

PHALEUCIUMS.   More properly Phaleucians. This was a poetic metre named after a Greek poet, Phalaecus. The phrasing of this sentence by Woolley is reminiscent of that quoted by the *OED* from James Shirley's *The Maid's Revenge* (1639).

PHILIPS, MRS.   Katherine Philips (1631–1664) was a poet and writer whose sobriquet was 'Matchless Orinda'. She translated the tragedy *Pompée* by Jean Corneille.

PIPKIN.   This is a round cooking pot, usually handled. In the main, it was earthenware, although the word might refer to a metal pan. Though pipkin sounds diminutive, the vessel could be large, a 'great pipkin'.

PIPPINS.   Apples.

PITH OF AN OX.   The pith is the spinal cord.

PLAISTER.   Plaisters or plasters were an adhesive salve spread on muslin or skin. By extension, the word came to describe the fabric that fixed the salve to the body rather than the salve itself.

POINT DE VENICE.   Lace made with a needle, needlepoint, as opposed to pillow lace or lace made with a bobbin. Such lace was often given a geographical descriptor and Venice was the place where the technique was first developed to a high degree.

POLE OF LING.   While jole was the term used for salmon, for ling (which was usually a salted and dried fish) the word was poll, i.e. head and shoulders (as we use it in poll tax). This might be variously spelled as poule or pole.

POMPION.   Pumpkin.

PORRINGER.   A small bowl of metal, wood or earthenware, sometimes with one or two handles at the side, from which porridge, broth, soup, etc. was eaten.

PORTIA.   Porcia, the daughter of Porcius Cato, was the wife of Marcus Brutus. She figures in Shakespeare's *Julius Caesar*. She was a strong upholder of republican virtues.

PORTION.   The money allocated to a person or an heir out of an estate: most usually referring to a marriage portion or dowry which was brought by a woman to a marriage contract.

POSSET. A hot drink made of milk curdled by the addition of an acid (wine, ale, citrus juice) and often spiced.

POTTLE. This is a measure equivalent to half a gallon or two quarts, used for corn and flour as well as liquids.

POUTS. A term for young birds.

POWDER'D-BEEF. To powder meat was to dry-cure it with salt or spices. This was done in powdering tubs, a frequent item in inventories.

PUMP WATER. The type of water is often specified in contemporary recipe books. In Woolley the terms fair water, spring water and pump water are encountered. Fair water means no more than clean water. The distinction between spring water and pump water is one of hardness. Pump water, being taken from far beneath the soil, is much harder and therefore would not be useful for soap. It may also taste more strongly. Spring water, or rain water, was softer.

QUEENS CLOSET, THE. *The Queens Closet Opened, Incomparable Secrets in Physick, Chirurgery, Preserving and Candying, … Transcribed from the true Copies of her Majesties own Receipt Books, by W.M., one of her late servants.* This book, which consisted of three parts, 'The Pearle of Practice', 'A Queens Delight', and 'The Compleat Cook', was first published in 1655 with repeated editions until the early eighteenth century.

RAISINS OF THE SUN. This phrase meant simply sun-dried grapes. It had been in use from medieval times to distinguish true raisins from raisins of Corinth, which were currants (and also sun-dried).

RAND. A side of fish; the head and shoulders were called the jole.

READ, DR. Probably Alexander Reid or Rhead (1586?–1641), anatomist and surgeon who wrote on anatomy and was lecturer at Barber-Surgeons' Hall from 1632.

REINS. These are the kidneys.

RIOLANUS, DR. This is Jean Riolan the Younger (1580–1657) a Parisian anatomist and supporter of Galenic theories. He therefore disputed with the Paracelsians and the new theories of circulation of the blood proposed by William Harvey.

ROCK-WORK. This describes the art of making rock-like forms out of shells, as well as out of sugar candy.

ROSE-STILL. Rose-water was distilled in a still as were all the other flower waters of the Restoration still-room.

ROSIN. The solid residue after distillation of spirits of turpentine from its crude state, used for sealing bungs and corks, etc.

ROWENS. The word rowan, rowen or rewain refers to the second crop of grass after the hay has been cut. Cheese made from this late crop (rowens) seems to have been softer than many.

ROYAL SOVERAIGN. The ship of this name (though spelled *Sovereign*) was a first-rate man-of-war that was not lost until 1696 when it was burned by accident.

RUNNET. A variant spelling of rennet.

SALADINE. A variant spelling of celandine; see celidony, above.

SALUST. Sallust was a Roman historian (86–35 BC). He wrote histories of Catiline and Jugurtha and of the period after the rule of Sulla. Sempronia was the wife of Scipio Aemilianus.

SALMASIUS. Claudius Salmasius, or Claude Saumaise (1588–1653) was a French classical scholar of great learning and influence. His protestantism inclined his career to Holland and northern Europe, and he was even involved in English affairs with his defence of the monarchy *Defensio regia pro Carolo I* (1649) which provoked a rather more impressive reply from Milton, *Pro populo anglicano defensio* (1651).

SANDERS. An epic might be written on sandalwood (sanders). There are three sorts, yellow, white and red, all coming from various trees of the order Santalaceae from India (though latterly from Africa and the Pacific as well). Red sandalwood or rubywood comes from the tree *Pterocarpus santalinus*. This is used in cookery, dyeing, for making a cosmetic powder, and as an astringent and tonic in medicine. It should not to be confused with *Santalum album*, the true, white, sandalwood. Red sanders is pharmacologically inert. The Victorian missionary John Williams was unfortunately eaten by the natives of Erromango (Vanuatu) in the Pacific because they had been so persecuted by white men in search of sandalwood that they conceived a hatred of all Europeans. *Encyclopaedia Britannica* comments that the sandalwood trade was more perilous than whaling due to the conflicts it engendered with aboriginal populations.

SAPPHO. A female Greek lyric poet of the seventh century BC.

SARSNET. Sarsnet or sarsenet was a fine silk fabric often, but not invariably, used for petticoats.

SCORDIUM. Water germander, *Teucrium scordium*, a herb which smells like garlic and has medicinal uses.

SCOTCH. Scotch or 'scorch' means to score a piece of meat or fish with the tip of a knife; nothing to do with Scotland.

SCRAPE SUGAR. Woolley says 'scrape sugar' on chicken pies as a form of finishing glaze to the pastry. The sugar is scraped because it was delivered to seventeenth-century kitchens in the form of tall, conical loaves that had to be scraped, chipped, cut or broken before it was fit for use.

SCRUPLE. A very small measure of weight, 20 grains.

SCUMMER. Also called a skimmer. It might be made out of wood or of brass and would be a flattened bowl or broad scoop with holes in it to let out the liquid or whey. John Evelyn records various forms of dish or trencher for lifting cream off the milk.

SCURVY-GRASS. The plant *Cochlearia officinalis*, whose leaves were infused as a preventative against scurvy.

SEA-WORMWOOD. *Artemisia maritima*; aromatic.

SEARCE. Searce or searse means to sift or sieve. It is also a noun. According to the *OED* our culinary term sieve was used mainly in agricultural contexts at this time.

SEARCLOTH. See cere-cloth.

SEMPRONIA. She was the daughter of Cornelia (see above) and wife of Scipio Aemilianus.

SET-WALL-ROOT. The root of the zedoary (setwall) from the Indies, *Curcuma zedoaria*, was used in many medicines and valued for its spicy, bitterish taste. Setwall is also a name for the garden plant, nay weed, valerian.

SHAMBLES. The shambles was the name given to a town's butchers' quarter, where the animals would also be slaughtered.

SIMPLES. A term indicating that a medicine is composed of a single herb or plant or ingredient, not one of those amazingly complex confections beloved of apothecaries.

SIPPET. A small piece of toasted or fried bread, usually served in soup or broth, or with meat, or used for dipping into gravy. Sippets were often prepared (sometimes out of puff pastry instead of bread) and arranged around the borders of a dish before sending it up.

SKIRRET. A root vegetable from the plant *Sium sisarum*, a species of water parsnip.

SLAT. The technical term for carving a pike, rehearsed in this very book, is 'splat'. However, here the word is correctly meant and printed and it means to split.

SLURT. The original meaning of the verb to slur was to smear or stain. This word is a variant, perhaps a simple misprint.

SMALLNESS OF YOUR BEER. Small beer was weak beer. Woolley mentions the preparation of the first wort when brewing at home. The wort was the liquor produced by boiling the malt and hops or other flavouring with water. This wort was then put to ferment with yeast. Were the first wort to be consumed, as she warns, then there will be nothing left to be mixed with the succeeding worts which, rather like replenishing brews at the tea-table, will be weaker.

SOUST, SOUC'D, SOUSED. To souse means to preserve in a pickle, for instance of diluted and spiced white wine or vinegar. A 'souse drink made of whey and salt' was another such preserving liquid.

SPECIES. Its use in the medical receipts seems to be 'composition of...' or 'element made up of...'.

SPIKE, OIL OF. The essential oil of French lavender (*Lavendula spica*).

SPOON-MEAT. The term is meant literally: food of a consistency that it may be eaten with a spoon. This may well have been conserves, creams and sweet confections, but it was also anything that had been reduced to a soft pulp, often, of course, fed to children and invalids. Thomas Carlyle, as ever, makes eloquent use of the word in his 'Did he, at one time, wear drivel-bibs, and live on spoon-meat?' (*OED*) In earlier centuries the distinction was the more telling because, if the food were not eaten with a spoon, it would be picked up with the fingers.

SPRING WATER. See pump water.

SPURGE. A plant of the genus *Euphorbia*: exuding a milky substance.

STAMP. To pound in a mortar, or to crush with the back of a knife or some other tool.

STEVENS, DR. Dr Stephens's Water was a stand-by of the contemporary apothecary. It was thought restorative and carminative, i.e. relieving flatulence. Recipes for this water survive from sixteenth-century books of secrets: for instance one may be found in Hugh Plat's *Delightes for Ladies*.

STRAND-MAY-POLE. There was always a maypole at the junction of Drury Lane and the Strand, roughly where the church St Mary-le-Strand now stands. It was removed during the

Commonwealth but re-erected at the Restoration and survived until 1718 (see Pepys Companion volume).

STROKINGS. The milk that is taken from the cow when stripping the udder at the end of milking. It is richer than other milk. It was sometimes called afterings. In *The Compleat Cook*, it says, 'Take a gallon of Stroakings, and a pint of Cream as it comes from the Cow, and put it together with a little Rennet,' in order to make angelot cheese. Instead, Woolley is advising the milkmaid to bolster the richness of her morning-milk cheese.

SUCCORY. Chicory (*Cichorium intybus*).

SULPITIA. Sulpicia was the daughter of Servius Sulpicius and related to Marcus Valerius Messalla Corvinus as well as being part of his literary circle (which included Tibullus and Horace). She was famed for her beauty and erudition and has left us six love poems dedicated to a young man sporting the Greek pseudonym Cerinthus.

SUPPER. See dinner.

SWINNOCK, MR. George Swinnock (1627–1673) was a nonconformist divine and fellow of Balliol College, Oxford with several works of devotion to his credit. His book *Christian Calling* was sold by Dorman Newman, the publisher and compiler of *The Gentlewomans Companion*.

TABLES. Tablets.

TAFFETY-TART. Taffety or taffeta was a word applied to a cream dish, taffeta cream, and to a tart. A suggestion is that the creams were so called because their lustrous surface matched the sheen of taffeta silk. However, it is difficult to make the link between a simple egg cream and a tart of highly-flavoured apple purée, though the recipe in Woolley gives the surface a lustrous sheen by being well iced. The *OED* connects the word in its culinary sense with the figurative usage, for example Shakespeare's 'taffata phrases, silken tearmes precise', when it means bombastic, florid, highly decorated.

THEMISTOCLES. An Athenian statesman (*c*. BC 524–c. 459).

TIFFANIES. Fine silks or linens.

TRENCHER. A piece of stale bread cut from a large oblong loaf used as a plate in the medieval and early modern period. The word derives from the French *trancher* (to slice, cut or hack) and indicated at root the surface upon which meat or food was sliced or cut. The bread trencher is thus a specialized form and in fact any flat board or plate used for this purpose could be called a trencher. By Woolley's time bread trenchers would be infrequent and most would have been of wood or of pewter.

TRIED SUET. The use of the word tried in this instance means prepared or processed.

TURNSOLE. The blue or violet colouring matter obtained from the plant *Crozophora tinctoria* and much used in the medieval and early modern periods.

TYNE. This seems to be a variant spelling of tin.

UNGUENTUM POPULEUM. More accurately, *Unguentum Populneum*, an ointment made principally from the buds of the black poplar tree.

UNICORNS-HORN. The horn of the rhinoceros. Quincy (1749) thought it was a fantastical remedy and worthless (see also Oriental Bezoar).

UNSTEAKY. The word steek means to stitch or to fasten and unsteek means to open. Thus she is using this adjective to describe the action of green ginger on the body.

USHER, BISHOP. James Usher (1581–1656), Archbishop of Armagh and important Anglican theologian, published *The Body of Divinity; or the Sum and Substance of the Christian Religion*, 'a hyper-Calvinistic work' in 1646.

VAILS. Perquisites. It was common for servants to have extra payments in kind over and above their wages. Often these might be clothes (hand-me-downs from the mistress perhaps). In the cook's case, it was fat from the kitchen that she sold to tallow-chandlers for candles. Woolley is pointing out that not all the fat should be sold on, certainly not that which has been melted and prepared for kitchen use.

VENICE-TURPENTINE. Common turpentine consisted of oleo-resins that exude from many types of conifers. Venice turpentine was the particular product of larch trees in the Tirol.

VERJUICE. Sour juice from unripe grapes or crab apples.

VERVINE. Vervain, *Verbena officinalis*.

VITRIOL. This is a sulphate of metal, i.e. metal acted upon by acid. Unqualified, it usually refers to sulphate of iron (copperas) – green vitriol. Oil of vitriol is concentrated sulphuric acid. Spirit of vitriol is a distilled essence of sulphuric acid.

VOITURE, MONSIEUR. Vincent Voiture (1598–1648) was a French poet and letter-writer whose works, although never published by the author himself, enjoyed great reputation in France for their style and phrasing.

WALM.   This is a bubble in boiling, a boiling-up, the heaving action of boiling.

WARDENS.   Pears, usually for cooking. The name derives, though no one knows why, from the abbey of Warden in Bedfordshire.

WESTPHALIA BACON AND HAM.   One of the great delicacies of northern Europe in the early modern period was bacon and ham cured in the manner of Westphalia in northern Germany. The hams were mildly salted and then smoked.

WHITELOF.   A whitlow or abscess on the finger.

WOOD-SORREL.   *Oxalis acetosella*: pleasantly sharp, like sorrel. John Evelyn includes it as a kitchen-garden plant.

WORT.   See 'smallness of your beer' above.

YOUTHS BEHAVIOUR, THE SECOND PART OF.   This refers to Robert Codrington's, *The Education of a Woman, The Second Part of Youths behaviour, or Decency of Conversation amongst Women* (1664), discussed in the introduction, above. There was a book with a similar title first published in English in 1641; it was a translation by Francis Hawkins (1628–1681).